M000249882

Derivatives Essentials

The Wiley Finance series contains books written specifically for finance and investment professionals as well as sophisticated individual investors and their financial advisors. Book topics range from portfolio management to e-commerce, risk management, financial engineering, valuation and financial instrument analysis, as well as much more. For a list of available titles, visit our Web site at www.WileyFinance.com.

Founded in 1807, John Wiley & Sons is the oldest independent publishing company in the United States. With offices in North America, Europe, Australia and Asia, Wiley is globally committed to developing and marketing print and electronic products and services for our customers' professional and personal knowledge and understanding.

Derivatives Essentials

An Introduction to Forwards, Futures, Options, and Swaps

ARON GOTTESMAN

WILEY

Published by John Wiley & Sons, Inc., Hoboken, New Jersey.
Published simultaneously in Canada.

Library of Congress Cataloging-in-Publication Data

Names: Gottesman, Aron A., author.
Title: Derivatives essentials : An introduction to forwards, futures, options and swaps / Aron Gottesman.
Description: Hoboken : Wiley, 2016. | Series: Wiley finance | Includes index.
Identifiers: LCCN 2016014397 (print) | LCCN 2016016290 (ebook) | ISBN 9781119163497 (hardback) | ISBN 9781119163572 (ePDF) | ISBN 9781119163565 (ePub)
Subjects: LCSH: Derivative securities.
Classification: LCC HG6024.A3 G68 2016 (print) | LCC HG6024.A3 (ebook) | DDC 332.64/57—dc23
LC record available at https://lccn.loc.gov/2016014397

Cover Image: © hywards/Shutterstock
Cover design: Wiley

Printed in the United States of America

V10012548_072619

For my wife Ronit and our children
Libby, Yakov, Raphi, Tzipora, and Kayla

Contents

Preface

This book provides an in-depth introduction to derivative securities. A derivative security is an agreement between two counterparties whose payoff depends on the value of an underlying asset. There is extensive interest in derivative securities due to their usefulness as tools through which investors can monetize views and transform exposures. Yet many that pursue an understanding of derivative securities can be frustrated with educational material that assumes the learner has sophisticated quantitative skills. Further, those with sophisticated quantitative skills can be frustrated with educational material that derives equations with little insight into the economic nature of derivative securities products and strategies.

This book focuses on helping you develop a meaningful understanding of derivative securities products and strategies and how to communicate your understanding both conceptually as well as through equations. You will learn about each product and strategy and the reasons for investing in them. You will learn about quantitative pricing and valuation models and will develop a deep understanding as to *why* the models represent price and value. You will learn of the great importance of the sensitivity measures known as the "Greeks" and learn how to use them to understand and characterize products and strategies.

Quantitative modeling is an important element of derivative securities, and this book will present quantitative models. However, this book does not assume that you have sophisticated quantitative or finance skills beyond the ability to add, subtract, multiply, divide, raise to a power, and rudimentary familiarity with time value of money concepts. Any other quantitative concept that is required to understand the material in this book will be introduced before it is required. Further, this book does not intend to provide comprehensive mathematical derivations nor provide quantitative overviews of each of the myriad of derivative securities variations in existence. Instead, the quantitative analysis in this book focuses on several key products through which we will explore conceptual and quantitative insights that are broadly applicable to other products and, most importantly, enable you to verbally communicate a deep understanding of products and strategies.

There are five parts to this book:

- Part One: Introduction to Forwards, Futures, and Options (Chapters 1–3)
- Part Two: Pricing and Valuation (Chapters 4–7)
- Part Three: The Greeks (Chapters 8–10)
- Part Four: Trading Strategies (Chapters 11–13)
- Part Five: Swaps (Chapters 14–15)

Part One introduces forwards, futures, and options. Forwards and futures are agreements that obligate counterparties to transact in the future. Options are agreements that provide one of the counterparties a right, and not an obligation, to transact in the future. In Part One you will learn about the key characteristics of forwards, futures, and options and each position's cash flows, payoffs, and P&L (profit and loss). You will also learn why forwards, futures, and options are described as zero-sum games and the concepts of moneyness and counterparty credit risk.

Part Two explores pricing and valuation of forwards and options. In Part Two you will learn to distinguish between price and value and explore models of price and value for each position, including the Black-Scholes and binomial option pricing models. You will also learn about the assumptions that these models make, risk-neutral valuation, and why the models represent price and value. You will also be introduced to the concepts of implied volatility and volatility surfaces.

Part Three explores the "Greeks," which are measures of product and strategy sensitivity to change in the determinants of their value. In Part Three you will learn how to define, calculate, and interpret the Greeks and why they can be inaccurate. You will also develop a deep understanding of how the Greeks can be used to understand and describe sensitivity; why a given Greek will be positive, negative, or zero; and why its magnitude can change.

Part Four explores trading strategies. In Part Four you will learn how to describe and implement price and volatility trading strategies, create synthetic positions, and implement protective, yield enhancing, and spread trading strategies. The trading strategies that will be explored in Part Four include straddles, strangles, protective puts, covered calls, collars, bull spreads, bear spreads, risk reversals, butterfly spreads, and condor spreads, among others. You will also learn advanced concepts related to moneyness and put-call parity.

Part Five introduces swaps. A swap is an exchange of cash flows between two counterparties over a number of periods of time. In an interest rate swap the counterparties exchange fixed and floating interest rates. In a credit default swap periodic payments of spread are exchanged for a payment contingent on a credit event. In a cross-currency swap the counterparties exchange interest payments in different currencies. In Part Five you will learn about the key characteristics of these swaps, their sensitivities and cash flows, and how they can be used to transform exposures.

Most of the chapters in this book build on the material in previous chapters. It is therefore important that you truly understand each chapter before advancing to the next. To allow you to test your understanding, there are more than 650 *Knowledge check* questions throughout the book, the solutions to which are provided in the appendix. The *Knowledge check* questions can be used to ensure absorption of the material both when you learn the material for the first time and also when you review.

I hope this book provides you with a deep understanding of derivative securities and an enjoyable and valuable learning experience!

Acknowledgments

I want to acknowledge the contribution of Bill Falloon of John Wiley & Sons. This book would not have been brought to completion without Bill's critical support. I also want to acknowledge Meg Freeborn, Michael Henton, and Chaitanya Mella of Wiley, Kevin Mirabile of Fordham University, and my colleagues at Pace University including Niso Abuaf, Lew Altfest, Neil Braun, Arthur Centonze, Burcin Col, Ron Filante, Natalia Gershun, Elena Goldman, Iuliana Ismailescu, Padma Kadiyala, Maurice Larraine, Sophia Longman, Ray Lopez, Ed Mantell, Matt Morey, Jouahn Nam, Richard Ottoo, Joe Salerno, Michael Szenberg, Carmen Urma, PV Viswanath, Tom Webster, Berry Wilson, and Kevin Wynne. I also want to acknowledge Niall Darby, Stephen Feline, Allegra Kettelkamp, John O'Toole, Patrick Pancoast, Carlos Remigio, Lisa Ryan, and the entire team at Intuition. I further want to acknowledge Moshe Milevsky, Eli Prisman, and Gordon Roberts of York University and Gady Jacoby of the University of Manitoba who helped spark my career. Thank you to my many students from whom I've learned tremendously. Finally, thank you to my wife Ronit, a woman of valor, and our children Libby, Yakov, Raphi, Tzipora, and Kayla for providing so much love and support.

About the Author

Aron Gottesman is Professor of Finance and the Chair of the Department of Finance and Economics at the Lubin School of Business at Pace University in Manhattan. He holds a PhD in Finance, an MBA in Finance, and a BA in Psychology, all from York University. He has published articles in academic journals including the *Journal of Financial Intermediation, Journal of Banking and Finance, Journal of Empirical Finance*, and the *Journal of Financial Markets*, among others, and has coauthored several books. Aron Gottesman's research has been cited in newspapers and popular magazines, including *The Wall Street Journal, The New York Times, Forbes Magazine,* and *Business Week*. He teaches courses on derivative securities, financial markets, and asset management. Aron Gottesman also presents workshops to financial institutions. His website can be accessed at www.arongottesman.com.

Derivatives Essentials

PART One

Introduction to Forwards, Futures, and Options

CHAPTER 1

Forwards and Futures

INTRODUCTION

A derivative security is an agreement between two counterparties whose payoff depends on the value of an underlying asset. In this chapter we will explore agreements that obligate counterparties to transact in the future, known as forward contracts and futures contracts.

After you read this chapter you will be able to

- Describe the key characteristics of a forward.
- Define and contrast the concepts of payoff and P&L.
- Describe a forward's cash flows, payoff, and P&L.
- Understand how equations and P&L diagrams can be used to describe a forward's cash flows.
- Understand when forwards earn profits, suffer losses, and break even.
- Explain why forwards are zero-sum games.
- Define counterparty credit risk and understand mechanisms through which it is managed and minimized.
- Describe futures contracts.
- Compare and contrast forwards and futures.

1.1 FORWARD CONTRACT CHARACTERISTICS

A forward contract is an agreement between two counterparties that obligates them to transact in the future. The key characteristics of a forward are as follows:

- One of the counterparties is referred to as the "long position" or "long forward," and the other counterparty is referred to as the "short position" or "short forward."
- The long forward is obligated to purchase an asset from the short forward at a future point in time. The short forward is obligated to sell the asset.

- The asset is known as the "underlying asset." The underlying asset can be any asset. Common examples include stocks, bonds, currencies, and commodities.
- The future point in time when the transaction occurs is known as the "expiration date." For example, a forward may have an expiration date that is three months after initiation.
- The price at which the underlying asset is purchased is called the "forward price." The forward price is set at initiation though the transaction only takes place in the future. For example, at initiation two counterparties may agree to a forward price of $100 and an expiration date that is in three months. The long forward is obligated to purchase the asset from the short forward for $100 in three months.
- All details are specified at initiation, including:
  - The counterparties
  - The underlying asset
  - The forward price
  - The expiration date

Hence, a forward is very similar to any transaction where an individual buys an asset from another individual, with the interesting twist that while the purchase price is set at initiation the transaction itself takes place at a future point in time. Figure 1.1 illustrates a forward.

For example, consider the following scenario:

- Initiation = July 15
- Expiration = September 15
- Underlying asset = one share
- Forward price = $100

Figure 1.2 illustrates this example.

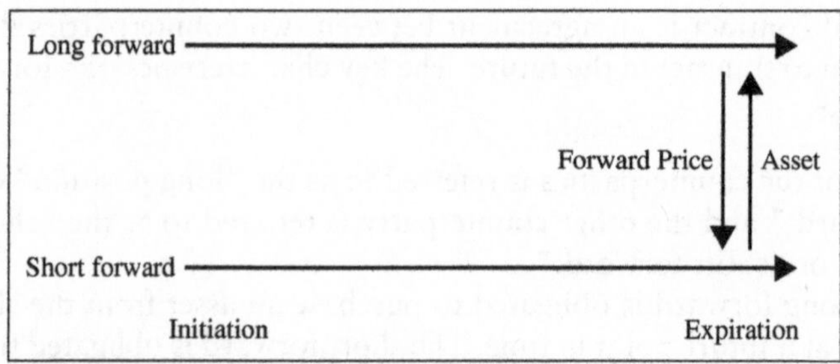

FIGURE 1.1 Forward contract cash flows

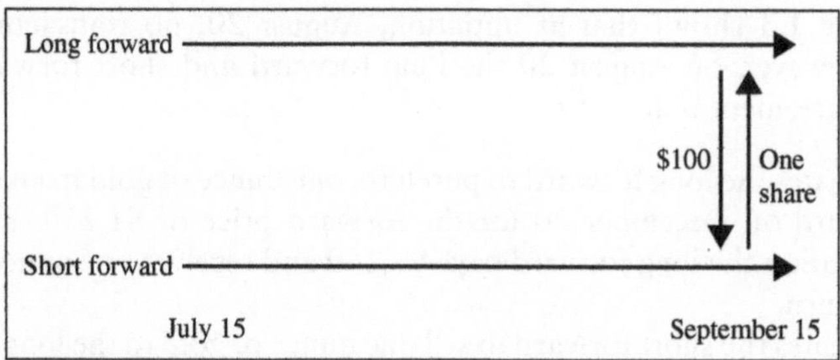

FIGURE 1.2 Forward contract cash flows example

Figure 1.2 shows that at initiation, July 15, no transaction takes place. Instead, on July 15 the long forward and short forward enter into an agreement that

- Obligates the long forward to purchase a single share from the short forward on September 15 for the forward price of $100. Hence, at expiration the long position pays $100 and receives one share in return.
- Obligates the short forward to sell a single share to the long forward on September 15 for the forward price of $100. Hence at expiration the short forward receives $100 and delivers one share in return.

Let's consider another example:

- Initiation = August 20
- Expiration = December 20
- Underlying asset = One ounce of gold
- Forward price = $1,250

Figure 1.3 illustrates this example.

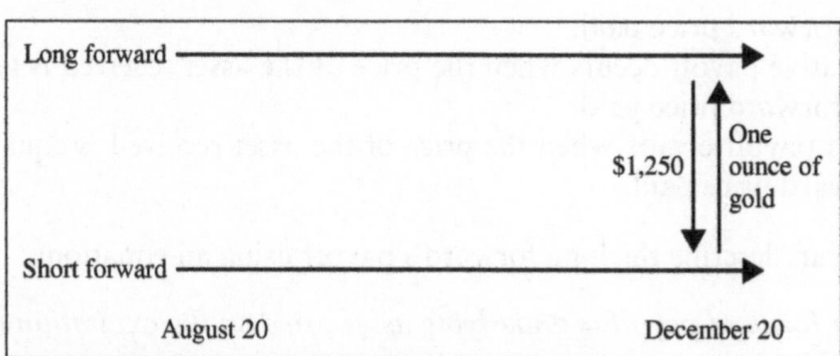

FIGURE 1.3 Forward contract cash flows example

Figure 1.3 shows that at initiation, August 20, no transaction takes place. However, on August 20 the long forward and short forward enter into an agreement that

- Obligates the long forward to purchase one ounce of gold from the short forward on December 20 for the forward price of $1,250. Hence, at expiration the long forward pays $1,250 and receives one ounce of gold in return.
- Obligates the short forward to sell one ounce of gold to the long forward on December 20 for the forward price of $1,250. Hence, at expiration the short forward receives $1,250 and delivers one ounce of gold in return.

Knowledge check

Q 1.1: What is a "forward contract"?
Q 1.2: What is the long forward position's obligation?
Q 1.3: What is the short forward position's obligation?
Q 1.4: What is the "expiration date"?
Q 1.5: What is the "forward price"?

1.2 LONG FORWARD PAYOFF

Payoff is the cash flow that occurs at expiration. A long forward is obligated to purchase the asset through paying the forward price at expiration. Hence, the long forward's payoff is the value of the underlying asset that it receives at expiration minus the forward price it pays. The value of the underlying asset at expiration is its market price at that time.

The long forward's payoff can be positive, negative, or zero:

- Positive payoff occurs when the price of the asset received is greater than the forward price paid.
- Negative payoff occurs when the price of the asset received is less than the forward price paid.
- Zero payoff occurs when the price of the asset received is equal to the forward price paid.

We can describe the long forward's payoff using an equation:

$$\textit{Long forward payoff} = \textit{underlying asset price on the expiration date} - \textit{forward price}$$

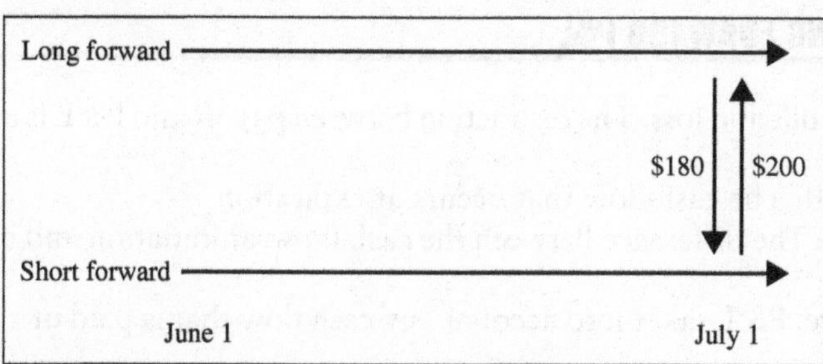

FIGURE 1.4 Long forward payoff example

This equation can be restated using notation rather than words. Let's define the following notation:

T = Expiration date
S_T = Underlying asset price at time T
F = Forward price

With this notation, we can rewrite the equation for the long forward's payoff:

$$\textit{Long forward payoff} = S_T - F$$

For example, consider the following scenario:

- Initiation = June 1
- Expiration = July 1
- Forward price = $180
- Underlying asset price on July 1 = $200

This scenario is illustrated in Figure 1.4.

In this example, the long forward's payoff is:

$$\begin{aligned}\textit{Long forward payoff} &= S_T - F \\ &= \$200 - \$180 \\ &= \$20\end{aligned}$$

Knowledge check

Q 1.6: What is "payoff"?
Q 1.7: What is the long forward's payoff?
Q 1.8: When does the long forward have a positive payoff?
Q 1.9: When does the long forward have a negative payoff?
Q 1.10: When does the long forward have zero payoff?

1.3 LONG FORWARD P&L

P&L is profit and loss. The distinction between payoff and P&L is as follows:

- Payoff: The cash flow that occurs at expiration
- P&L: The difference between the cash flows at initiation and expiration

Hence, P&L takes into account any cash flow that is paid or received at initiation.

A long forward's payoff and P&L are identical. After all, the long forward does not pay nor receive a cash flow at initiation. The equation for a long forward's P&L is therefore identical to the equation for the long forward's payoff:

$$\textit{Long forward P\&L} = \textit{Long forward payoff} = S_T - F$$

The long forward may experience a profit, suffer a loss, or break even:

- Profit occurs when the price of the asset received is greater than the forward price paid.
- Loss occurs when the price of the asset received is less than the forward price paid.
- Breakeven occurs when the price of the asset received is equal to the forward price paid.

We can describe the long forward's breakeven point using an equation:

$$\textit{Long forward breakeven point} : S_T = F$$

For example, consider the following scenario:

- Initiation = May 10
- Expiration = July 15
- Forward price = $1,500
- Underlying asset price on July 15 = $1,250

This scenario is illustrated in Figure 1.5.

In this example, the long forward's P&L is:

$$\begin{aligned} \textit{Long forward P\&L} &= S_T - F \\ &= \$1,250 - \$1,500 \\ &= -\$250 \end{aligned}$$

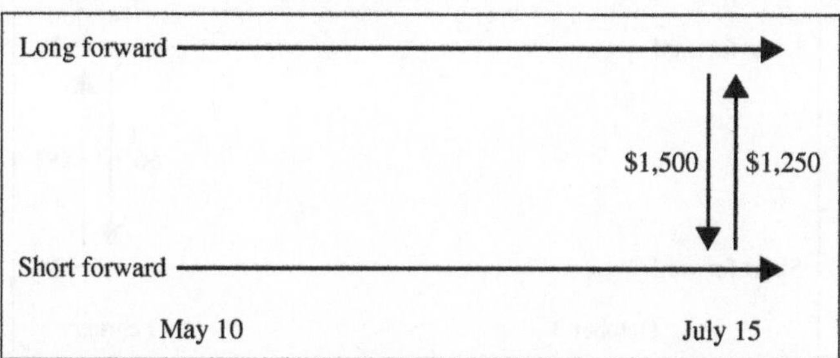

FIGURE 1.5 Long forward P&L example

Knowledge check

Q 1.11: What is "P&L"?
Q 1.12: What is the long forward's P&L?
Q 1.13: When does the long forward earn a profit?
Q 1.14: When does the long forward suffer a loss?
Q 1.15: When does the long forward break even?

1.4 SHORT FORWARD PAYOFF

A short forward is obligated to sell an asset at expiration in return for which it receives the forward price. Hence, the short forward's payoff at expiration is the forward price received minus the price of the asset it delivers. The short forward's payoff can be positive, negative, or zero:

- Positive payoff occurs when the forward price received is greater than the price of the asset delivered.
- Negative payoff occurs when the forward price received is less than the price of the asset delivered.
- Zero payoff occurs when the forward price received is equal to the price of the asset delivered.

The short forward's payoff can be expressed as:

$$\textit{Short forward payoff} = F - S_T$$

For example, consider the following scenario:

- Initiation = October 3
- Expiration = February 1
- Forward price = $65
- Underlying asset price on February 1 = $82

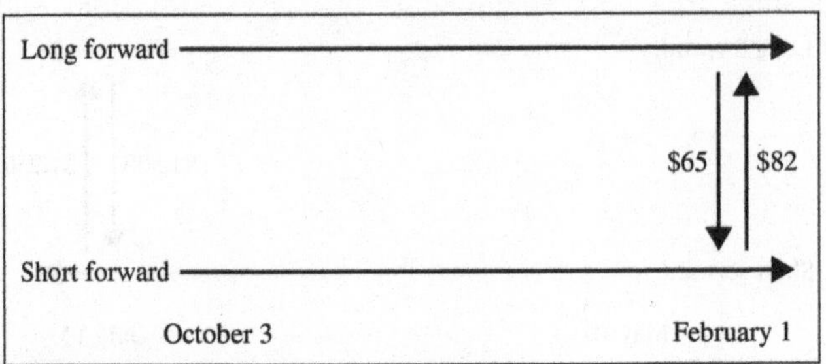

FIGURE 1.6 Short forward payoff example

This scenario is illustrated in Figure 1.6.
In this example, the short forward's payoff is:

$$\begin{aligned} \textit{Short forward payoff} &= F - S_T \\ &= \$65 - \$82 \\ &= -\$17 \end{aligned}$$

Knowledge check

Q 1.16: What is the short forward's payoff?
Q 1.17: When does the short forward have a positive payoff?
Q 1.18: When does the short forward have a negative payoff?
Q 1.19: When does the short forward have zero payoff?

1.5 SHORT FORWARD P&L

P&L is the difference between the cash flows that occur at initiation and expiration. A short forward's P&L is equal to its payoff as the only cash flow associated with a short forward is the payoff that takes place at expiration. Therefore, the equation for the short forward's P&L is identical to the equation for the short forward's payoff:

$$\textit{Short forward P\&L} = \textit{Short forward payoff} = F - S_T$$

The short forward may experience a profit, suffer a loss, or break even:

- Profit occurs when the forward price received is greater than the price of the asset delivered.

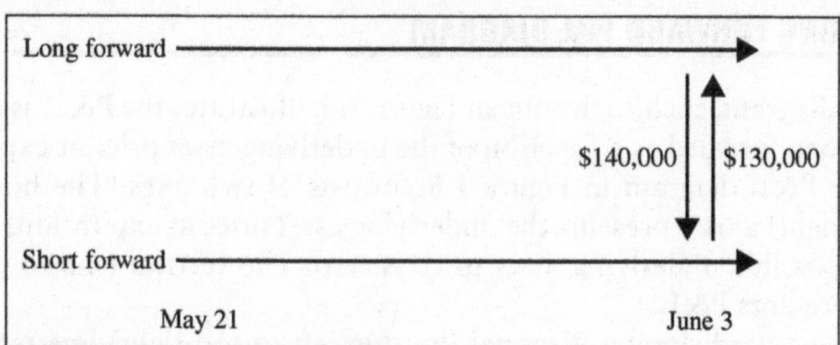

FIGURE 1.7 Short forward P&L example

- Loss occurs when the forward price received is less than the price of the asset delivered.
- Breakeven occurs when the forward price received is equal to the price of the asset delivered.

We can describe the short forward's breakeven point using an equation:

$$\textit{Short forward breakeven point} : S_T = F$$

The short forward's breakeven point is identical to the long forward's breakeven point.

For example, consider the following scenario:

- Initiation = May 21
- Expiration = June 3
- Forward price = $140,000
- Underlying asset price on June 3 = $130,000

This scenario is illustrated in Figure 1.7.

In this example, the short forward's P&L is:

$$\begin{aligned} \textit{Short Forward P\&L} &= F - S_T \\ &= \$140,000 - \$130,000 \\ &= \$10,000 \end{aligned}$$

Knowledge check

Q 1.20: What is the short forward's P&L?
Q 1.21: When does the short forward earn a profit?
Q 1.22: When does the short forward suffer a loss?
Q 1.23: When does the short forward break even?

1.6 LONG FORWARD P&L DIAGRAM

A P&L diagram, such as the one in Figure 1.8, illustrates the P&L associated with a long forward as a function of the underlying asset price at expiration.

The P&L diagram in Figure 1.8 consists of two axes: The horizontal (left to right) axis represents the underlying asset price at expiration, S_T. The lowest possible underlying asset price is zero. The vertical (top to bottom) axis represents P&L.

The upward sloping diagonal (bottom-left to top-right) line represents the P&L as a function of the underlying asset price. P&L depends on the underlying asset price:

- If the underlying asset price is less than the forward price, then the P&L is negative and the long forward suffers a loss.
- If the underlying asset price is greater than the forward price, then the P&L is positive and the long forward earns a profit.
- If the underlying asset price is equal to the forward price, then the P&L is zero and the long forward is at its breakeven point.

For example, consider the following scenario:

- Initiation = June 1
- Expiration = July 1
- Forward price = $75

On June 1 we do not know what the underlying asset price will be on July 1. The P&L diagram in Figure 1.9 depicts the range of potential P&L that the long forward may experience on July 1. The potential payoffs will

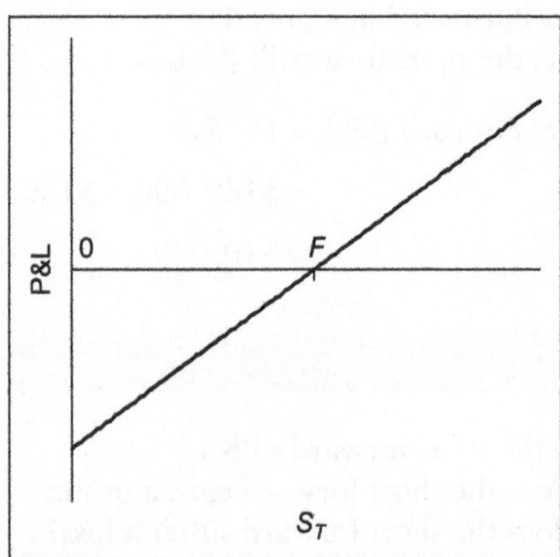

FIGURE 1.8 Long forward P&L diagram

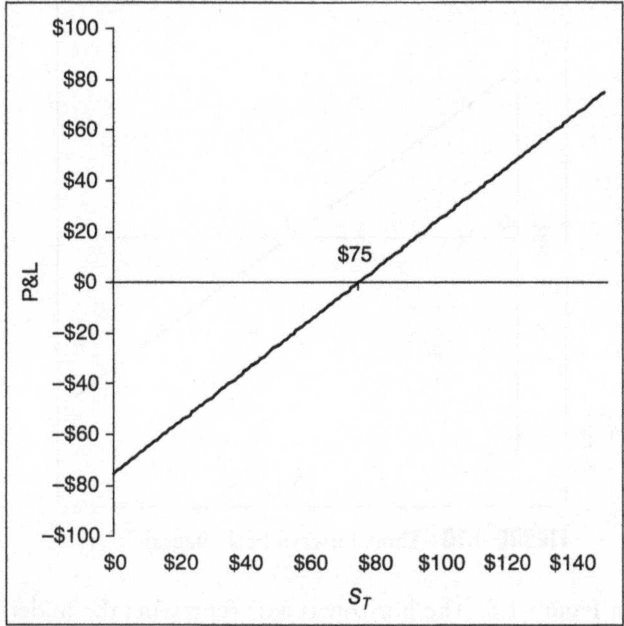

FIGURE 1.9 Long forward P&L diagram

depend on the value of the underlying asset price on July 1. If the underlying asset price is greater than the forward price of $75, then the P&L will be positive. If the underlying asset price is less than $75, then the P&L will be negative. If the underlying asset price is $75, then the P&L will be zero.

Knowledge check

Q 1.24: What does the horizontal axis of a P&L diagram represent?
Q 1.25: What does the vertical axis of a P&L diagram represent?
Q 1.26: What does a long forward's P&L diagram look like?
Q 1.27: What is the positive P&L range for the long forward?
Q 1.28: What is the negative P&L range for the long forward?

1.7 SHORT FORWARD P&L DIAGRAM

Figure 1.10 presents the P&L diagram for a short forward position.

The axes associated with the short forward's P&L diagram in Figure 1.10 are identical to the axes used for the long forward's P&L

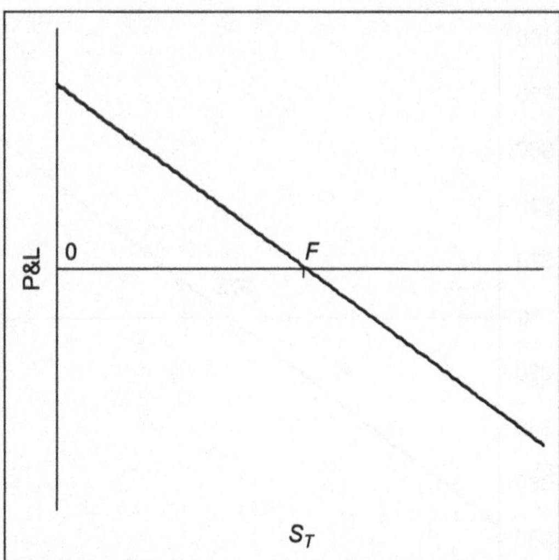

FIGURE 1.10 Short forward P&L diagram

diagram in Figure 1.8. The horizontal axis represents the underlying asset price at expiration. The vertical axis represents P&L. The downward sloping diagonal line (top-left to bottom-right) represents the short forward's P&L, which depends on the underlying asset price:

- If the underlying asset price is less than the forward price, then the P&L is positive and the short forward earns a profit.
- If the underlying asset price is greater than the forward price, then the P&L is negative and the short forward suffers a loss.
- If the underlying asset price is equal to the forward price, then the P&L is zero and the short forward is at its breakeven point.

The short forward's breakeven point is identical to the long forward's breakeven point. For the long forward the breakeven point is the point where, as the underlying asset price increases, the long forward switches from loss to profit, while for the short forward the breakeven point is the point where it switches from profit to loss.

For example, consider the following scenario:

- Initiation = December 1
- Expiration = January 12
- Forward price = \$60

On December 1 we do not know what the underlying asset price will be on January 12. The P&L diagram in Figure 1.11 depicts the range of

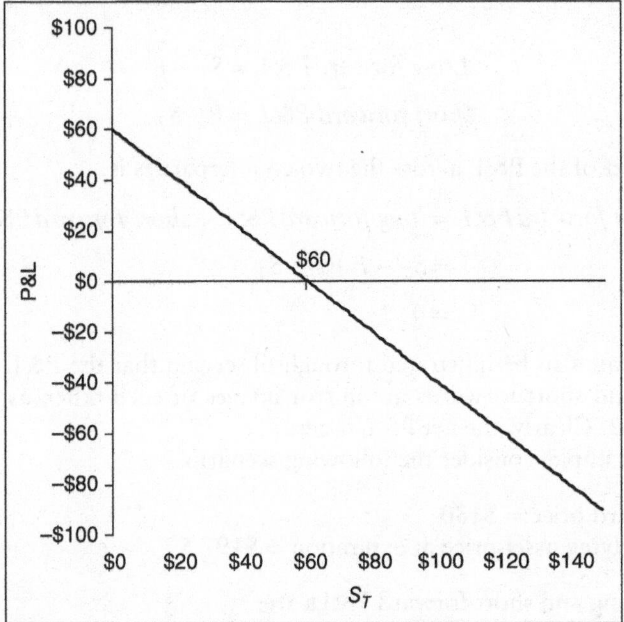

FIGURE 1.11 Short forward P&L diagram

potential P&L that the short forward may experience on January 12. The potential payoffs will depend on the underlying asset price on January 12. If the underlying asset price is less than $60, then the P&L will be positive. If the underlying asset price is greater than $60, then the P&L will be negative. If the underlying asset price is $60, then the P&L will be zero.

Knowledge check

Q 1.29: What does a short forward's P&L diagram look like?
Q 1.30: What is the positive P&L range for the short forward?
Q 1.31: What is the negative P&L range for the short forward?

1.8 FORWARDS ARE ZERO-SUM GAMES

Forwards are zero-sum games. This means that any profit that one of the counterparties receives is exactly equal to the loss that the other counterparty suffers. This is evident from the P&L associated with long and short forwards:

$$Long\ forward\ P\&L = S_T - F$$
$$Short\ forward\ P\&L = F - S_T$$

The net of the P&L across the two counterparties is:

$$\begin{aligned} Net\ forward\ P\&L &= long\ forward\ P\&L + short\ forward\ P\&L \\ &= S_T - F + F - S_T \\ &= 0 \end{aligned}$$

This can also be illustrated through observing that the P&L diagrams for long and short forwards are mirror images of each other, as shown in Figure 1.12. Clearly, the net P&L is zero.

For example, consider the following scenario:

- Forward price = \$180
- Underlying asset price at expiration = \$197.5

The long and short forward P&Ls are:

$$\begin{aligned} Long\ forward\ P\&L &= S_T - F \\ &= \$197.5 - \$180 \\ &= \$17.5 \end{aligned}$$

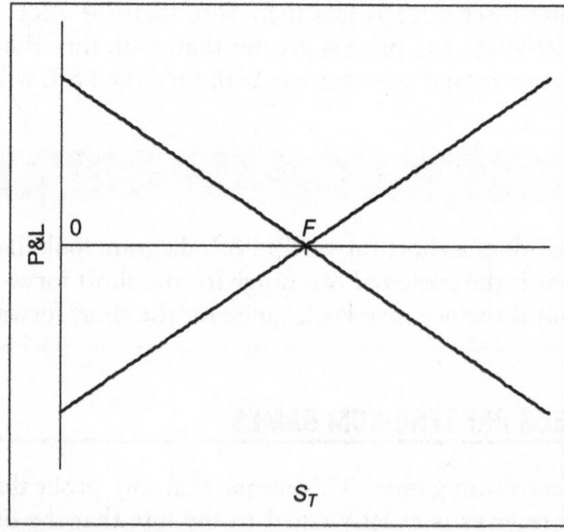

FIGURE 1.12 Forward contract as a zero-sum game

$$
\begin{aligned}
\textit{Short forward P\&L} &= F - S_T \\
&= \$180 - \$197.5 \\
&= -\$17.5
\end{aligned}
$$

The net P&L across the long and short forwards is:

$$
\begin{aligned}
\textit{Net forward P\&L} &= \textit{long forward P\&L} + \textit{short forward P\&L} \\
&= \$17.5 - \$17.5 \\
&= 0
\end{aligned}
$$

Knowledge check

Q 1.32: What is a "zero-sum game"?
Q 1.33: Why is a forward a zero-sum game?

1.9 COUNTERPARTY CREDIT RISK

An investor that enters into either a long or short forward has an obligation that it must satisfy:

- The long forward is obligated to purchase an asset from the short forward in the future.
- The short forward is obligated to sell an asset to the long forward in the future.

Each of the counterparties must fulfill its obligation whether it results in a positive or negative payoff. A counterparty that has earned a positive payoff is relying on the other counterparty to fulfill its obligation. Should the other counterparty fail to do so, the counterparty that has earned the positive payoff will lose the payoff and therefore suffer a loss. The risk of suffering a loss because one's counterparty does not fulfill its obligations is called "counterparty credit risk."

For example, consider the following forward:

- Forward price = $500
- Underlying asset price = $550

In this scenario, the payoffs to the long and short forwards are:

$$\begin{aligned}\textit{Long forward payoff} &= S_T - F \\ &= \$550 - \$500 \\ &= \$50\end{aligned}$$

$$\begin{aligned}\textit{Short forward payoff} &= F - S_T \\ &= \$500 - \$550 \\ &= -\$50\end{aligned}$$

In this scenario the long forward has a positive payoff and the short forward has a negative payoff. Should the short forward not satisfy its obligations, then the long forward will lose its positive payoff of $50. Therefore, the long forward faces counterparty credit risk.

Market participants work to manage and minimize counterparty credit risk. A number of mechanisms are used to do so, examples of which include the following:

- Careful screening of potential counterparties.
- Careful measurement of the counterparty credit risk exposure associated with a given counterparty.
- Legal contracts that carefully specify the terms of the agreement to allow for legal solutions should one of the counterparties fail to fulfill its obligations.
- Netting agreements. Netting is the idea that when two counterparties owe each other money the two cash flows are netted so that the counterparty that owes more than it is owed is the only one that makes a payment. This avoids situations where one of the counterparties fulfills its obligations while the other counterparty does not.
- Margin requirements. Margin requirements refer to requirements that counterparties put up cash when entering into agreements. Margin acts as collateral and assures each of the counterparties that positive payoffs will be received even if the other counterparty is unable or unwilling to fulfill its obligation. The amount of margin that is required can vary as a function of the underlying asset volatility and the characteristics of the given counterparty.
- Periodic cash resettlement. To alleviate the buildup of large payoffs, the counterparties may agree to early payments based on the expected payoff, known as "cash resettlement."

- Central counterparty clearing houses. A central counterparty clearing house (CCP) is an organization that can become the counterparty to each of the original counterparties to a derivatives transaction.

The process through which a CCP becomes the counterparty to each of the original counterparties is as follows: Two counterparties enter into an agreement with each other. Then, through a process known as "novation," the CCP becomes the counterparty to each of the original counterparties. Once this occurs the original counterparties are no longer obligated to each other. Instead, each of the original counterparties now has the CCP as its counterparty. Both of the original counterparties are now obligated to the CCP, and the CCP is obligated to each of the original counterparties in return.

Market participants perceive CCPs as low-risk counterparties as they maintain high credit ratings. Therefore, there is low counterparty credit risk when one's counterparty is a CCP. The CCP engages in extensive risk management to minimize its counterparty credit risk exposure including demanding margin, third-party guarantees, reserve funds, and other mechanisms.

Knowledge check

Q 1.34: What is counterparty credit risk?
Q 1.35: What mechanisms are used to manage and minimize counterparty credit risk?
Q 1.36: What is a CCP?
Q 1.37: Why do market participants perceive a CCP as a low-risk counterparty?

1.10 FUTURES CONTRACTS

While the expressions "forward contract" and "futures contract" may sound similar, forward contracts and futures contracts are distinct agreements. Their key difference is as follows:

- Forward contracts are traded over-the-counter (OTC). OTC trading takes place through networks of dealers that are employed by financial institutions. OTC trading does not take place on an exchange.

- Futures contracts are standardized forward contracts that trade on exchanges. Because futures contracts trade on exchanges they are heavily standardized and regulated. Derivatives exchanges in the United States are regulated by the Commodities Futures Trading Commission (CFTC).[1]

In a forward contract, the price at which the asset is purchased is called the "forward price." In contrast, in a futures contract the price at which the asset is purchased is called the "futures price."

The CME Group is a prominent example of a company that owns several exchanges that trade futures, as well as other products. The exchanges owned by the CME Group include:

- Chicago Board of Trade (CBOT)
- Chicago Mercantile Exchange (CME)
- Commodity Exchange (COMEX)
- New York Mercantile Exchange (NYMEX)

Underlying assets associated with futures contracts that trade on the CME Group include:[2]

- Commodity futures (e.g., agriculture, energy, metals)
- FX futures
- Interest rate futures
- Equity index futures
- Other futures products

The CME Group only trades equity index futures contracts, not single stock futures contracts. The U.S. exchange that trades single stock futures contracts is OneChicago.[3]

Knowledge check

Q 1.38: What is a "futures contract"?
Q 1.39: How is a futures contract similar to a forward contract?

---

[1]See www.cftc.gov
[2]Please see www.cmegroup.com/trading/products for a full listing of contracts that trade through the CME Group.
[3]See www.onechicago.com

Q 1.40: How is a futures contract different than a forward contract?
Q 1.41: What is "Over-the-Counter (OTC)"?
Q 1.42: What is the "futures price"?
Q 1.43: Does the CME Group trade single stock futures?
Q 1.44: What does the OneChicago exchange trade?
Q 1.45: What organization regulates derivatives exchanges in the United States?

KEY POINTS

- A forward contract is an agreement between two counterparties that obligates them to transact in the future. On the expiration date the long forward is obligated to purchase the underlying asset and the short forward is obligated to sell. The forward price at which the transaction takes place is agreed upon at initiation.
- Payoff is the cash flow that occurs at expiration. The long forward's payoff is the underlying asset price minus the forward price. The short forward's payoff is the forward price minus the underlying asset price.
- P&L is the difference between the cash flows at initiation and expiration. In a forward, P&L is equal to payoff.
- A forward's cash flows can be described using equations and P&L diagrams. A P&L diagram illustrates the P&L associated with a long forward as a function of the underlying asset price at expiration.
- Both long and short forwards break even when the underlying asset price is equal to the forward price.
- Forwards are zero-sum games, as any profit that one of the counterparties receives is equal to the loss that the other counterparty suffers.
- The counterparties to a forward face counterparty credit risk exposure. Mechanisms that are used to manage and minimize counterparty credit risk include careful screening of counterparties, use of legal contracts, netting agreements, margin requirements, periodic cash resettlement, and the use of central counterparty clearing houses (CCPs).
- Forward contracts are traded over-the-counter (OTC) through a network of dealers. Futures contracts are standardized forward contracts that trade on exchanges. Because futures contracts trade on exchanges, they are heavily standardized and regulated.

CHAPTER 2

Call Options

INTRODUCTION

Options are agreements between two counterparties that provide one of the counterparties a right, but not an obligation, to transact in the future. There are two types of option contracts: Call options that provide the right to purchase and put options that provide the right to sell. In this chapter we will explore call options in-depth. In the subsequent chapter we will turn to put options.

After you read this chapter you will be able to

- Describe the key characteristics of a call option.
- Explain the decision to exercise a call option.
- Describe a call option's cash flow, payoffs, and P&L.
- Understand how equations and P&L diagrams can be used to describe call option cash flows.
- Understand when call options earn profits, suffer losses, and break even.
- Explain why call options are zero-sum games.
- Explain the concept of "moneyness" and understand when a call option is in-the-money, at-the-money, and out-of-the-money.
- Understand when it makes sense to exercise a call option early.
- Compare and contrast forwards/futures and call options.

2.1 CALL OPTION CHARACTERISTICS

A call option is an agreement between two counterparties in which one of the counterparties has the right to purchase an underlying asset from the other counterparty in the future. The characteristics of a call option are as follows:

- The two counterparties to a call option are the long call and the short call.

- A call option gives the long call the right, but not the obligation, to purchase an underlying asset from the short call in the future. Hence, the long call can choose in the future whether or not to exercise its right to purchase. The expression "exercise" means "take advantage of."
- The short call is obligated to sell the underlying asset to the long call should the long call exercise its right to purchase.
- The long call is also referred to as the "buyer" and the short call is also referred to as the "writer" or the "seller" of the call option.
- The price at which the long call has the right to purchase the underlying asset is known as the "strike price." Another commonly used name for the strike price is the "exercise price."
- It is advantageous to have a right and not an obligation. Hence, the long call must pay the short call a fee for providing the right. The fee is known as the "call premium." The call premium is paid at initiation. Other names for the call premium are the "call price" or simply the "premium."
- We can distinguish between a European-style and an American-style call option. In a European-style call option the right to exercise is only at expiration. In an American-style call option the long call has the right to exercise either at expiration or before expiration. Both American-style and European-style call options trade in the United States.
- The asset can be any asset. Examples of assets include stocks, bonds, currencies and commodities.
- All details are specified at initiation, including:
    - The counterparties
    - The underlying asset
    - The strike price
    - The call premium
    - The expiration date
    - Whether the option is American-style or European-style
- Options can trade either OTC (over-the-counter) or through an exchange. Hence, options are described as OTC options or exchange-traded options. A prominent example of an options exchange is the Chicago Board Options Exchange (CBOE).[1]

Figure 2.1 illustrates a European-style call option's cash flows. The exchange of strike price for the asset will only take place should the long call exercise its right to purchase. Since Figure 2.1 illustrates a European-style call option it can only be exercised at expiration. American-style options can be exercised either at expiration or before expiration.

[1] See www.CBOE.com

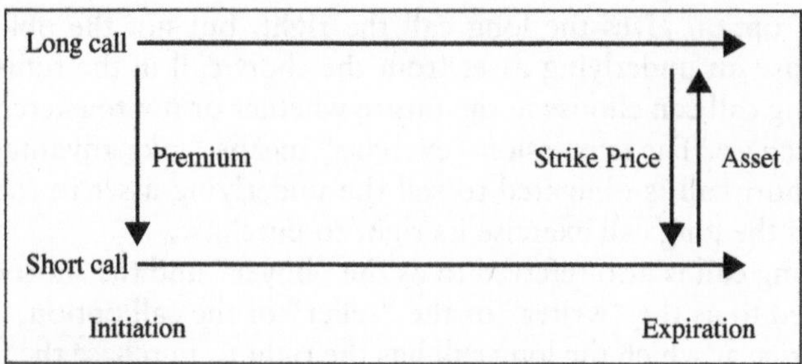

FIGURE 2.1 European-style call option cash flows

For example, consider the following scenario:

- European-style call option
- Initiation = July 15
- Expiration date = September 15
- Premium = $2
- Underlying asset = one share
- Strike price = $40

Figure 2.2 illustrates this example. As Figure 2.2 demonstrates:

- At initiation, July 15, the long call pays a $2 premium to the short call.
- On September 15 the long call has the right to purchase one share for $40. The purchase will only take place should the long call exercise its right to purchase.

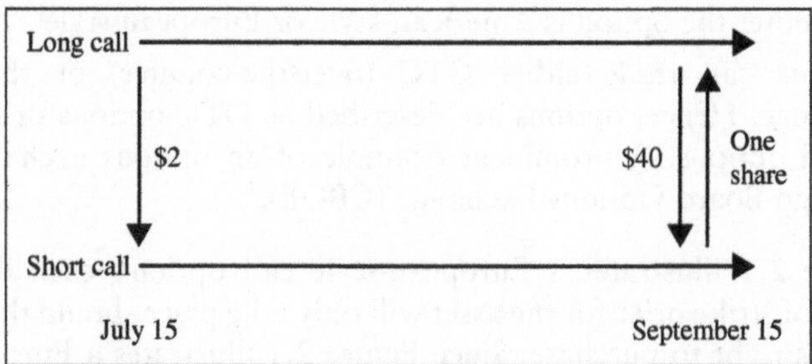

FIGURE 2.2 European-style call option cash flows example

Knowledge check

Q 2.1: What is a call option?
Q 2.2: What does the long call have the right to do?
Q 2.3: What is the short call's obligation?
Q 2.4: What does "exercise" mean in the context of options?
Q 2.5: What is the "strike price"?
Q 2.6: What is the "exercise price"?
Q 2.7: What is the "call premium"?
Q 2.8: What is the "call price"?
Q 2.9: Which position is the "buyer" of a call option?
Q 2.10: Which position is the "writer" of a call option?
Q 2.11: Which position is the "seller" of a call option?
Q 2.12: When does the long call position pay the premium to the short call position?
Q 2.13: What is an "American-style" option?
Q 2.14: What is a "European-style" option?
Q 2.15: Do options trade on exchanges or OTC?

2.2 LONG CALL PAYOFF

Payoff is the cash flow that occurs at expiration. The long call can either exercise or not exercise. The payoff associated with a long call is, therefore, the following:

- If the long call exercises then the payoff is the difference between the price of the underlying asset that the long call receives and the strike price that it pays.
- If the long call does not exercise then the payoff is zero as no transaction takes place.

Let's explore the equation for the payoff at expiration associated with a long call. Let's define the following notation:

T = Expiration date
S_T = Underlying asset price at time T
K = Strike price

TABLE 2.1 Call option exercise decision and long call payoff

Relationship between S_T and K	The exercise decision at expiration	Long call payoff
$S_T > K$	The option will be exercised, as S_T that the long call can receive is greater than the strike price K.	$S_T - K$
$S_T \leq K$	The option will not be exercised, as S_T that the long call can receive is less than or equal to the strike price K.	0

The long call's payoff and its relationship to the underlying asset price are detailed in Table 2.1. The long call's payoff will never be less than zero. Instead, the long call earns the larger of two possible payoffs, either $S_T - K$ or zero.

The difference between the underlying asset price and the strike price is the call option's "intrinsic value." A call option only has intrinsic value when the underlying asset price is greater than the strike price. Otherwise, the intrinsic value of a call option is zero.

An equation that describes the payoff to the long call is:

$$\textit{Long call payoff} = \max(S_T - K, 0)$$

The output of the max( ) function is the larger of the two values on either side of the comma within the function.

Consider the following example:

- Strike price = \$125
- Underlying asset price at expiration = \$135

The payoff is:

$$\begin{aligned}\textit{Long call payoff} &= \max(S_T - K, 0)\\ &= \max(\$135 - \$125, 0)\\ &= \$10\end{aligned}$$

Consider another example:

- Strike price = \$823
- Underlying asset price at expiration = \$721

The payoff is:

$$\begin{aligned} \textit{Long call payoff} &= \max(S_T - K,\ 0) \\ &= \max(\$721-\$823,\ 0) \\ &= 0 \end{aligned}$$

The payoff of zero indicates that the long call will not exercise the option.

Knowledge check

Q 2.16: When will the long call exercise the call option?
Q 2.17: When will the long call not exercise the call option?
Q 2.18: What is the long call's payoff should it exercise?
Q 2.19: What is the long call's payoff should it not exercise?
Q 2.20: What is a call option's intrinsic value?
Q 2.21: When does a call option have intrinsic value?
Q 2.22: What equation describes the long call's payoff?

2.3 LONG CALL P&L

P&L is the difference between the cash flows that occur at initiation and expiration. Hence, P&L takes into account the premium that is paid by the long call at initiation.

In Chapter 1 we learned that a forward's P&L is equal to its payoff as there is no premium associated with a forward at initiation. A call option's payoff is not equal to its P&L. Instead, the long call's P&L takes into account the premium that it pays upfront.

The long call's P&L and its relationship to the underlying asset price are detailed in Table 2.2. The notation c_0 is defined as follows:

c_0 = Call premium paid by long call to the short call at initiation

The long call option's P&L at expiration can be expressed as:

$$\textit{Long call P\&L} = \max(S_T - K,\ 0) - c_0$$

A positive value for the long call's P&L represents profit, and a negative value represents loss.

TABLE 2.2 Call option exercise decision and long call payoff and P&L

Relationship between S_T and K	The exercise decision at expiration	Long call payoff	Long call P&L
$S_T > K$	The option will be exercised, as S_T that the long call can receive is greater than the strike price K.	$S_T - K$	$S_T - K - c_0$
$S_T \leq K$	The option will not be exercised, as S_T that the long call can receive is less than or equal to the strike price K.	0	$-c_0$

Consider the following example:

- Strike price = \$145
- Underlying asset price at expiration = \$154
- Call premium paid at initiation = \$8

The P&L is:

$$\begin{aligned} \textit{Long Call P\&L} &= \max(S_T - K,\ 0) - c_0 \\ &= \max(\$154 - \$145,\ 0) - \$8 \\ &= \$1 \end{aligned}$$

Consider another example:

- Strike price = \$112.50
- Underlying asset price = \$113.00
- Call premium paid at initiation = \$7

The P&L is:

$$\begin{aligned} \textit{Long Call P\&L} &= \max(S_T - K,\ 0) - c_0 \\ &= \max(\$113 - \$112.5,\ 0) - \$7 \\ &= -\$6.5 \end{aligned}$$

Knowledge check

Q 2.23: How does the long call's P&L differ from its payoff?
Q 2.24: What is the long call's P&L should it exercise?
Q 2.25: What is the long call's P&L should it not exercise?
Q 2.26: What equation describes the long call's P&L?

2.4 SHORT CALL PAYOFF

A short call is obligated to sell the underlying asset to the long call should the long call exercise its right to purchase. The short call has no choice in the matter, because whether the transaction takes place or not completely depends on the long call's decision. The long call's choices at expiration, and their impact on the short call's payoff, are as follows:

- The long call exercises: The long call will exercise at expiration when the underlying asset price is greater than the strike price. In this scenario the price of the underlying asset that the short call must deliver is greater than the strike price that the short call receives, and the short call's payoff is negative.
- The long call does not exercise: If the underlying asset price is less than the strike price, the long call will not exercise, and the short call's payoff is zero.

Table 2.3 presents the payoff to the short call at expiration. The short call's payoff will never be greater than zero. Instead, the short call earns the smaller of two possible payoffs, either $K - S_T$ or zero.

The short call's payoff can be expressed as:

$$\textit{Short call payoff} = \min(K - S_T,\ 0)$$

The output of the min( ) function is the smaller of the two values on either side of the comma within the function.

Consider the following example:

- Strike price = \$125
- Underlying asset price at expiration = \$135

TABLE 2.3 Call option exercise decision and short call payoff

Relationship between S_T and K	The exercise decision at expiration	Short call payoff
$S_T > K$	The option will be exercised, as S_T that the long call can receive is greater than the strike price K.	$K - S_T$
$S_T \leq K$	The option will not be exercised, as S_T that the long call can receive is less than or equal to the strike price K.	0

The payoff is:

$$\begin{aligned} \textit{Short call payoff} &= \min(K - S_T,\ 0) \\ &= \min(\$125 - \$135,\ 0) \\ &= -\$10 \end{aligned}$$

Consider another example:

- Strike price = \$823
- Underlying asset price at expiration = \$721

The payoff is:

$$\begin{aligned} \textit{Short call payoff} &= \min(K - S_T,\ 0) \\ &= \min(\$823 - \$721,\ 0) \\ &= 0 \end{aligned}$$

Knowledge check

Q 2.27: What is the short call's payoff should the long call exercise?
Q 2.28: What is the short call's payoff should the long call not exercise?
Q 2.29: What equation describes the short call's payoff?

2.5 SHORT CALL P&L

We've seen that the payoff associated with a short call is either zero or negative. If so, when does the short call profit? The answer is that the short call's P&L takes into account the premium that the short call receives at initiation. The short call's P&L and its relationship to the long call's exercise decision are summarized in Table 2.4.

The short call's P&L at expiration can be expressed as:

$$\textit{Short call P\&L} = \min(K - S_T,\ 0) + c_0$$

A positive value for the short call's P&L represents profit while a negative value represents loss.

TABLE 2.4 Call option exercise decision and short call payoff and P&L

Relationship between S_T and K	The exercise decision at expiration	Short call payoff	Short call P&L
$S_T > K$	The option will be exercised, as S_T that the long call can receive is greater than the strike price K.	$K - S_T$	$K - S_T + c_0$
$S_T \leq K$	The option will not be exercised, as S_T that the long call can receive is less than or equal to the strike price K.	0	c_0

Consider the following example:

- Strike price = \$145
- Underlying asset price = \$154
- Call premium paid at initiation = \$8

The short call's P&L is:

$$\begin{aligned} \textit{Short call P\&L} &= \min(K - S_T,\ 0) + c_0 \\ &= \min(\$145 - \$154,\ 0) + \$8 \\ &= -\$1 \end{aligned}$$

Consider another example:

- Strike price = \$112.50
- Underlying asset price = \$113.00
- Call premium paid at initiation = \$7

The short call's P&L is:

$$\begin{aligned} \textit{Short call P\&L} &= \min(K - S_T,\ 0) + c_0 \\ &= \min(\$112.5 - \$113,\ 0) + \$7 \\ &= \$6.5 \end{aligned}$$

Knowledge check

Q 2.30: How does the short call's P&L differ from its payoff?
Q 2.31: What is the short call's P&L should the long call exercise?
Q 2.32: What is the short call's P&L should the long call not exercise?
Q 2.33: What equation describes the short call's P&L?

2.6 LONG CALL P&L DIAGRAM

A P&L diagram, such as the one shown in Figure 2.3, is used to illustrate the P&L associated with a long call as a function of the underlying asset price at expiration.

The long call's breakeven point is where the price of the underlying asset that is received is equal to the combination of both the premium and strike price paid:

$$\textit{Long call breakeven:} S_T = K + c_0$$

For example, consider the following scenario:

- Initiation = June 1
- Expiration = July 1
- Strike price = $75
- Call premium = $10

On June 1 we do not know what the underlying asset price will be on July 1. The P&L diagram in Figure 2.4 depicts the range of potential P&L that the long call may experience on July 1. If the underlying asset price is less than $75 then the P&L will be −$10 representing a loss equal to the premium paid. The breakeven point occurs when the underlying asset price is $75 + $10 = $85.

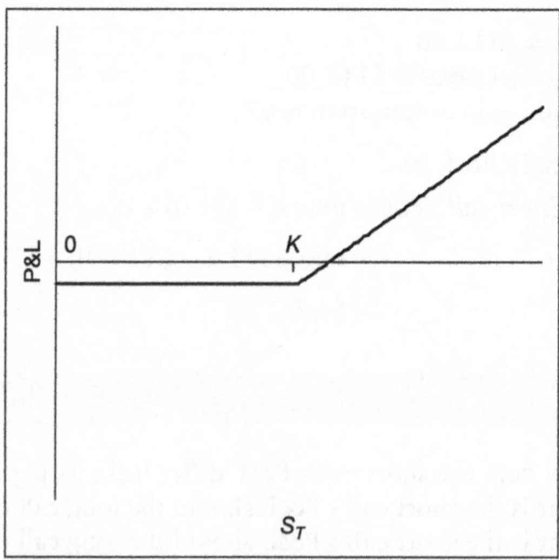

FIGURE 2.3 Long call P&L diagram

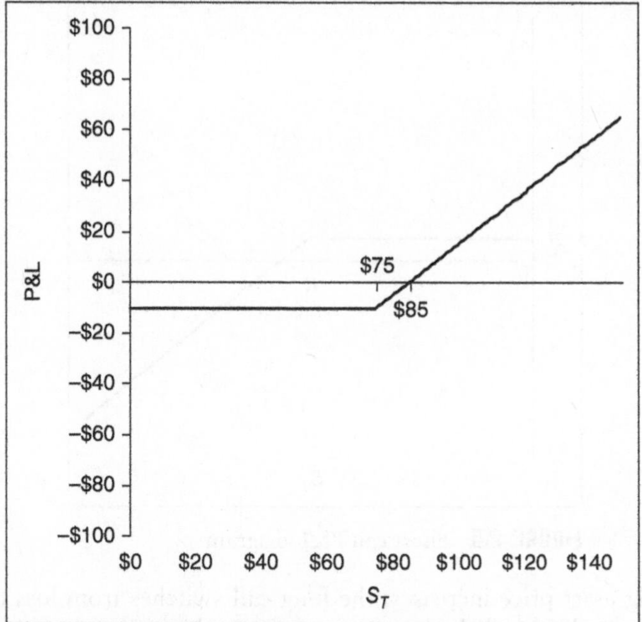

FIGURE 2.4 Long call P&L diagram example

Knowledge check

Q 2.34: What does a long call's P&L diagram look like?
Q 2.35: What is the positive P&L range for the long call?
Q 2.36: What is the negative P&L range for the long call?
Q 2.37: What is the long call's breakeven point?

2.7 SHORT CALL P&L DIAGRAM

A P&L diagram, such as the one shown in Figure 2.5, can be used to illustrate the P&L associated with a short call as a function of the underlying asset price at expiration.

The short call's breakeven point is where the price of the underlying asset that is delivered is equal to the combination of both the premium and strike price received:

$$\textit{Short call breakeven}: S_T = K + c_0$$

The short call's breakeven point is identical to the long call's breakeven point. For the long call the breakeven point is the point where, as the

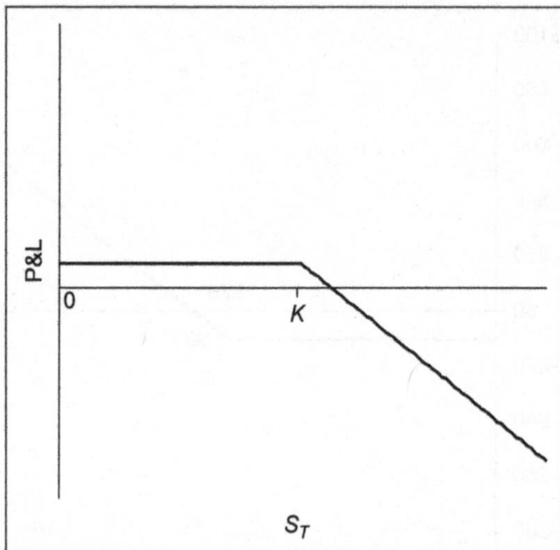

FIGURE 2.5 Short call P&L diagram

underlying asset price increases, the long call switches from loss to profit, while for the short call the breakeven point is the point where it switches from profit to loss.

For example, consider the following scenario:

- Initiation = December 1
- Expiration = January 12
- Strike price = $60
- Call premium = $9

On December 1 we do not know what the underlying asset price will be on January 12. The P&L diagram in Figure 2.6 depicts the range of potential P&L that the short call may experience on January 12. The potential payoffs will depend on the underlying asset price on January 12. If the underlying asset price is less than $60, then the P&L will be $9, equal to the premium received by the short call. The breakeven point occurs when the underlying asset price is $60 + $9 = $69.

Knowledge check

Q 2.38: What does a short call's P&L diagram look like?
Q 2.39: What is the positive P&L range for the short call?
Q 2.40: What is the negative P&L range for the short call?
Q 2.41: What is the short call's breakeven point?

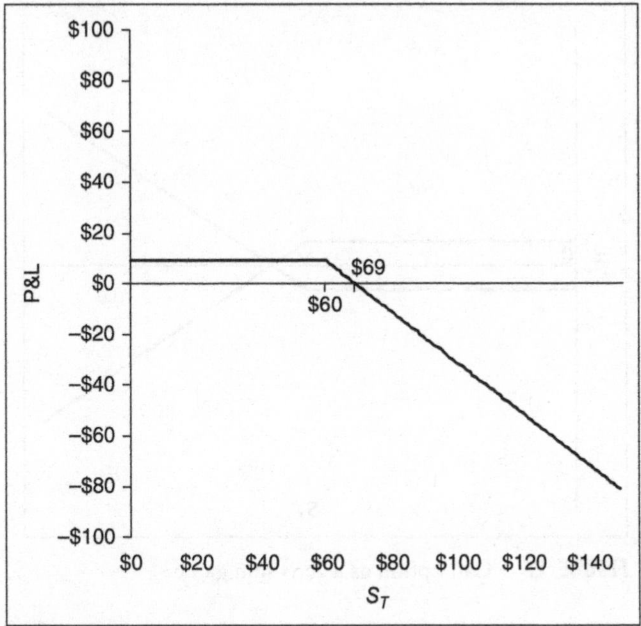

FIGURE 2.6 Short call P&L diagram

2.8 CALL OPTIONS ARE ZERO-SUM GAMES

Call options are zero-sum games. This means that any profit that one of the counterparties receives is exactly equal to the loss that the other counterparty suffers. This is true whether or not the long call exercises, as shown in Table 2.5.

This can also be illustrated through observing that the P&L diagrams for long and short calls are mirror images of each other: The net P&L across the long and short calls is zero, as shown in Figure 2.7.

TABLE 2.5 Long and short call P&L and net P&L

Relationship between S_T and K	Long call P&L	Short call P&L	Net P&L
$S_T > K$	$S_T - K - c_0$	$K - S_T + c_0$	0
$S_T \leq K$	$-c_0$	c_0	0

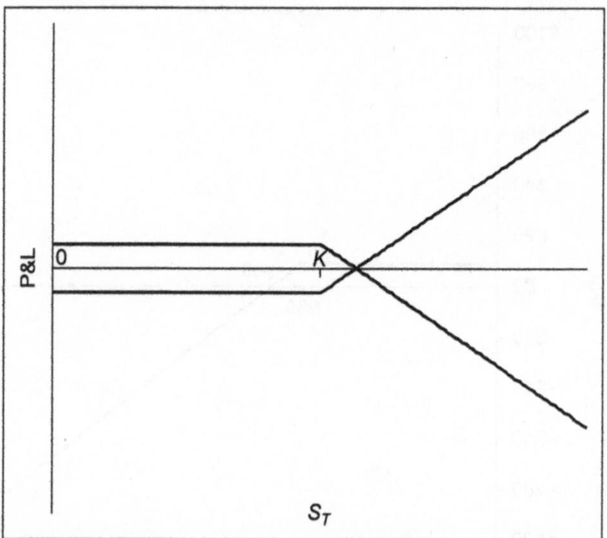

FIGURE 2.7 Call option as a zero-sum game

For example, consider the following scenario:

- Call premium = $5
- Strike price = $75
- Underlying asset price at expiration = $85

The P&L is:

$$\begin{aligned}
\textit{Long call P\&L} &= \max(S_T - K,\ 0) - c_0 \\
&= \max(\$85 - \$75,\ 0) - \$5 \\
&= \$5 \\
\textit{Short call P\&L} &= \min(K - S_T,\ 0) + c_0 \\
&= \min(\$75 - \$85,\ 0) + \$5 \\
&= -\$5
\end{aligned}$$

The net P&L across the long and short calls is:

$$\begin{aligned}
\textit{Net call P\&L} &= \textit{long call P\&L} + \textit{short call P\&L} \\
&= \$5 - \$5 \\
&= 0
\end{aligned}$$

Knowledge check

Q 2.42: Why is a call option a zero-sum game?

2.9 CALL OPTION MONEYNESS

"Moneyness" is whether a long option position will earn a positive payoff if it exercises. The moneyness of an option is one of the following:

- In-the-money (ITM)
- Out-of-the-money (OTM)
- At-the-money (ATM)

Let's explore each:

- ITM: An option is ITM when the long position will earn a positive payoff if it exercises the option. A call option is ITM when the value of the underlying asset is greater than the strike price.
- OTM: An option is OTM when the long position will earn a negative payoff if it exercises the option. A call option is OTM when the value of the underlying asset is less than the strike price. A long call will not exercise an OTM option to avoid the negative payoff.
- ATM: An option is ATM if the long position will earn a payoff of zero if it exercises the option. A call option is ATM when the value of the asset is equal to the strike price. The long call is indifferent about choosing to exercise an ATM option since the long call earns a payoff of zero whether it exercises or not.

Table 2.6 describes the relationship between the underlying asset price and the strike price, moneyness, and call option payoffs.

TABLE 2.6 Call option moneyness and long and short call payoff

Relationship between S_T and K	Call moneyness	Long call payoff	Short call payoff
$S_T > K$	ITM	$S_T - K$	$K - S_T$
$S_T = K$	ATM	0	0
$S_T < K$	OTM	0	0

Some notes:

- The moneyness of an option is a function of the payoff that the long position will experience should it exercise. It is not a function of profitability. Hence, whether a long position, a short position, or a third party, each determines an option's moneyness through determining the long position's payoff should it exercise.
- Since moneyness is a function of the long position choosing to exercise, the concept of moneyness does not apply to forwards and futures contracts where both counterparties face obligations and neither of the counterparties gets to choose whether to exercise.
- As an option progresses from OTM to ATM to ITM, its moneyness is described as increasing.
- When the underlying asset price is much higher than the strike price, the call option is described as deep-ITM. When the underlying asset price is much lower than the strike price, the call option is described as deep-OTM. These uses of the expression "deep" are subjective, and there is no formal designation of a call option as deep-ITM or deep-OTM.
- The expression "near-the-money" is used when the underlying asset price is in the vicinity of the strike price. The use of the expression is subjective and is not a formal designation.

Knowledge check

Q 2.43: What is "moneyness"?
Q 2.44: What is "ITM"?
Q 2.45: What is "ATM"?
Q 2.46: What is "OTM"?
Q 2.47: When is a call option ITM?
Q 2.48: When is a call option ATM?
Q 2.49: When is a call option OTM?
Q 2.50: Why isn't the concept of "moneyness" used in the context of forwards/futures?

2.10 EXERCISING A CALL OPTION EARLY

A long position in an American-style call option has the right to exercise early. But does it make sense to do so?

To explore this question, note that holding a call option is valuable for two reasons:

- Intrinsic value: The difference between the underlying asset price and the strike price
- Optionality value: The value of having the right to decide whether to exercise or not[2]

A call option only has intrinsic value when the underlying asset price is greater than the strike price (i.e., when ITM). Otherwise, the intrinsic value of a call option is zero. A call option has optionality value regardless of its moneyness.

Observe that there are both an advantage and disadvantages to early exercise, as follows:

- Disadvantage: Early exercise destroys the optionality value of the option. Having the ability to decide is valuable. But once an investor exercises the option early, the investor destroys the ability to decide in the future whether to exercise. Hence, early exercise is disadvantageous.
- Disadvantage: Early exercise means that the strike price will have to be paid earlier. The earlier a payment takes place, the higher the payment is in present value terms. Hence, early exercise is disadvantageous.
- Advantage: Early exercise means the investor receives any income that flows from the underlying asset. For example, consider a situation where the underlying asset is a share that pays a dividend at some point in time between initiation and expiration. The dividend is only paid to those that hold title to the share before the ex-dividend date.[3] If the investor exercises the option before the ex-dividend date, the investor will hold title to the share and will therefore receive its dividend. Otherwise, the investor will not receive the dividend.

Early exercise of an American-style call option makes sense if the advantage of doing so outweighs the disadvantages. Otherwise, the investor should not exercise early. If the disadvantages outweigh the advantage one should not exercise early even if one wishes to liquidate the position and/or remove the exposure. Instead, one should sell the position, as when one sells the position, one does not destroy its optionality value nor force early payment of the strike price.

Two important implications of these arguments are as follows:

---

[2]Another name for optionality value is "time value."

[3]The ex-dividend date is the date used to identify which shareholders receive a dividend. Dividends are only paid to those holding title before the ex-dividend date.

- The premium associated with an American-style call option will only be greater than the premium associated with a European-style call option if early exercise may make sense. Otherwise, an American-style call option should only be exercised at expiration and therefore is, effectively, identical to a European-style call option. For example, we expect that American-style and European-style options on non-dividend paying underlying assets will have identical premiums.
- The ability to exercise early can be valuable when the underlying asset pays a dividend. An investor that fails to exercise early when it should has failed to take advantage of a right for which it has paid. Dividend option arbitrage is the strategy of selling call options where the underlying assets pay dividends to naïve investors that fail to take advantage of their ability to exercise early when they should. This allows the short call to receive a premium whose level reflects the value associated with allowing the long call to exercise early, without the early exercise actually taking place.

Knowledge check

Q 2.51: What are the disadvantages associated with early exercise of a call option?

Q 2.52: What is optionality value?

Q 2.53: What is the advantage associated with early exercise of a call option?

Q 2.54: When are the premiums of otherwise identical American-style and European-style call options equal to each other?

Q 2.55: What is dividend option arbitrage?

2.11 COMPARISON OF CALL OPTIONS AND FORWARDS/FUTURES

Table 2.7 compares call options and forwards/futures based on the following characteristics:

- Does the position have a right or an obligation?
- Will the position be buying or selling?
- Does the agreement require the position to pay or receive a premium at initiation?

TABLE 2.7 Comparison of forwards/futures and call option positions

	Long forward/futures	Short forward/futures	Long call option	Short call option
Right or obligation	Obligation	Obligation	Right	Obligation
Buy or sell	Buy	Sell	Buy	Sell
Premium	None	None	Paid	Received
Name for purchase price	Forward: Forward price Futures: Futures price		Strike price or exercise price	
Payoff at expiration	$S_T - F$	$F - S_T$	$\max(S_T - K, 0)$	$\min(K - S_T, 0)$
Positive payoff range	$S_T > F$	$S_T < F$	$S_T > K$	None
Negative payoff range	$S_T < F$	$S_T > F$	None	$S_T > K$
Zero payoff point	$S_T = F$	$S_T = F$	$S_T = K$	$S_T = K$
P&L at expiration	$S_T - F$	$F - S_T$	$\max(S_T - K, 0) - c_0$	$\min(K - S_T, 0) + c_0$
Profit range	$S_T > F$	$S_T < F$	$S_T - K - c_0 > 0$	$K - S_T + c_0 > 0$
Loss range	$S_T < F$	$S_T > F$	$S_T - K - c_0 < 0$	$K - S_T + c_0 < 0$
Breakeven point	$S_T = F$	$S_T = F$	$S_T = K + c_0$	$S_T = K + c_0$
ITM range	Concept of moneyness not applicable		$S_T > K$	
ATM point			$S_T = K$	
OTM range			$S_T < K$	

- What is the name of the purchase price at which the transaction will take place in the future?
- What is the payoff associated with the position?
- When is the payoff positive, negative, and zero?
- What is the P&L associated with the position?
- When does the position earn a profit, suffer a loss, and break even?
- When is the option ITM, ATM, and OTM? Note that the concept of moneyness is not applicable to forwards and futures.

Knowledge check

Q 2.56: In what ways are long and short forwards/futures and calls similar?

Q 2.57: In what ways do long and short forwards/futures and calls differ?

KEY POINTS

- A call option is an agreement between two counterparties in which one of the counterparties has the right to purchase an underlying asset from the other counterparty in the future. The long call has the right to purchase. The short call is obligated to sell the underlying asset to the long call should the long call exercise its right to purchase. The price at which the transaction will take place is agreed-upon at initiation and is known as the strike price or exercise price. The long call pays a premium at initiation in order to obtain its right.
- Call options trade both OTC and through exchanges. Call options are either American-style or European-style. In a European-style call option the right to exercise is only at expiration. In an American-style call option the long call has the right to exercise earlier as well.
- At expiration the long call will exercise its right to purchase when the underlying asset price is greater than the strike price. Its payoff is therefore the larger of either zero or the underlying asset price minus the strike price. The short call's payoff is the smaller of either zero or the strike price minus the underlying asset price.
- The long call's P&L at expiration is its payoff minus the call premium paid at initiation. The short call's P&L at expiration is its payoff plus the call premium received at initiation.
- Call option payoff and P&L at expiration can be described using equations and P&L diagrams. A P&L diagram illustrates the P&L at expiration as a function of the underlying asset price at expiration.

- Both long and short call options break even when the underlying asset price is equal to the strike price plus the premium.
- Call options are zero-sum games, as any profit that one of the counterparties receives is equal to the loss that the other counterparty suffers.
- "Moneyness" is whether the long position to an option will exercise or not. The moneyness of an option is described as being either in-the-money (ITM), out-of-the-money (OTM), or at-the-money (ATM). A call option is ITM when the long call will earn a positive payoff through exercising the option, OTM when the long call will not exercise as it would earn a negative payoff, and ATM when it will earn zero payoff.
- An investor should exercise an American-style call option if the advantage of receiving a more valuable asset outweighs the disadvantages of loss of optionality value and paying the strike price earlier.

CHAPTER 3

Put Options

INTRODUCTION

In this chapter we will explore put options. A put option is an agreement between two counterparties in which one of the counterparties has the right to sell an underlying asset to the other counterparty in the future. A put option is distinct from a call option, as a put option provides the right to sell while a call option provides the right to purchase.

After you read this chapter you will be able to

- Describe the key characteristics of a put option.
- Explore the decision whether to exercise a put option or not.
- Describe a put option's cash flows, payoff, and P&L.
- Understand how equations and P&L diagrams can be used to describe put option payoff and P&L.
- Understand when put options earn profits, suffer losses, and break even.
- Explain why put options are zero-sum games.
- Understand when a put option is in-the-money (ITM), at-the-money (ATM), and out-of-the-money (OTM).
- Understand when it makes sense to exercise a put option early.
- Compare and contrast forwards/futures, call options, and put options.

3.1 PUT OPTION CHARACTERISTICS

A put option is an agreement between two counterparties in which one of the counterparties has the right to sell an underlying asset to the other counterparty in the future. A put option is similar to a call option with one key difference: While both a call option and a put option provide the long position a right, a call option provides the right to purchase while a put option provides the right to sell.

Characteristics of a put option are as follows:

- The two counterparties to a put option are the long put and the short put.
- The price at which the long put has the right to sell the asset is known as the strike price or exercise price.
- A put option gives the long put the right, but not the obligation, to sell an underlying asset to the short put in the future. Hence, the long put can choose in the future whether or not to exercise its right to sell.
- The short put is obligated to purchase the underlying asset from the long put should the long put exercise its right to sell.
- The long put is also referred to as the "buyer" of the put option. The short put is also referred to as the "writer" or "seller" of the put option.
- The long put must pay a fee to the short put for providing the right. The fee is known as the "put premium." The put premium is paid at initiation. Other names for the put premium are the "put price" or simply the "premium."
- A European-style put option provides the long put the right to exercise only at expiration. An American-style put option provides the right to exercise either at expiration or before expiration. Both American-style and European-style put options trade in the United States.
- Put options trade both OTC and through exchanges.
- All details are specified at initiation, including:
  - The counterparties
  - The underlying asset
  - The strike price
  - The put premium
  - The expiration date
  - Whether the option is American-style or European-style

Figure 3.1 illustrates a European-style put option's cash flows. The exchange of strike price for the asset will only take place should the long put exercise its right to sell. Figure 3.1 illustrates a European-style put option, which can only be exercised at expiration. American-style options can be exercised either at expiration or before expiration.

For example, consider the following scenario:

- European-style put option
- Initiation = July 15
- Expiration date = September 15
- Premium = $1

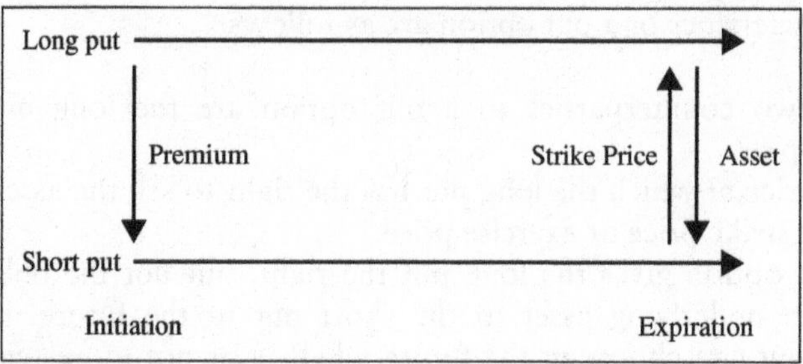

FIGURE 3.1 European-style put option cash flows

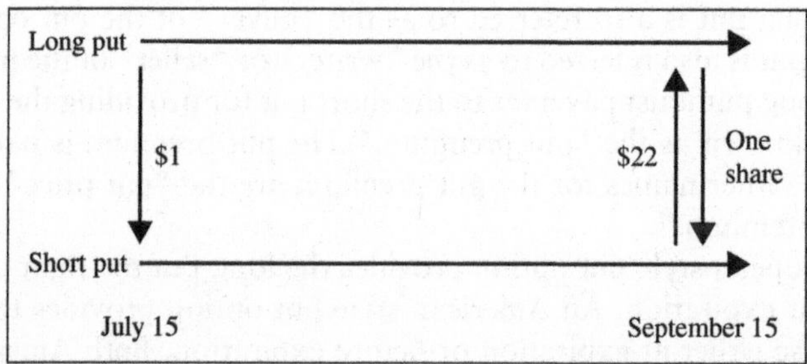

FIGURE 3.2 European-style put option cash flows example

- Underlying asset = one share
- Strike price = $22

Figure 3.2 illustrates this example.
As Figure 3.2 demonstrates:

- At initiation, July 15, the long put pays a $1 premium to the short put.
- On September 15 the long put has the right to sell one share for $22. The sale will only take place should the long put exercise its right to sell.

Knowledge check

Q 3.1: What is a put option?
Q 3.2: How is a put option different from a call option?
Q 3.3: What does the long put have the right to do?
Q 3.4: What is the short put's obligation?
Q 3.5: What is the "put premium"?

Q 3.6: What is the "put price"?
Q 3.7: Which position is the "buyer" of a put option?
Q 3.8: Which position is the "writer" of a put option?
Q 3.9: Which position is the "seller" of a put option?
Q 3.10: When does the long put position pay the premium to the short put position?

3.2 LONG PUT PAYOFF

The payoff associated with a long put is a function of whether the long put exercises its right:

- If the long put exercises the payoff is the difference between the strike price that the long put receives and the price of the underlying asset that it delivers.
- If the long put does not exercise the payoff is zero as no transaction takes place.

Let's explore the equation for the payoff at expiration associated with a long put. Let's define the following notation:

T = Expiration date
S_T = Underlying asset price at time T
K = Strike price

Table 3.1 details whether the long put will exercise and the resulting payoffs as a function of the relationship between the underlying asset price and the strike price. The payoff to the long put will never be less than

TABLE 3.1 Put option exercise decision and long put payoff

Relationship between S_T and K	The exercise decision at expiration	Long put payoff
$S_T \geq K$	The option will be not be exercised, as the strike price K that the long put can receive is less than or equal to S_T that it must deliver.	0
$S_T < K$	The option will be exercised, as the strike price K that the long put can receive is greater than S_T that it must deliver.	$K - S_T$

zero. Instead, the long put earns the larger of two possible payoffs: $K - S_T$ or zero.

The difference between the strike price and the underlying asset price is the put option's "intrinsic value." A put option only has intrinsic value when the underlying asset price is less than the strike price. Otherwise, the intrinsic value of a put option is zero.

An equation that describes the payoff to the long put is:

$$\textit{Long put payoff} = \max(K - S_T,\ 0)$$

Consider the following example:

- Strike price = \$22
- Underlying asset price at expiration = \$32

The payoff is:

$$\begin{aligned}\textit{Long put payoff} &= \max(K - S_T,\ 0)\\ &= \max(\$22 - \$32,\ 0)\\ &= 0\end{aligned}$$

Consider another example:

- Strike price = \$25
- Underlying asset price at expiration = \$23

The payoff is:

$$\begin{aligned}\textit{Long put payoff} &= \max(K - S_T,\ 0)\\ &= \max(\$25 - \$23,\ 0)\\ &= \$2\end{aligned}$$

Knowledge check

Q 3.11: When will the long put exercise the put option?
Q 3.12: When will the long put not exercise the put option?
Q 3.13: What is the long put's payoff should it exercise?
Q 3.14: What is the long put's payoff should it not exercise?
Q 3.15: What is a put option's intrinsic value?
Q 3.16: When does a put option have intrinsic value?
Q 3.17: What equation describes the long put's payoff?

3.3 LONG PUT P&L

To calculate the long put's P&L we have to take into account the premium that it pays at initiation. The long put's P&L and its relationship to the underlying asset price are detailed in Table 3.2. The notation p_0 is defined as follows:

p_0 = Put premium paid by long put to the short put at initiation.

The long put's P&L at expiration can be expressed as:

$$\textit{Long put P\&L} = \max(K - S_T,\ 0) - p_0$$

A positive value for the long put's P&L represents profit and a negative value represents loss.

Consider the following example:

- Strike price = \$122
- Underlying asset price at expiration = \$133
- Put premium paid at initiation = \$7

The P&L is:

$$\begin{aligned}\textit{Long put P\&L} &= \max(K - S_T,\ 0) - p_0 \\ &= \max(\$122 - \$133, 0) - \$7 \\ &= -\$7\end{aligned}$$

TABLE 3.2 Put option exercise decision and long put payoff and P&L

Relationship between S_T and K	The exercise decision at expiration	Long put payoff	Long put P&L
$S_T \geq K$	The option will be not be exercised, as the strike price K that the long put can receive is less than or equal to S_T that it must deliver.	0	$-p_0$
$S_T < K$	The option will be exercised, as the strike price K that the long put can receive is greater than S_T that it must deliver.	$K - S_T$	$K - S_T - p_0$

Consider another example:

- Strike price = \$118.50
- Underlying asset price at expiration = \$109
- Put premium paid at initiation = \$7

The P&L is:

$$\begin{aligned} \textit{Long put P\&L} &= \max(K - S_T,\ 0) - p_0 \\ &= \max(\$118.5 - \$109, 0) - \$7 \\ &= \$2.5 \end{aligned}$$

Knowledge check

Q 3.18: How does the long put's P&L differ from its payoff?
Q 3.19: What is the long put's P&L should it exercise?
Q 3.20: What is the long put's P&L should it not exercise?
Q 3.21: What equation describes the long put's P&L?

3.4 SHORT PUT PAYOFF

The short put is obligated to purchase the underlying asset from the long put should the long put exercise its right to sell. The payoff to the short put depends on whether the long put exercises or not:

- The long put exercises: The long put will exercise at expiration when the underlying asset price is less than the strike price. In this scenario the price of the underlying asset that the short put receives is less than the strike price that it pays.
- The long put does not exercise: If the underlying asset price is greater than the strike price, the long put will not exercise.

The payoff to the short put is presented in Table 3.3. The short put's payoff will never be greater than zero. The short put earns the smaller two possible payoffs, $S_T - K$ or zero.

The short put's payoff at expiration can be expressed as:

$$\textit{Short put payoff} = \min(S_T - K,\ 0)$$

TABLE 3.3 Put option exercise decision and short put payoff

Relationship between S_T and K	The exercise decision at expiration	Short put payoff
$S_T \geq K$	The option will be not be exercised, as the strike price K that the long put can receive is less than or equal to S_T that it must deliver.	0
$S_T < K$	The option will be exercised, as the strike price K that the long put can receive is greater than S_T that it must deliver.	$S_T - K$

Consider the following example:

- Strike price = \$115
- Underlying asset price at expiration = \$125

The payoff is:

$$\begin{aligned} \textit{Short put payoff} &= \min(S_T - K,\ 0) \\ &= \min(\$125 - \$115, 0) \\ &= 0 \end{aligned}$$

Consider another example:

- Strike price = \$33
- Underlying asset price at expiration = \$31

The payoff is:

$$\begin{aligned} \textit{Short put payoff} &= \min(S_T - K,\ 0) \\ &= \min(\$31 - \$33,\ 0) \\ &= -\$2 \end{aligned}$$

Knowledge check

Q 3.22: What is the short put's payoff should the long put exercise?
Q 3.23: What is the short put's payoff should the long put not exercise?
Q 3.24: What equation describes the short put's payoff?

3.5 SHORT PUT P&L

To calculate the short put's P&L, we have to take into account the premium that the short put receives at initiation. The short put's P&L and its relationship to the long put's exercise decision at expiration are shown in Table 3.4.

The short put's P&L at expiration can be expressed as:

$$\textit{Short put P\&L} = \min(S_T - K,\ 0) + p_0$$

A positive value for the short put's P&L represents profit while a negative value represents loss.

Consider the following example:

- Strike price = \$125
- Price of the underlying asset = \$134
- Put premium paid at initiation = \$8

The P&L is:

$$\begin{aligned}\textit{Short put P\&L} &= \min(S_T - K,\ 0) + p_0 \\ &= \min(\$134 - \$125,\ 0) + \$8 \\ &= \$8\end{aligned}$$

Consider another example:

- Strike price = \$102.50
- Underlying asset price = \$100
- Put premium paid at initiation = \$7

TABLE 3.4 Put option exercise decision and short put payoff and P&L

Relationship between S_T and K	The exercise decision at expiration	Short put payoff	Short put P&L
$S_T \geq K$	The option will be not be exercised, as the strike price K that the long put can receive is less than or equal to S_T that it must deliver.	0	p_0
$S_T < K$	The option will be exercised, as the strike price K that the long put can receive is greater than S_T that it must deliver.	$S_T - K$	$S_T - K + p_0$

The P&L is:

$$Short\ put\ P\&L = \min(S_T - K,\ 0) + p_0$$
$$= \min(\$100 - \$102.5,\ 0) + \$7$$
$$= \$4.5$$

Knowledge check

Q 3.25: How does the short put's P&L differ from its payoff?
Q 3.26: What is the short put's P&L should the long put exercise?
Q 3.27: What is the short put's P&L should the long put not exercise?
Q 3.28: What equation describes the short put's P&L?

3.6 LONG PUT P&L DIAGRAM

A P&L diagram, such as the one show in Figure 3.3, can be used to illustrate the P&L associated with a long put as a function of the underlying asset price at expiration.

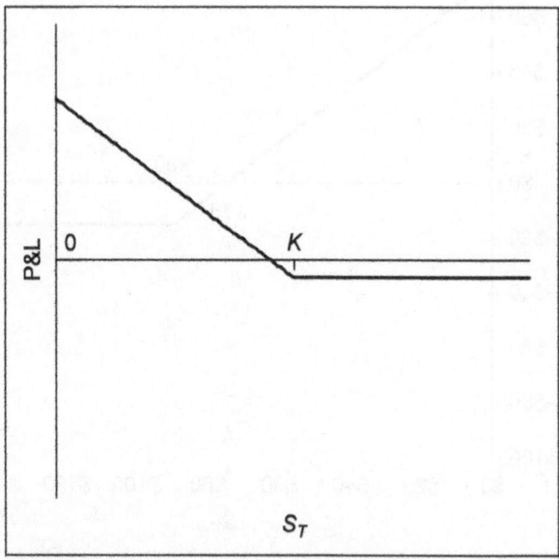

FIGURE 3.3 Long put P&L diagram

The long put's breakeven point occurs when the price of the underlying asset price delivered is equal to the combination of the strike received minus the premium paid at initiation. The breakeven point is:

$$\textit{Long put breakeven}: S_T = K - p_0$$

For example, consider the following scenario:

- Initiation = June 1
- Expiration = July 1
- Strike price = \$90
- Put premium = \$15

On June 1 we do not know what the underlying asset price will be on July 1. The P&L diagram in Figure 3.4 depicts the range of potential P&L that the long put may experience on July 1. If the underlying asset price is greater than \$90, then the P&L will be −\$15, representing a loss equal to the premium paid. The breakeven point occurs when the underlying asset price is \$90 − \$15 = \$75.

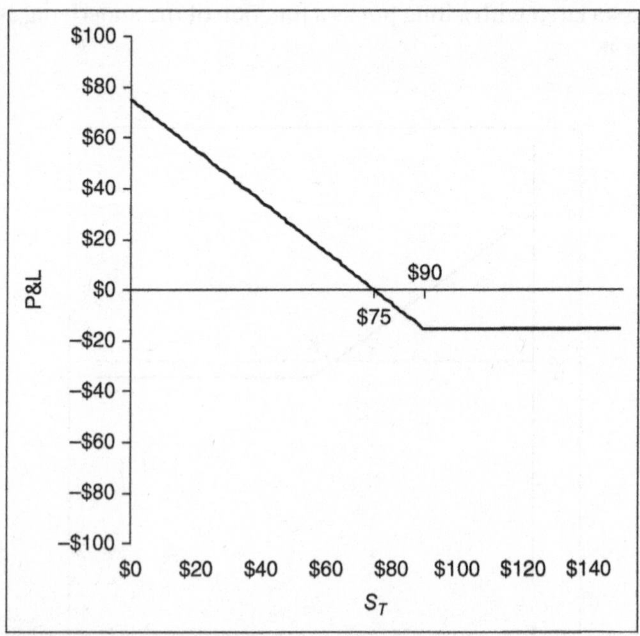

FIGURE 3.4 Long put P&L diagram example

Knowledge check

Q 3.29: What does a long put's P&L diagram look like?
Q 3.30: What is the positive P&L range for the long put?
Q 3.31: What is the negative P&L range for the long put?
Q 3.32: What is the long put's breakeven point?

3.7 SHORT PUT P&L DIAGRAM

A P&L diagram, such as the one shown in Figure 3.5, can be used to illustrate the P&L associated with a short put as a function of the underlying asset price at expiration.

The short put's breakeven point occurs where the price of the underlying asset received is equal to the combination of the strike paid minus the premium received at initiation. The short put's breakeven point is:

$$\textit{Short put breakeven}: S_T = K - p_0$$

The short put's breakeven point is identical to the long put's breakeven point. For the long put the breakeven point is the point where, as the underlying asset price increases, the long put switches from profit to loss, while for the short put the breakeven point is the point where it switches from loss to profit.

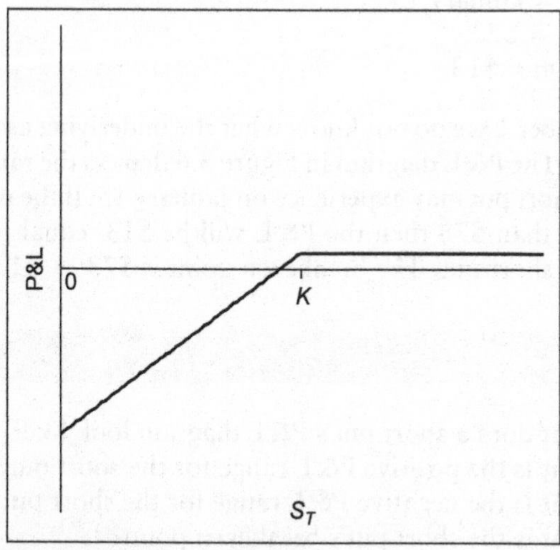

FIGURE 3.5 Short put P&L diagram

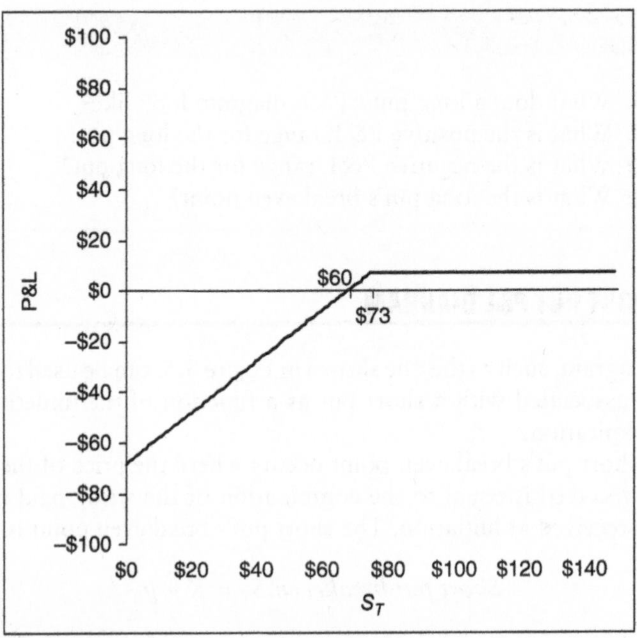

FIGURE 3.6 Short put P&L diagram example

For example, consider the following scenario:

- Initiation = November 1
- Expiration = January 15
- Strike price = $73
- Put premium = $13

On November 1 we do not know what the underlying asset price will be on January 15. The P&L diagram in Figure 3.6 depicts the range of potential P&L that the short put may experience on January 15. If the underlying asset price is greater than $73 then the P&L will be $13, equal to the premium received by the short put. The breakeven point is $73 − $13 = $60.

Knowledge check

Q 3.33: What does a short put's P&L diagram look like?
Q 3.34: What is the positive P&L range for the short put?
Q 3.35: What is the negative P&L range for the short put?
Q 3.36: What is the short put's breakeven point?

3.8 PUT OPTIONS ARE ZERO-SUM GAMES

Put options are zero-sum games as the net P&L is always zero. This is shown in Table 3.5.

This is also illustrated in Figure 3.7, which shows that the P&L diagrams for long and short puts are mirror images of each other. The net P&L across the long and short puts is zero.

For example, consider the following scenario:

- Put premium = \$5
- Strike price = \$75
- Underlying asset price at expiration = \$85

TABLE 3.5 Long and short put P&L and net P&L

Relationship between S_T and K	Long put P&L	Short put P&L	Net P&L
$S_T \geq K$	$-p_0$	p_0	0
$S_T < K$	$K - S_T - p_0$	$S_T - K + p_0$	0

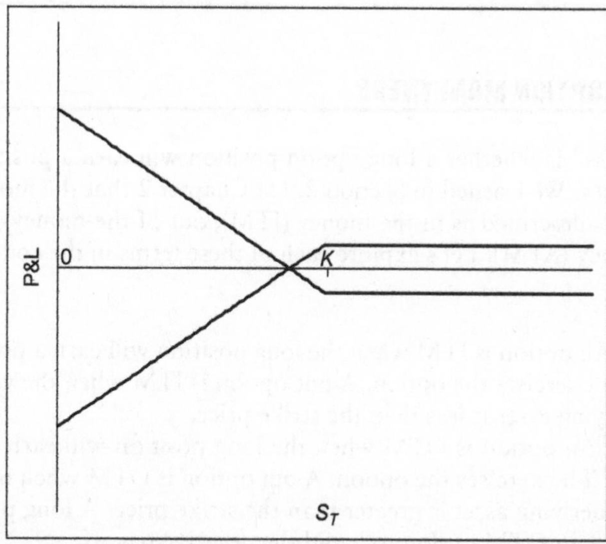

FIGURE 3.7 Put option as a zero-sum game

The P&L is:

$$
\begin{aligned}
\textit{Long put P\&L} &= \max(K - S_T,\ 0) - p_0 \\
&= \max(\$75 - \$85,\ 0) - \$5 \\
&= -\$5 \\
\textit{Short put P\&L} &= \min(S_T - K,\ 0) + p_0 \\
&= \min(\$85 - \$75,\ 0) + \$5 \\
&= \$5
\end{aligned}
$$

The net P&L across the long and short puts is:

$$
\begin{aligned}
\textit{Net put P\&L} &= \textit{long put P\&L} + \textit{short put P\&L} \\
&= -\$5 + \$5 \\
&= 0
\end{aligned}
$$

Knowledge check

Q 3.37: Why is a put option a zero-sum game?

3.9 PUT OPTION MONEYNESS

"Moneyness" is whether a long option position will earn a positive payoff if it exercises. We learned in Section 2.9 of Chapter 2 that the moneyness of an option is described as in-the-money (ITM), out-of-the-money (OTM), or at-the-money (ATM). Let's explore each of these terms in the context of put options:

- ITM: An option is ITM when the long position will earn a positive payoff if it exercises the option. A put option is ITM when the value of the underlying asset is less than the strike price.
- OTM: An option is OTM when the long position will earn a negative payoff if it exercises the option. A put option is OTM when the value of the underlying asset is greater than the strike price. A long put will not exercise an OTM option to avoid the negative payoff.
- ATM: An option is ATM if the long position will earn a payoff of zero if it exercises the option. A put option is ATM when the value of the asset

TABLE 3.6 Put option moneyness and long and short put payoff

Relationship between S_T and K	Moneyness	Long put payoff	Short put payoff
$S_T > K$	OTM	0	0
$S_T = K$	ATM	0	0
$S_T < K$	ITM	$K - S_T$	$S_T - K$

is equal to the strike price. The long put is indifferent about choosing to exercise an ATM option since the long put earns a payoff of zero whether it exercises or not.

Table 3.6 describes the relationship between the underlying asset price and the strike price, moneyness, and put option payoffs.

Knowledge check

Q 3.38: When is a put option ITM?
Q 3.39: When is a put option ATM?
Q 3.40: When is a put option OTM?

3.10 EXERCISING A PUT OPTION EARLY

A long position in an American-style put option has the right to exercise the option early. The advantage and disadvantages associated with early exercise of an American-style put option are as follows:

- Disadvantage: Optionality value is the value of having the right to decide whether to exercise or not. Early exercise destroys the optionality value of a put option. Hence, early exercise is disadvantageous.
- Disadvantage: The value of the underlying asset that the long put delivers will be higher if it exercises before the underlying asset pays income. For example, consider a situation where the underlying asset is a share that pays a dividend at some point in time between initiation and expiration. Stocks are worth more before their ex-dividend date as only those who hold the stock before the ex-dividend date receive the dividend. Hence, if the investor exercises the option before the ex-dividend date they will have to deliver a more valuable underlying asset. Hence, early exercise is disadvantageous.

- Advantage: Early exercise means the long put receives the strike price earlier. The earlier a payment is received, the higher the payment received in present value terms. Hence, early exercise is advantageous.

An investor should exercise an American-style put option if the advantage outweighs the disadvantages. Otherwise, the investor should not exercise.

We can contrast early exercise of put options to call options. In Section 2.10 of Chapter 2 we learned that European-style and American-style call options have identical premiums when the underlying asset pays no income, as early exercise is disadvantageous. In contrast, American-style put option premiums are higher than European-style put option premiums when the underlying asset does not pay income, as early exercise may be advantageous.

Knowledge check

Q 3.41: What are the disadvantages associated with early exercise of a put option?

Q 3.42: What is the advantage associated with early exercise of a put option?

Q 3.43: What is the relationship between the premiums of otherwise identical American-style and European-style put options?

3.11 COMPARISON OF PUT OPTIONS, CALL OPTIONS, AND FORWARDS/FUTURES

Table 2.7 of Chapter 2 compared the characteristics of call options and forwards/futures. Table 3.7 expands the comparison to include put options.

Knowledge check

Q 3.44: In what ways are long and short forwards/futures, calls, and puts similar?

Q 3.45: In what ways do long and short forwards/futures, calls, and puts differ?

TABLE 3.7 Comparison of forwards/futures, call option, and put option positions

	Long forward/ futures	Short forward/ futures	Long call option	Short call option	Long put option	Short put option
Right or obligation	Obligation	Obligation	Right	Obligation	Right	Obligation
Buy or sell	Buy	Sell	Buy	Sell	Sell	Buy
Premium	None	None	Paid	Received	Paid	Received
Name for purchase price	Forward: Forward price Futures: Futures price		Strike price or exercise price		Strike price or exercise price	
Payoff	$S_T - F$	$F - S_T$	$\max(S_T - K, 0)$	$\min(K - S_T, 0)$	$\max(K - S_T, 0)$	$\min(S_T - K, 0)$
Positive payoff range	$S_T > F$	$S_T < F$	$S_T > K$	None	$S_T < K$	None
Negative payoff range	$S_T < F$	$S_T > F$	None	$S_T > K$	None	$S_T < K$
Zero payoff point	$S_T = F$	$S_T = F$	$S_T = K$	$S_T = K$	$S_T = K$	$S_T = K$
P&L at expiration	$S_T - F$	$F - S_T$	$\max(S_T - K, 0) - c_0$	$\min(K - S_T, 0) + c_0$	$\max(K - S_T, 0) - p_0$	$\min(S_T - K, 0) + p_0$
Profit range	$S_T > F$	$S_T < F$	$S_T - K - c_0 > 0$	$K - S_T + c_0 > 0$	$K - S_T - p_0 > 0$	$S_T - K + p_0 < 0$
Loss range	$S_T < F$	$S_T > F$	$S_T - K - c_0 < 0$	$K - S_T + c_0 < 0$	$K - S_T - p_0 < 0$	$S_T - K + p_0 > 0$
Breakeven point	$S_T = F$	$S_T = F$	$S_T = K + c_0$	$S_T = K + c_0$	$S_T = K - p_0$	$S_T = K - p_0$
ITM range	Concept of moneyness not applicable		$S_T > K$		$S_T < K$	
ATM point			$S_T = K$		$S_T = K$	
OTM range			$S_T < K$		$S_T > K$	

KEY POINTS

- A put option is an agreement between two counterparties in which one of the counterparties has the right to sell an underlying asset to the other counterparty in the future. The long put has the right to sell. The short put is obligated to purchase the underlying asset from the long put should the long put exercise its right to sell. The strike price at which the transaction will take place is agreed-upon at initiation. The long put pays a premium at initiation in order to obtain its right.
- Put options trade both OTC and through exchanges. Put options are either American-style or European-style.
- At expiration the long put will exercise its right to sell when the underlying asset price is less than the strike price. Its payoff is therefore the larger of either zero or the strike price minus the underlying asset price. The short put's payoff is the smaller of either zero or the underlying asset price minus the strike price.
- The long put's P&L at expiration is its payoff minus the put premium paid at initiation. The short put's P&L at expiration is its payoff plus the put premium received at initiation.
- Both long and short put options break even when the underlying asset price is equal to the strike price minus the premium.
- Put options are zero-sum games, as any profit that one of the counterparties receives is exactly equal to the loss that the other counterparty suffers.
- A put option is ITM when the long put will earn a positive payoff through exercising the option, OTM when the long put will not exercise as it would earn a negative payoff, and ATM if the long put will earn a payoff of zero if it exercises the option.
- An investor should exercise an American-style put option if the advantage of receiving the strike price earlier is more valuable than both the loss of optionality value and the need to deliver a more expensive asset.

PART

Two

Pricing and Valuation

CHAPTER 4

Useful Quantitative Concepts

INTRODUCTION

In the first three chapters of this book, we've been introduced to forwards, futures, and options. In the next few chapters we will learn about pricing, valuation, and sensitivity concepts. To comprehend these concepts it is essential to be familiar with several quantitative concepts related to interest rates, time value of money, volatility, and probability distributions. In this chapter we will explore these concepts.

After you read this chapter you will be able to

- Explain compounding conventions.
- Explain continuous compounding.
- Calculate future value and present value.
- Understand how to use the exponential function.
- Understand how to use the natural logarithm function.
- Identify continuously compounded interest rates.
- Estimate volatility using historical standard deviation.
- Interpret volatility.
- Calculate annualized standard deviation.
- Use the standard normal cumulative distribution function.
- Explain z-scores.

This chapter does not assume that you have sophisticated quantitative skills beyond the ability to add, subtract, multiply, divide, and raise to a power, or finance skills beyond rudimentary familiarity with the concept of time value of money. This chapter will introduce you to the quantitative concepts that you will need to comprehend the pricing, valuation, and sensitivity concepts that will be presented in subsequent chapters.

4.1 COMPOUNDING CONVENTIONS

Consider the following scenario: An investor wishes to invest \$1,000 for one year with a financial institution that offers to investors a stated interest rate of 5%. This stated interest rate suggests that the value of the individual's position at the end of the year will be \$1,050, as the following calculation shows:

$$\textit{Future value after one year} = \$1{,}000 \times 105\% = \$1{,}050$$

This scenario is illustrated in Figure 4.1. The \$50 increase in value is reflective of the 5% interest rate received. This scenario is simple and easy to understand: The stated rate is 5%, and the investor receives exactly 5%, or \$50, of the invested amount.

In practice, understanding interest rates and the time value of money is rarely so simple. Continuing our example, imagine a situation where the financial institution indicates that the interest rate is 5% for a one year investment, but also adds the following: The stated interest rate of 5% assumes the investor will invest for six months at 2.5% (half of 5%) and then immediately withdraw the proceeds and reinvest at 2.5% for another six months.

The future value is:

$$\begin{aligned}\textit{Future value after six months} &= \$1{,}000 \times 102.5\% \\ &= \$1{,}025 \\ \textit{Future value after one year} &= \$1{,}025 \times 102.5\% \\ &= \$1{,}050.625\end{aligned}$$

The original \$1,000 grows into \$1,025 after six months. The \$1,025 is then immediately reinvested and grows into \$1,050.625 after one year,

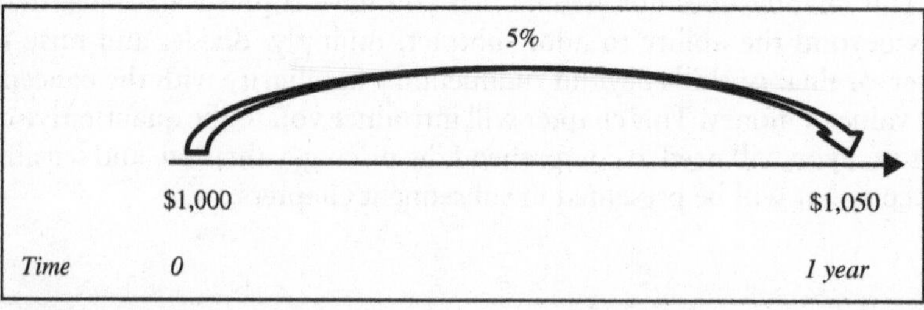

FIGURE 4.1 Growth of an investment that receives 5% over one year

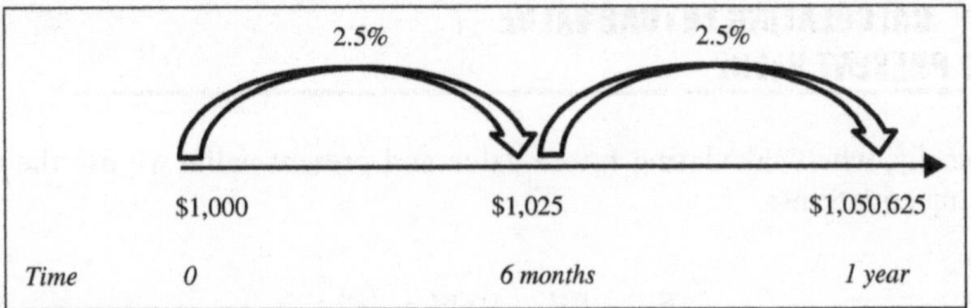

FIGURE 4.2 Growth of an investment that receives 2.5% for two six-month periods

as illustrated in Figure 4.2. While the stated rate is 5%, the investor earns $50.625, representing a 5.0625% effective interest rate.

The convention in financial markets is to communicate interest rates assuming withdrawal and reinvestment a certain number of times per year. The "compounding frequency" is the frequency with which a stated interest rate is assumed to be invested during a given year. In our first scenario, the interest rate of 5% was communicated assuming annual compounding. In our second scenario, the interest rate was communicated assuming semi-annual compounding. This convention means that when communicating a stated interest rate, one must indicate the frequency with which the interest rate is compounded.

In different markets different compounding conventions are used. For example, in the U.S. bond market the typical assumption is that yields are compounded semi-annually. In analysis of forwards, futures, and options neither annual nor semi-annual compounding is typically assumed. Instead, the typical assumption is that interest rates are compounded an *infinite* number of times per year. Hence the investment is assumed to be reinvested an infinite number of times per year, earning each time at an infinitesimally low interest rate equal to the stated rate divided by infinity. An interest rate that is compounded an infinite number of times per year is referred to as a "continuously compounded" interest rate.

Knowledge check

Q 4.1: What is the "compounding frequency"?

Q 4.2: How frequently are interest rates typically assumed to be compounded in analysis of forwards, futures, and options?

Q 4.3: What is a continuously compounded interest rate?

4.2 CALCULATING FUTURE VALUE AND PRESENT VALUE

Typically, when calculating future value and present value we use the following equations:

$$FV = PV \cdot \left(100\% + \frac{r}{m}\right)^{m \cdot t}$$

$$PV = \frac{FV}{\left(100\% + \frac{r}{m}\right)^{m \cdot t}}$$

where

FV = future value
PV = present value
r = interest rate
m = compounding frequency per year
t = years until the cash flow is received

For example, consider a scenario where the future value is \$3,500, the future point in time is in 30 years, the interest rate is 2%, and the compounding frequency is twelve times per year. The present value is:

$$PV = \frac{FV}{\left(100\% + \frac{r}{m}\right)^{m \cdot t}}$$
$$= \frac{\$3,500}{\left(100\% + \frac{2\%}{12}\right)^{12 \cdot 30}}$$
$$= \$1,921.80$$

Since in derivatives markets we assume the interest rate is compounded an infinite number of times per year (i.e., continuously compounded), this means that m is equal to infinity (∞). It is difficult to implement calculations when one of the inputs is infinity! Fortunately, there is another method through which we can calculate present value and future value when interest rates are continuously compounded that does not require us to input infinity into an equation. This method uses a function that is known as the "exponential function."

4.2.1 The exponential function

Before learning how to calculate future value and present value using the exponential function, let's explore the function itself. Like any function, a number is input into the exponential function, and it provides an output. The formal notation for the exponential function is:

$$Output = e^{Input}$$

The exponential function can be implemented using Excel through inputting values into Excel's EXP( ) function. For example, an input of 1 into the exponential function results in:

$$\begin{aligned} Output &= e^{Input} \\ &= e^{1} \\ &= \text{EXP}(1) \\ &= 2.7182 \end{aligned}$$

As another example, an input of −0.5 into the exponential function results in:

$$\begin{aligned} Output &= e^{Input} \\ &= e^{-0.5} \\ &= \text{EXP}(-0.5) \\ &= 0.6065 \end{aligned}$$

Three notable characteristics of the exponential function are as follows:

$$e^{A} \cdot e^{B} = e^{A+B}$$
$$e^{0} = 1$$
$$\frac{1}{e^{A}} = e^{-A}$$

4.2.2 Time value of money when interest rates are continuously compounded

When the stated interest rate is continuously compounded, the methods through which we calculate future value and present value are:

$$FV = PV \cdot e^{r \cdot t}$$
$$PV = FV \cdot e^{-r \cdot t}$$

In these equations, r is the continuously compounded interest rate.

Consider the following example: The future value of a cash flow to be received in 2.5 years is \$20,000. The continuously compounded interest rate is 5%. What is the present value of the cash flow? The answer is:

$$\begin{aligned} PV &= FV \cdot e^{-r \cdot t} \\ &= \$20,000 \cdot e^{-5\% \cdot 2.5} \\ &= \$20,000 \cdot \text{EXP}(-5\% \cdot 2.5) \\ &= \$17,649.94 \end{aligned}$$

Let's consider another example: The present value of a cash flow is \$2.54. The continuously compounded interest rate is 2.18%. What is the future value of the cash flow in 4.5 years? The answer is:

$$\begin{aligned} FV &= PV \cdot e^{r \cdot t} \\ &= \$2.54 \cdot e^{2.18\% \cdot 4.5} \\ &= \$2.54 \cdot \text{EXP}(2.18\% \cdot 4.5) \\ &= \$2.80 \end{aligned}$$

Knowledge check

Q 4.4: How is present value calculated if the interest rate is not continuously compounded?

Q 4.5: How is future value calculated if the interest rate is not continuously compounded?

Q 4.6: What function in Excel is used for exponential function calculations?

Q 4.7: To what is $e^A \cdot e^B$ equal?

Q 4.8: To what is e^0 equal?

Q 4.9: To what is $\frac{1}{e^A}$ equal?

Q 4.10: How is present value calculated if the interest rate is continuously compounded?

Q 4.11: How is future value calculated if the interest rate is continuously compounded?

4.3 IDENTIFYING CONTINUOUSLY COMPOUNDED INTEREST RATES

In the previous section we learned how to calculate future value and present value when interest rates are continuously compounded. It is also useful to know how to reverse the process: If we know the present value and future value, we can identify the continuously compounded interest rate. To do so we have to first learn about another function known as the "natural logarithm function." Once we understand this function, we can then learn how it can be used to identify the continuously compounded interest rate.

4.3.1 The natural logarithm function

The inverse of the exponential function is the natural logarithm function. The formal notation for the natural logarithm function is:

$$Output = \ln(Input)$$

Since the natural logarithm function is the inverse of the exponential function it follows:

$$A = \ln(e^A)$$

The natural logarithm function can be implemented using Excel through inputting values into Excel's LN( ) function. Consider the following example: If e^A is equal to 20, to what is A equal? The answer is:

$$\begin{aligned} A &= \ln(e^A) \\ &= \text{LN}(20) \\ &= 2.9957 \end{aligned}$$

4.3.2 Using the natural logarithm function to identify continuously compounded interest rates

We can use the natural logarithm function to identify the continuously compounded interest rate if we know the present and future values. After all, we know that:

$$FV = PV \cdot e^{r \cdot t}$$

It follows that:

$$e^{r \cdot t} = \frac{FV}{PV}$$

We apply the natural logarithm to both sides of the above equation, resulting in the following:

$$r \cdot t = \ln\left(\frac{FV}{PV}\right)$$

We isolate the continuously compounded interest rate through dividing both sides of the above equation by t, resulting in the following equation for the continuously compounded interest rate:

$$r = \frac{\ln\left(\frac{FV}{PV}\right)}{t}$$

For example, the future value of a cash flow to be received in ten years is \$10,000. The present value of the cash flow is \$6,000. What is the continuously compounded interest rate? The answer is:

$$r = \frac{\ln\left(\frac{FV}{PV}\right)}{t}$$

$$= \frac{\ln\left(\frac{\$10,000}{\$6,000}\right)}{10}$$

$$= 5.11\%$$

Knowledge check

Q 4.12: What is the inverse of the exponential function?
Q 4.13: What function in Excel is used for natural logarithm function calculations?
Q 4.14: How is the continuously compounded interest rate identified when the present and future values are known?

4.4 VOLATILITY AND HISTORICAL STANDARD DEVIATION

Volatility is the degree to which asset returns are dispersed over time. A common method through which one can measure volatility for a given asset is through estimating the historical standard deviation of the asset's return. As the word "historical" communicates, historical standard deviation estimates standard deviation over a historical period of time.

In this section we will learn how to calculate historical standard deviation. In the next sections we will learn how to interpret standard deviation and calculate annualized standard deviation.[1]

The calculation of historical standard deviation requires five steps, as follows:

- Step 1: Calculate the average return over the sample period.
- Step 2: Calculate the amount by which each return observation deviates from the average return.
- Step 3: Calculate the square of each deviation.
- Step 4: Calculate the average of the squared deviations. The average of the squared deviations is known as the variance.
- Step 5: Calculate the square root of the variance to find the standard deviation.

There are two types of historical standard deviation one can calculate: population standard deviation and sample standard deviation.

- Population standard deviation: Standard deviation calculated using an entire population of observations
- Sample standard deviation: Standard deviation calculated using a sample from a larger population

Historical standard deviation is typically calculated using a sample of the asset's return history; hence, we typically calculate sample standard deviation.

When calculating sample standard deviation, one calculates the average in step 4 through summing together the squared deviations and dividing by the number of observations minus one. Conversely, population standard deviation simply divides by the number of observations.

Let's explore the calculation of historical standard deviation using the following example: Consider a situation where the daily returns listed in Table 4.1 are observed for a hypothetical security over a 15-day period.

Let's calculate the historical standard deviation. Since our 15 days of returns are a sample of the asset's return history, we will calculate the sample standard deviation.

Table 4.2 presents the calculation of standard deviation and shows that the standard deviation is 1.2907%.

[1]In Section 5.9 of Chapter 5 we will learn another method through which volatility can be estimated known as "implied volatility."

TABLE 4.1 15-day sample

Day	Daily Return
1	1.06%
2	−0.23%
3	0.01%
4	1.50%
5	1.23%
6	−0.34%
7	−0.02%
8	−2.54%
9	−1.50%
10	2.50%
11	0.21%
12	−0.05%
13	−0.96%
14	1.34%
15	1.14%

TABLE 4.2 Calculation of historical standard deviation

Day	Daily Return	Deviation	Squared Deviation
1	1.06%	0.8367%	0.0070%
2	−0.23%	−0.4533%	0.0021%
3	0.01%	−0.2133%	0.0005%
4	1.50%	1.2767%	0.0163%
5	1.23%	1.0067%	0.0101%
6	−0.34%	−0.5633%	0.0032%
7	−0.02%	−0.2433%	0.0006%
8	−2.54%	−2.7633%	0.0764%
9	−1.50%	−1.7233%	0.0297%
10	2.50%	2.2767%	0.0518%
11	0.21%	−0.0133%	0.0000%
12	−0.05%	−0.2733%	0.0007%
13	−0.96%	−1.1833%	0.0140%
14	1.34%	1.1167%	0.0125%
15	1.14%	0.9167%	0.0084%
Avg. daily return =	0.2233%	Variance =	0.0167%
		Standard deviation =	1.2907%

Details of the steps used to calculate the standard deviation are as follows:

- Step 1: Calculate the average return over the sample period. To calculate the average return, we sum together the return observations and divide by the number of observations. The sum of the return observations is 3.35%, and the number of observations is fifteen. Hence, the average daily return is:

$$\frac{3.35\%}{15} = 0.2233\%$$

- Step 2: Calculate the amount by which each return observation deviates from the average return. To calculate the deviation, we subtract the average return (calculated in step 1) from the given return observation. For example, the day one daily return is 1.06%. Subtracting the average daily return of 0.2233% from 1.06% results in the deviation for day one of:

$$1.06\% - 0.2233\% = 0.8367\%$$

- Step 3: Calculate the square of each deviation. We calculate the square of the deviations by taking the deviations (calculated in step 2) and raising them to the power of two. For example, the square of the day one deviation is:

$$0.8367\%^2 = 0.0070\%$$

- Step 4: Calculate the variance. The variance is the average squared deviation. To calculate the average squared deviation, we sum together the squared deviations (calculated in step 3) and divide by the number of observations minus one. The sum of the squared deviations observations is 0.2332%, and the number of observations is fifteen. Hence, the average squared deviation is:

$$\frac{0.2332\%}{15 - 1} = 0.0167\%$$

- Step 5: Calculate the square root of the variance to find the standard deviation. Since the variance is 0.0167%, the square root of the variance is:

$$\sqrt{0.0167\%} = 1.2907\%$$

We can conclude that the standard deviation of the daily returns is 1.2907%.

The calculations through which we estimate historical standard deviation can be expressed as:

$$\sigma = \sqrt{\frac{\sum_{i=1}^{n} (r_i - \bar{r})^2}{n-1}}$$

where

σ = standard deviation
$\bar{r}$ = average return = $\sum_{i=1}^{n} \frac{r_i}{n}$
r_i = return observation i
n = number of observations

Sample standard deviation can be calculated using the STDEV.S( ) function in Excel:

$$\sigma = \text{STDEV.S}(1.06\%, -0.23\%, 0.01\%, 1.50\%, 1.23\%, -0.34\%, -0.02\%, -2.54\%, -1.50\%, 2.50\%, 0.21\%, -0.05\%, -0.96\%, 1.34\%, 1.14\%) = 1.2907\%$$

Knowledge check

Q 4.15: What is volatility?
Q 4.16: What does historical standard deviation measure?
Q 4.17: What are the steps through which to calculate historical standard deviation?
Q 4.18: What is population standard deviation?
Q 4.19: What is sample standard deviation?
Q 4.20: How do the calculations of sample and population standard deviations differ?
Q 4.21: What is variance?
Q 4.22: What is the equation for historical sample standard deviation?
Q 4.23: Which function do we use to calculate sample standard deviation in Excel?

4.5 INTERPRETATION OF STANDARD DEVIATION

At the simplest level, we can compare standard deviations of different investments to explore their relative riskiness. Investments with higher standard deviations are characterized as riskier. Hence:

- An investment with higher standard deviation than another is riskier, as its returns are more widely dispersed.
- As the standard deviation of a given investment increases or decreases over time, this indicates that the given investment has become riskier or less risky, respectively, than before.

At a more sophisticated level, we can use standard deviation together with average return to develop deeper understanding of the riskiness of an asset. If we assume that an asset's returns are normally distributed, we can take advantage of the following facts about normally distributed returns:

- There is a 50% probability that the return will be greater than the average return.
- There is a 50% probability that the return will be less than the average return.
- There is a 68.27% probability that the return will fall between one standard deviation above and below the average return.
- There is a 95.45% probability that the return will fall between two standard deviations above and below the average return.
- There is a 99.73% probability that the return will fall between three standard deviations above and below the average return.

For example, consider the following scenario:

- $\bar{r} = 10\%$
- $\sigma = 20\%$

Since the average return is 10% and the standard deviation is 20%, we can conclude:

- There is a 50% probability that the return will be greater than the average return of 10% and a 50% probability that the return will be less than the average return of 10% (illustrated in Figure 4.3).

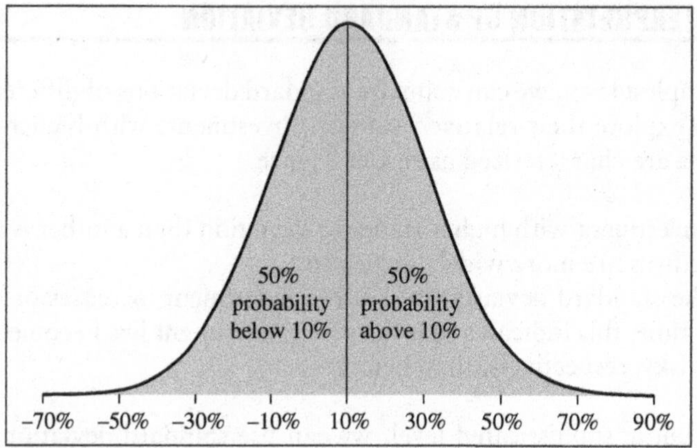

FIGURE 4.3 Probability of return above or below the average return

- There is a 68.27% probability that the return will fall between −10% and 30% (illustrated in Figure 4.4). This is because:
  - One standard deviation below the average return is equal to 10% − 20% = −10%.
  - One standard deviation above the average return is equal to 10% + 20% = 30%.
- There is a 95.45% probability that the return will fall between −30% and 50% (illustrated in Figure 4.5). This is because:
  - Two standard deviations below the average return is equal to 10% − 2 × 20% = −30%.

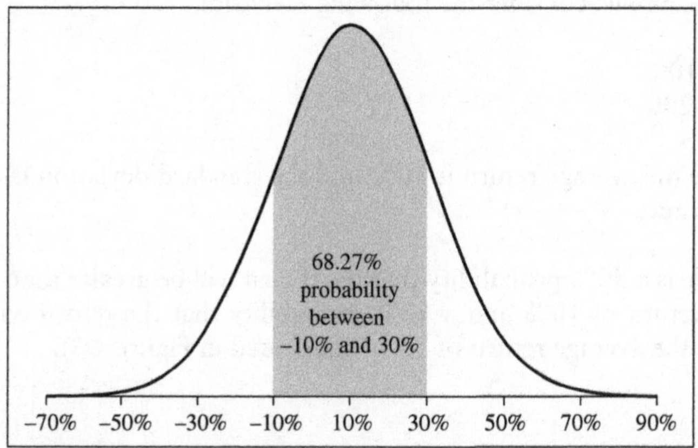

FIGURE 4.4 Probability of return within one standard deviation of the average return

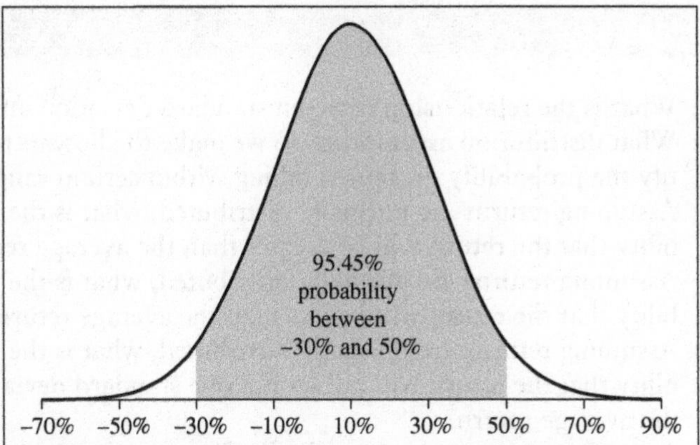

FIGURE 4.5 Probability of return within two standard deviations of the average return

- Two standard deviations above the average return is equal to 10% + 2 × 20% = 50%.

- There is a 99.73% probability that the return will fall between –50% and 70% (illustrated in Figure 4.6). This is because:
  - Three standard deviations below the average return is equal to 10% – 3 × 20% = –50%.
  - Three standard deviations above the average return is equal to 10% + 3 × 20% = 70%.

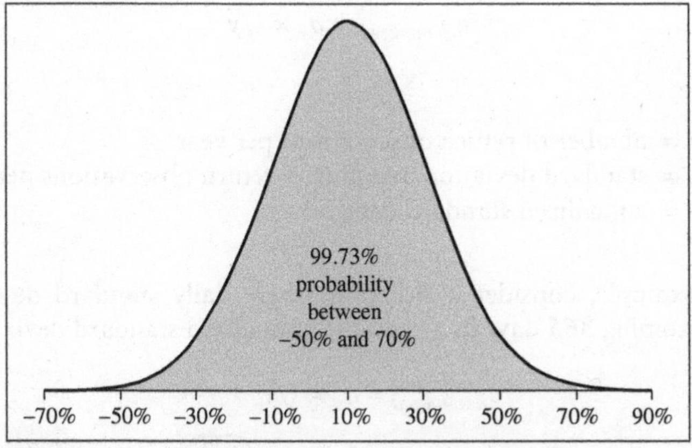

FIGURE 4.6 Probability of return within three standard deviations of the average return

Knowledge check

Q 4.24: What is the relationship between standard deviation and risk?
Q 4.25: What distribution assumption do we make to allow us to identify the probability of returns falling within certain ranges?
Q 4.26: Assuming returns are normally distributed, what is the probability that the return will be greater than the average return?
Q 4.27: Assuming returns are normally distributed, what is the probability that the return will be less than the average return?
Q 4.28: Assuming returns are normally distributed, what is the probability that the return will fall within one standard deviation of the average return?
Q 4.29: Assuming returns are normally distributed, what is the probability that the return will fall within two standard deviations of the average return?
Q 4.30: Assuming returns are normally distributed, what is the probability that the return will fall within three standard deviations of the average return?

4.6 ANNUALIZED STANDARD DEVIATION

The return observations used to calculate standard deviation may be daily, weekly, or monthly returns. Yet models typically require the input of the standard deviation of annual returns, known as the annualized standard deviation. To convert any standard deviation into the annualized standard deviation, we use the following equation:

$$\sigma_{annualized} = \sigma_y \times \sqrt{y}$$

where

y = number of return observations per year
σ_y = standard deviation assuming y return observations per year
$\sigma_{annualized}$ = annualized standard deviation

For example, consider a situation where daily standard deviation is 1.5%. Assuming 365 days in a year, the annualized standard deviation is:

$$\begin{aligned}\sigma_{annualized} &= \sigma_y \times \sqrt{y} \\ &= 1.5\% \times \sqrt{365} \\ &= 28.66\%\end{aligned}$$

Knowledge check

Q 4.31: What is annualized standard deviation?
Q 4.32: How does one calculate annualized standard deviation?

4.7 THE STANDARD NORMAL CUMULATIVE DISTRIBUTION FUNCTION

In this section we will explore the standard normal cumulative distribution function. The standard normal cumulative distribution function can allow us to identify the probability that the return will fall below a given return, assuming the following:

- Returns are normally distributed
- The average return is zero
- The standard deviation of returns is 100%

The standard normal cumulative distribution function requires an input and provides an output. The formal notation for the standard normal cumulative distribution function is:

$$Output = \mathrm{N}(Input)$$

The input and output are as follows:

- Input: A given return that is input into the function
- Output: The probability that the return will fall below the given return

The standard normal cumulative distribution function is implemented using the NORM.S.DIST( ) function in Excel. The NORM.S.DIST( ) function requires two inputs:

- The first input is the given return. In other words, the given return for which we are trying to find the probability of the return falling below.
- The second input is simply the number "1." This tells the NORM.S .DIST( ) function to calculate the cumulative distribution.

For example, for a given asset the average return is zero and the standard deviation is 100%. What is the probability of the return falling below a given return of 10%?

We use the standard normal cumulative distribution function to identify that the probability that returns fall below the given return of 10% is:

$$\begin{aligned}\text{Probability of returns below } 10\% &= \text{N}(10\%)\\ &= \text{NORM.S.DIST}(10\%, 1)\\ &= 53.98\%\end{aligned}$$

Here's another example: For a given stock the average return is zero and the standard deviation is 100%. What is the probability of the return falling below a given return of –5%?

We use the standard normal cumulative distribution function to identify that the probability that returns fall below the given return of –5% is:

$$\begin{aligned}\text{Probability of returns below } -5\% &= \text{N}(-5\%)\\ &= \text{NORM.S.DIST}(-5\%, 1)\\ &= 48.01\%\end{aligned}$$

The probability that the return falls *above* a given return is equal to 1 – N( ). Further:

$$1 - \text{N}(A) = \text{N}(-A)$$

For example, we can identify the probability of the return falling above a given return of –5%, assuming the average return is zero and the standard deviation is 100%:

$$\begin{aligned}\text{Probability of returns above } -5\% &= 1 - \text{N}(-5\%)\\ &= 1 - \text{NORM.S.DIST}(-5\%, 1)\\ &= 51.99\%\end{aligned}$$

Further:

$$\begin{aligned}1 - \text{NORM.S.DIST}(-5\%, 1) &= \text{NORM.S.DIST}(-(-5\%), 1)\\ &= 51.99\%\end{aligned}$$

Knowledge check

Q 4.33: What function in Excel is used to implement the standard normal cumulative distribution function?

Q 4.34: What does the standard normal cumulative distribution function assume?

Q 4.35: How do we identify the probability of return below a given return?
Q 4.36: How do we identify the probability of return above a given return?
Q 4.37: What is the relationship between $1 - N(A)$ and $N(-A)$?

4.8 THE Z-SCORE

While the standard normal cumulative distribution function is useful, the fact that it assumes that the average return is zero and the standard deviation is 100% is problematic. After all, typically the average return is *not* zero, and the standard deviation is *not* 100%.

When the average return is not zero and the standard deviation is not 100%, one can still use the standard normal cumulative distribution function to calculate the probability of the return falling below a given return. To do so, we first calculate the "z-score" for the given return:

$$\textit{z-score} = \frac{\textit{given return} - \textit{average return}}{\textit{standard deviation of return}}$$

We then input the z-score into the standard normal cumulative distribution function to calculate the probability of returns falling below the given return.

For example, consider an asset with an average return of 15% and standard deviation of 30%. What is the probability of the return falling below 65%? The answer is:

$$\begin{aligned}\textit{z-score} &= \frac{\textit{given return} - \textit{average return}}{\textit{standard deviation of return}}\\ &= \frac{65\% - 15\%}{30\%}\\ &= 166.67\%\\ \text{Probability of returns below } 65\% &= \text{N}(166.67\%)\\ &= \text{NORM.S.DIST}(166.67\%, 1)\\ &= 95.22\%\end{aligned}$$

Let's consider another example. As in the previous example, consider an asset with an average return of 15% and standard deviation of 30%. What is the probability of returns falling below 5%? The answer is:

$$z\text{-}score = \frac{given\ return - average\ return}{standard\ deviation\ of\ return}$$

$$= \frac{5\% - 15\%}{30\%}$$

$$= -33.33\%$$

$$\text{Probability of returns below } 5\% = \text{N}(-33.33\%)$$

$$= \text{NORM.S.DIST}(-33.33\%, 1)$$

$$= 36.94\%$$

Knowledge check

Q 4.38: What is a "z-score"?

Q 4.39: How can we use the standard normal cumulative distribution function for any average return and standard deviation?

KEY POINTS

- The compounding frequency is the frequency with which a stated interest rate is assumed to be invested during a given year.
- In analysis of forwards, futures, and options, the typical assumption is that interest rates are compounded an infinite number of times per year, known as "continuously compounded" interest rates.
- Future value and present value can be calculated using the exponential function when interest rates are continuously compounded.
- Continuously compounded interest rates can be identified from present and futures values using the natural logarithm function.
- Volatility is the degree to which asset returns are dispersed over time. Volatility can be measured using historical standard deviation.
- Historical standard deviation is the square root of the average squared deviation of returns from the average return.
- Investments with higher standard deviation are characterized as riskier. Further, assuming normal distribution, we can use standard deviation to identify the probability that returns will fall within various ranges.
- Annualized standard deviation can be calculated through multiplying the standard deviation associated with a given period by the square root of the frequency of the return observations per year.

- The standard normal cumulative distribution function can identify the probability that the return will fall below a given return assuming returns are normally distributed, the average return is zero, and the standard deviation of returns is 100%.
- When the average return is not zero and the standard deviation is not 100%, one can calculate the probability of the return falling below a given return through inputting the z-score into the standard normal cumulative distribution function. The z-score is calculated through subtracting the average return from the given return and dividing the resulting value by the standard deviation.

CHAPTER 5

Introduction to Pricing and Valuation

INTRODUCTION

This chapter introduces the pricing and valuation of forwards and options. The expressions "price" and "value" may superficially seem similar. In reality, however, "price" is the price at which counterparties agree to transact, while "value" is the value of holding a given position.

After you read this chapter, you will be able to

- Understand the concepts of forward price and forward value.
- Understand the concepts of strike price and option value.
- Compare and contrast price and value concepts across forwards and options.
- Describe the determinants of forward value and forward price.
- Calculate forward value and forward price.
- Describe the determinants of option value.
- Calculate option value using the Black-Scholes model.
- Understand the assumptions that underlie the Black-Scholes model.
- Explain implied volatility.
- Describe volatility term structures, smiles, skews, and surfaces.

The scope of this chapter

The purpose of this chapter is to provide an understanding of pricing and valuation and introduce the methods through which pricing and valuation are implemented. There are numerous variations of forwards, futures, and options, and this chapter is not intended to provide a comprehensive quantitative overview of each. Instead, we will focus on the following key products:

- Forwards where the underlying asset does not provide income, such as a dividend or coupon
- European-style call options and put options where the underlying asset does not provide income

While limited to these products, this chapter will provide conceptual and quantitative insights into the determinants of value and price and the impact of changes in these determinants. This chapter can also be a foundation for the exploration of quantitative pricing and valuation techniques for a wide variety of products.

Note as well that this chapter focuses on presenting equations that show *how* price and value are calculated. In the subsequent chapter we will delve into these equations to develop insight as to *why* they represent price and value.

5.1 THE CONCEPTS OF PRICE AND VALUE OF A FORWARD CONTRACT

"Price" is the price at which counterparties agree to transact, while "value" is the value of holding a given position. Let's explore the concepts of price and value in the context of a forward:

- Forward price: The price at which the long forward is obligated to purchase the underlying asset from the short forward. The forward price is determined at initiation and does not change.
- Forward value: The value of holding a position in a forward at a given point in time during the life of the forward.

A forward is designed to have zero value at initiation. To ensure this, a forward price is chosen that is agreeable, or "fair," to both counterparties. It is "fair" because at initiation neither of the counterparties perceive their position to have positive value (i.e., an asset) or negative value (i.e., a liability). There is only one price that is fair to both counterparties. In this chapter we will learn how to estimate this forward price.

While the forward is designed to have zero value at initiation, after initiation the determinants of forward value will, inevitably, change. As we will learn in detail in this chapter, the determinants of a forward's value are the underlying asset price, the forward price, the time to expiration, and the continuously compounded risk-free interest rate. Changes in one or more of these determinants will inevitably benefit one of the counterparties and harm the other. Forward value will no longer be zero. Instead, the forward value will be one of the following:

- Asset: The forward value of the counterparty that benefits from changes in the determinants of value will now be positive (an asset).
- Liability: The forward value of the counterparty that is harmed by changes in the determinants of value will now be negative (a liability).

For example, consider a forward that obligates the long forward to purchase an underlying asset from the short forward in three months for $103:

- The forward price is $103. This is the forward price chosen that is "fair" to both counterparties.
- At initiation, the forward value is zero for both the long and short positions.
- The long forward's value will either increase above or decrease below zero as the determinants of value change.
- Since a forward is a zero-sum game, the positive forward value of one of the positions will always be exactly offset by the negative forward value of the other position.

In this chapter we will learn how to estimate forward value.

Knowledge check

Q 5.1: What is "price"?
Q 5.2: What is "value"?
Q 5.3: What do we call the "price" of a forward?
Q 5.4: What do we call the "value" of a forward?
Q 5.5: When is the forward price determined?
Q 5.6: How is the forward price determined?
Q 5.7: Does the forward price change during the life of the forward?
Q 5.8: What is the forward value at initiation?
Q 5.9: Does the forward value change during the life of the forward?
Q 5.10: When is a forward an asset?
Q 5.11: When is a forward a liability?
Q 5.12: What is the relationship between the long and short forward values?

5.2 THE CONCEPTS OF PRICE AND VALUE OF AN OPTION

We've seen that "price" is the price at which counterparties transact, while "value" is the value of holding a given position. In an option, the price is called the strike price, while the value is called the option value:

- Strike price: The price at which the long position has the right to transact the underlying asset with the short position. The strike price is determined at initiation and does not change.

- Option value: The value of holding a position in an option at a given point in time during the life of the option.

Unlike a forward, an option is not designed to have zero value at initiation. Option value is positive for the long position (which has the right to exercise) and negative for the short position (which is obligated to transact should the long position exercise). Hence, option value is an asset for the long position and a liability for the short position.

During the life of an option its value will change as the determinants of value change. As we will learn in detail in this chapter, the determinants of an option's value are the underlying asset price, the strike price, the underlying asset volatility, the time to expiration, and the continuously compounded risk-free interest rate. Further, since an option is a zero-sum game, the positive option value of the long position will always be exactly offset by the negative option value of the short position.

The option premium reflects the amount that the two counterparties believe is "fair," given the terms of the option agreement. The premium should be equal to the option's value. If differences between the premium and option value occur, this suggests that the market is mispricing the premium.

For example, consider a call option that provides the long call the right to purchase 100 ounces of gold from the short call in three months for $110,000. The long call pays a call premium of $13,000 upfront in order to have this right. In this example:

- The strike price at which the two counterparties will transact in the future should the long call exercise its right to purchase is $110,000.
- At initiation, the call premium is $13,000. This indicates that the market values the long call's right to purchase at $13,000. Hence, at initiation, the long call has an asset valued at $13,000, while the short call position has a liability valued at $13,000.
- As time progresses, the option value can increase or decrease as the determinants of option value change.

A potential source of confusion is the use of the terms "call price" and "put price." These terms *do not* refer to the strike price. Instead, they are alternative names for the premium. Another potential source of confusion is that another name for the strike price is "exercise price."

Knowledge check

Q 5.13: What do we call the "price" of an option?
Q 5.14: What do we call the "value" of an option?

Q 5.15: When is the strike price determined?
Q 5.16: Does the strike price change during the life of the option?
Q 5.17: Is an option designed to have zero value at initiation?
Q 5.18: What is the relationship between an option's premium and value?
Q 5.19: For which counterparty is the option value an asset?
Q 5.20: For which counterparty is the option value a liability?
Q 5.21: What is the relationship between the long call's value and the short call's value?

5.3 COMPARISON OF PRICE AND VALUE CONCEPTS FOR FORWARDS AND OPTIONS

Table 5.1 compares price and value concepts for forwards and options.

TABLE 5.1 Comparison of price and value concepts for forwards and options

	Forward	Option
What is the price called?	Forward price	Strike price or exercise price
When is the price determined?	Initiation	Initiation
Does the price change during its life?	No	No
What is the value called?	Forward value	Option value: Option premium/price should be equal to option value.
What is the value at initiation?	Zero	Not zero: Asset for the long position and liability for the short position.
Is there only one possible price?	Yes, the price that ensures that the forward value is zero at initiation.	No, any strike price can be chosen. The strike price chosen will impact the option premium.
What is the long position's value post-initiation?	Either positive (an asset) or negative (a liability): Value will fluctuate.	Positive (an asset): Value will fluctuate.
What is the short position's value post-initiation?	Either positive (an asset) or negative (a liability): Value will fluctuate.	Negative (a liability): Value will fluctuate.
Is it a zero-sum game?	Yes	Yes

Knowledge check

Q 5.22: In what ways are price and value concepts similar and different for forwards and options?

5.4 FORWARD VALUE

Forward value is the value of holding a position in a forward at a given point in time during the life of the forward. While forward value will be zero at initiation, after initiation forward value will either be positive (an asset) or negative (a liability). Let's explore an equation through which one can calculate forward value. In the next chapter we will explore *why* this equation represents forward value.

The value of a forward is, by design, zero at initiation. Following initiation, the value of the forward from the long forward's perspective is:

$$f_t = S_t - F \cdot e^{-r_t \cdot (T-t)}$$

where

f_t = Long forward value
F = Forward price
t = Valuation date
T = Expiration date
$T - t$ = Years between the valuation date and the expiration date
S_t = Underlying asset price on the valuation date
r_t = Continuously compounded risk-free interest rate on the valuation date

This equation is from the long forward's perspective. Forwards are zero-sum games. Hence, the short forward's value is $-f_t$, the negative of the long forward's value.

We see that the determinants of forward value are:

- The underlying asset price on the valuation date
- The forward price
- The risk-free interest rate on the valuation date
- The time to expiration

In Chapters 8–10 we will explore forward value sensitivity to changes in the determinants of forward value.

Consider the following example: An investor has entered into a long forward. The forward has 0.25 years remaining until expiration. The continuously compounded risk-free interest rate is 8%. The forward price is \$1,000. The underlying asset price is \$950. What is the forward value? Is the forward an asset or a liability? The answer is:

$$\begin{aligned} f_t &= S_t - F \cdot e^{-r_t \cdot (T-t)} \\ &= \$950 - \$1{,}000 \cdot e^{-8\% \cdot 0.25} \\ &= -\$30.20 \end{aligned}$$

Hence, the long forward's value is –\$30.20 and the short forward's value is \$30.20. Since the long forward value is negative and the short forward value is positive the long forward has a liability and the short forward has an asset.

Let's consider another example: An investor has entered into a long forward. The forward has 1.25 years remaining until expiration. The continuously compounded risk-free interest rate is 2%. The forward price associated is \$90. The underlying asset price is \$95. What is the forward value? Is the forward an asset or a liability? The answer is:

$$\begin{aligned} f_t &= S_t - F \cdot e^{-r_t \cdot (T-t)} \\ &= \$95 - \$90 \cdot e^{-2\% \cdot 1.25} \\ &= \$7.22 \end{aligned}$$

Hence, the long forward's value is \$7.22 and the short forward's value is –\$7.22. Since the long forward value is positive and the short forward value is negative, the long forward has an asset and the short forward has a liability.

Knowledge check

Q 5.23: How do we calculate long forward value?
Q 5.24: How do we calculate short forward value?

5.5 FORWARD PRICE

Forward price is the price at which the long forward is obligated to purchase the underlying asset from the short forward at the expiration of the forward. The forward price is set at initiation and does not change over the life of the forward. Let's explore the equation through which one can calculate the forward price. In the next chapter we will learn *why* this equation represents forward price.

The forward price that is set at initiation should be equal to:

$$F = S_0 \cdot e^{r_0 \cdot (T - t_0)}$$

where

F = Forward price
t_0 = Initiation date
T = Expiration date
$T - t_0$ = Years between the initiation date and the expiration date
S_0 = Underlying asset price on the initiation date
r_0 = Continuously compounded risk-free interest rate on the initiation date

We see that the determinants of forward price are:

- The underlying asset price on the initiation date
- The risk-free interest rate on the initiation date
- The time to expiration

This equation helps us understand what the forward price *should* be. In other words, it represents the *theoretical* forward price. In reality, the two counterparties will negotiate a forward price, and the negotiated forward price may differ from the theoretical forward price.

Consider the following example: A forward contract obligates the long forward to purchase an underlying asset from the short forward in three years. The underlying asset price at initiation is \$85, and the continuously compounded risk-free interest rate is 5%. What is the forward price? The answer is:

$$\begin{aligned} F &= S_0 \cdot e^{r_0 \cdot (T - t_0)} \\ &= \$85 \cdot e^{5\% \cdot 3} \\ &= \$98.76 \end{aligned}$$

Let's consider another example: A forward contract obligates the long forward to purchase an underlying asset from the short forward in one month. The underlying asset price at initiation is \$1,000, and the continuously compounded risk-free interest rate is 2%. What is the forward price? The answer is:

$$\begin{aligned} F &= S_0 \cdot e^{r_0 \cdot (T - t_0)} \\ &= \$1,000 \cdot e^{2\% \cdot \frac{1}{12}} \\ &= \$1,001.67 \end{aligned}$$

Knowledge check

Q 5.25: How do we calculate forward price?

5.6 OPTION VALUE: THE BLACK-SCHOLES MODEL

Option value is the value of holding a position in an option at a given point in time during the life of the option. Let's explore equations through which one can calculate an option's value.

The option valuation equations that we will explore can be used to determine the option value at any point in time during an option's life. They can also be used to determine the fair premium at initiation.

The academics that initially derived these equations are Fischer Black, Myron Scholes, and Robert Merton.[1] These equations are therefore known as the "Black-Scholes-Merton model" or the "Black-Scholes model." In the subsequent chapter we will learn to understand *why* this model represents option value.

The value of a long call option and long put option are:

$$c_t = S_t \cdot \mathrm{N}(d_1) - K \cdot e^{-r_t \cdot (T-t)} \cdot \mathrm{N}(d_2)$$
$$p_t = K \cdot e^{-r_t \cdot (T-t)} \cdot \mathrm{N}(-d_2) - S_t \cdot \mathrm{N}(-d_1)$$

where

$$d_1 = \frac{\ln\left(\frac{S_t}{K}\right) + \left(r_t + \frac{\sigma_t^2}{2}\right) \cdot (T-t)}{\sigma_t \cdot \sqrt{T-t}}$$

$$d_2 = d_1 - \sigma_t \cdot \sqrt{T-t}$$

[1]Please see F. Black and M. Scholes "The Pricing of Options and Corporate Liabilities," *The Journal of Political Economy* 81, no. 3 (1973): 637–659 and R. C. Merton, "Theory of Rational Option Pricing," *Bell Journal of Economics and Management Science* 4, no. 1 (1973): 141–183.

and

c_t = Long call value
p_t = Long put value
K = Strike price
t = Valuation date
T = Expiration date
$T - t$ = Years between the valuation date and the expiration date
S_t = Underlying asset price on the valuation date
r_t = Continuously compounded risk-free interest rate on the valuation date
σ_t = Underlying asset volatility on the valuation date
N( ) = The standard normal cumulative distribution function

"Underlying asset volatility" is the volatility of the returns of the underlying asset on the valuation date.

We see that the determinants of option value are:

- The underlying asset price on the valuation date
- The strike price
- The underlying asset volatility on the valuation date
- The risk-free interest rate on the valuation date
- The time to expiration

In Chapters 8–10 we will learn about option value sensitivity to changes in the determinants of option value.

Since options are zero-sum games, the short position's value is simply the negative of the long call's value; and, therefore, short call value is $-c_t$ and short put value is $-p_t$.

Knowledge check

Q 5.26: How do we calculate long call value?
Q 5.27: How do we calculate short call value?
Q 5.28: How do we calculate long put value?
Q 5.29: How do we calculate short put value?
Q 5.30: To what is d_1 equal?
Q 5.31: To what is d_2 equal?

5.7 CALCULATING THE BLACK-SCHOLES MODEL

The Black-Scholes model is quite complex. In this section we will explore a four-step process through which option value can be calculated using the Black-Scholes model. The process varies somewhat for each position, as detailed in Table 5.2.

As Table 5.2 indicates, the first two steps are identical for all positions: identification of the inputs (step 1) and calculation of d_1 and d_2 (step 2). Step 3 depends on whether the position is a call or a put. Step 4 is different for each position.

Consider the following example: An investor holds a long call that gives the right to purchase an underlying asset for \$800 in one year. The current underlying asset price is \$1,000. The continuously compounded risk-free interest rate is 5%. The underlying asset volatility is 25%. What is the option's value?

Let's use the four-step process to answer this question, as follows:

- Step 1: Identify the inputs:

$$\begin{aligned} S_t &= \$1{,}000 \\ K &= \$800 \\ r_t &= 5\% \\ T-t &= 1 \\ \sigma_t &= 25\% \end{aligned}$$

- Step 2: Calculate d_1 and d_2:

$$d_1 = \frac{\ln\left(\frac{S_t}{K}\right) + \left(r_t + \frac{\sigma_t^2}{2}\right) \cdot (T-t)}{\sigma_t \cdot \sqrt{T-t}}$$

$$= \frac{\ln\left(\frac{\$1,000}{\$800}\right) + \left(5\% + \frac{25\%^2}{2}\right) \cdot 1}{25\% \cdot \sqrt{1}}$$

$$= 1.2176$$

TABLE 5.2 Option value calculation process

	Long call	Short call	Long put	Short put
Step 1	Identify the inputs: S_t, K, r_t, σ_t, and $T-t$			
Step 2	Calculate d_1 and d_2			
Step 3	Calculate $N(d_1)$ and $N(d_2)$		Calculate $N(-d_1)$ and $N(-d_2)$	
Step 4	Calculate c_t	Calculate $-c_t$	Calculate p_t	Calculate $-p_t$

$$\begin{aligned} d_2 &= d_1 - \sigma_t \cdot \sqrt{T-t} \\ &= 1.2176 - 25\% \cdot \sqrt{1} \\ &= 0.9676 \end{aligned}$$

- Step 3: Calculate $N(d_1)$ and $N(d_2)$:

$$\begin{aligned} N(d_1) &= \text{NORM.S.DIST}(1.2176, 1) \\ &= 0.8883 \\ N(d_2) &= \text{NORM.S.DIST}(0.9676, 1) \\ &= 0.8334 \end{aligned}$$

- Step 4: Calculate c_t:

$$\begin{aligned} c_t &= S_t \cdot N(d_1) - K \cdot e^{-r_t \cdot (T-t)} \cdot N(d_2) \\ &= \$1,000 \cdot 0.8883 - \$800 \cdot e^{-5\% \cdot 1} \cdot 0.8334 \\ &= \$254.13 \end{aligned}$$

Let's consider another example: An investor holds a long put that gives the right to sell an underlying asset for $95 in 0.25 years. The current underlying asset price is $85. The continuously compounded risk-free interest rate is 2%. The underlying asset volatility is 65%. What is the option value?

We once again break the answer into four steps.

- Step 1: Identify the inputs:

$$\begin{aligned} S_t &= \$85 \\ K &= \$95 \\ r_t &= 2\% \\ T - t &= 0.25 \\ \sigma_t &= 65\% \end{aligned}$$

- Step 2: Calculate d_1 and d_2:

$$\begin{aligned} d_1 &= \frac{\ln\left(\frac{S_t}{K}\right) + \left(r_t + \frac{\sigma_t^2}{2}\right) \cdot (T-t)}{\sigma_t \cdot \sqrt{T-t}} \\ &= \frac{\ln\left(\frac{\$85}{\$95}\right) + \left(2\% + \frac{65\%^2}{2}\right) \cdot 0.25}{65\% \cdot \sqrt{0.25}} \\ &= -0.1643 \end{aligned}$$

$$
\begin{aligned}
d_2 &= d_1 - \sigma_t \cdot \sqrt{T-t} \\
&= -0.1643 - 65\% \cdot \sqrt{0.25} \\
&= -0.4893
\end{aligned}
$$

- Step 3: Calculate $\text{N}(-d_1)$ and $\text{N}(-d_2)$:

$$
\begin{aligned}
\text{N}(-d_1) &= \text{NORM.S.DIST}(-(-0.1643), 1) \\
&= 0.5653 \\
\text{N}(-d_2) &= \text{NORM.S.DIST}(-(-0.4893), 1) \\
&= 0.6877
\end{aligned}
$$

- Step 4: Calculate p_t:

$$
\begin{aligned}
p_t &= K \cdot e^{-r_t \cdot (T-t)} \cdot \text{N}(-d_2) - S_t \cdot \text{N}(-d_1) \\
&= \$95 \cdot e^{-2\% \cdot 0.25} \cdot 0.6877 - \$85 \cdot 0.5653 \\
&= \$16.96
\end{aligned}
$$

Knowledge check

Q 5.32: What are the steps through which we calculate long call value?
Q 5.33: What are the steps through which we calculate short call value?
Q 5.34: What are the steps through which we calculate long put value?
Q 5.35: What are the steps through which we calculate short put value?

5.8 BLACK-SCHOLES MODEL ASSUMPTIONS

Quantitative models make assumptions to allow the simplification of the complexity of reality into equations. This applies to the Black-Scholes model as well. Key assumptions that underlie the Black-Scholes model include:

- Options are European-style and not American-style.
- The underlying asset pays no income.
- There are no "frictions" such as transaction costs or taxes.
- The risk-free interest rate is known and constant.
- The underlying asset volatility is known and constant.
- Returns are normally distributed.

All of these assumptions can be problematic. Many options are American-style, not European-style. Many options are written on underlying assets that pay income. There are frequently significant frictions. The risk-free rate and volatility are unlikely to be constant. Returns may not be normally distributed.

Clearly, there are many ways that these assumptions can be violated. The models that we have explored are baseline models. There are many variations and advancements of the Black-Scholes model to allow one to address situations where the assumptions do not hold. A popular alternative to the Black-Scholes model is the binomial option pricing model, which we will explore in Chapter 7.

Knowledge check

Q 5.36: What are the key assumptions of the Black-Scholes model?
Q 5.37: In what ways are the assumptions of the Black-Scholes model problematic?
Q 5.38: Are there alternatives to the Black-Scholes model?

5.9 IMPLIED VOLATILITY

To implement the Black-Scholes model we input five variables and the model outputs option value as illustrated in Table 5.3.

Interestingly, we can reverse-engineer the Black-Scholes model to identify the underlying asset volatility. After all, when an option trades on a market we know its premium. Through reverse-engineering of the Black-Scholes model, we can input the premium and output the underlying asset volatility, as illustrated in Table 5.4. This output is referred to as "implied volatility."

Estimation of implied volatility can be challenging. While academics have derived equations that approximate implied volatility,[2] professional data sources identify the implied volatility using sophisticated numerical analysis techniques such as the Newton-Raphson method.

[2]For example, see C. J. Corrado and T. W. Miller, "A Note on a Simple, Accurate Formula to Compute Implied Standard Deviations," *Journal of Banking & Finance* 20 (1996): 595–603.

TABLE 5.3 Option value as the output of the Black-Scholes model

Inputs	Black-Scholes	Output
Underlying asset price Strike price Risk-free interest rate Time to expiration Underlying asset volatility	→	Option value

TABLE 5.4 Implied volatility as the output of the reverse-engineered Black-Scholes model

Inputs	Reverse-Engineered Black-Scholes	Output
Underlying asset price Strike price Risk-free interest rate Time to expiration Option premium	→	Implied volatility

5.9.1 Volatility term structure

A "volatility term structure" is a graph of the implied volatility across time to expiration. Figure 5.1 presents an example of a volatility term structure. The horizontal axis is time to expiration, while the vertical axis is the annualized implied volatility. As Figure 5.1 shows, implied volatility differs across different times to expiration. In this example, the term structure is characterized by higher implied volatility for longer times to expiration. In practice, the term structure may slope upwards, downwards, or fluctuate.

Why does the implied volatility vary over time to expiration? An explanation is that the market forms different expectations of the underlying asset volatility across different periods in the future. After all, implied volatility reflects the market's expectation of the underlying asset volatility between initiation and expiration of the given option from which it is extracted. One's expectations of volatility can differ across different periods in the future.

The volatility term structure is a useful tool through which to learn about the market's expectation of underlying asset volatility in the future. For example, an upward sloping volatility term structure indicates that the market expects volatility to increase, while a downward sloping volatility term structure indicates that the market expects volatility to decrease.

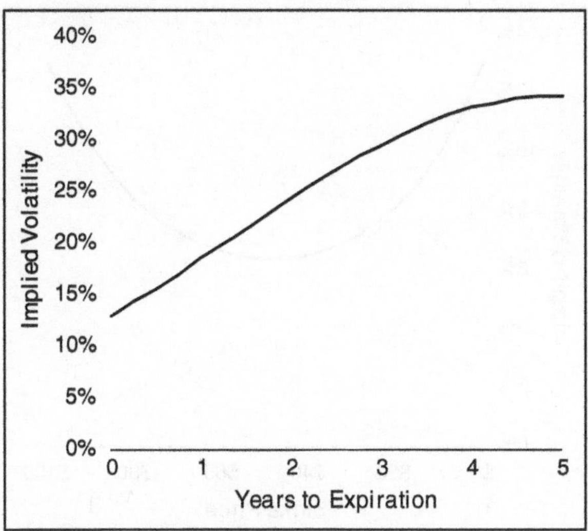

FIGURE 5.1 Volatility term structure example

5.9.2 Volatility smile and volatility skew

A "volatility smile" or "volatility skew" is a graph of implied volatility across strike prices.[3] The terms "smile" and "skew" describe the shapes one may observe when looking at a graph of implied volatility across strike prices. Figure 5.2 presents a volatility smile example and Figure 5.3 presents a volatility skew example. While these are common shapes, other shapes, such as frowns, can be observed as well.

The existence of volatility smiles and skews is interesting. After all, the Black-Scholes model requires the input of the underlying asset volatility into the model and outputs the premium. The implication is that when we reverse the process we should output the same implied volatility regardless of the strike price. The existence of volatility smiles and skews show that, in fact, the implied volatility varies as a function of the strike price. This effect may occur because the Black-Scholes model is imperfect. Alternatively, it may occur because the key input used to identify implied volatility—the premium—is incorrectly valued by the market.

5.9.3 Volatility surface

One may wish to explore both the volatility term structure and the volatility smile/skew simultaneously. To do so, one can use a three-dimensional graph

[3]The volatility skew is also referred to as the "volatility smirk."

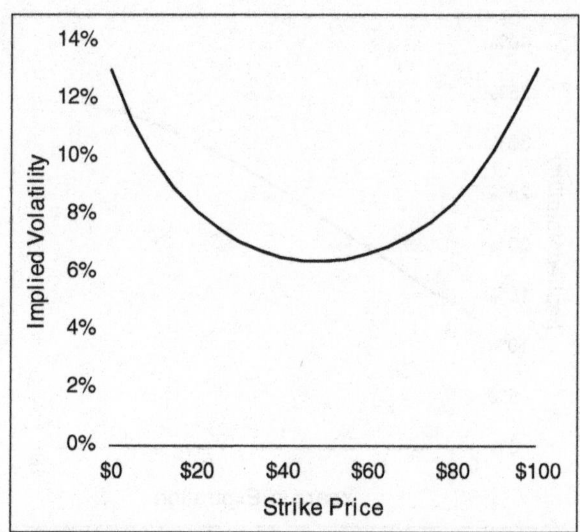

FIGURE 5.2 Volatility smile example

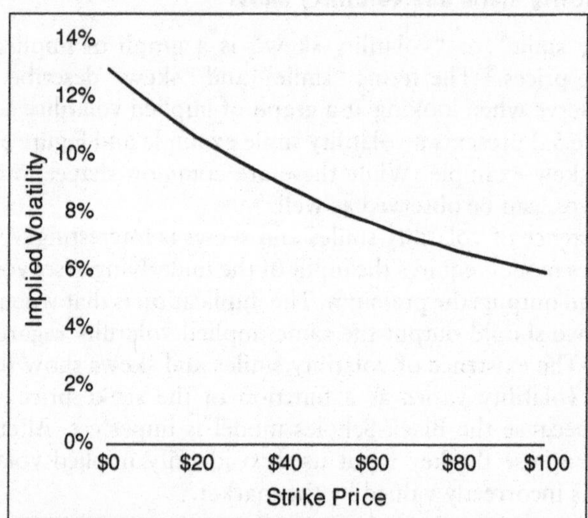

FIGURE 5.3 Volatility skew example

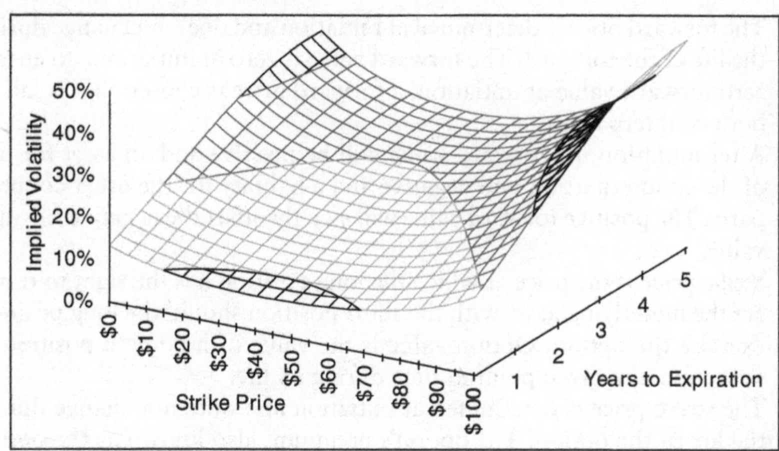

FIGURE 5.4 Volatility surface example

of implied volatility across both time to expiration and strike price, referred to as a "volatility surface." Figure 5.4 presents an example of a volatility surface.

Knowledge check

Q 5.39: What is implied volatility?
Q 5.40: How is the implied volatility identified?
Q 5.41: What is a volatility term structure?
Q 5.42: Why is a volatility term structure interesting?
Q 5.43: What does an upward sloping volatility term structure indicate?
Q 5.44: What does a downward sloping volatility term structure indicate?
Q 5.45: What is a volatility smile?
Q 5.46: What is a volatility skew?
Q 5.47: What is a volatility surface?
Q 5.48: Why are volatility smiles and skews interesting?

KEY POINTS

- Forward price is the price at which the long forward is obligated to purchase the underlying asset from the short forward at expiration. Forward value is the value of holding a position in a forward at a given point in time during its life.

- The forward price is determined at initiation and does not change during the life of the forward. The forward value is zero at initiation. To ensure zero forward value at initiation, a forward price is chosen that is fair to both counterparties.
- After initiation the forward value will be positive and an asset for one of the counterparties, and negative and a liability for the other counterparty. The positive forward value will exactly offset the negative forward value.
- Strike price is the price at which the long position has the right to transact the underlying asset with the short position should the long position exercise the option. Option value is the value of holding a position in an option at a given point in time during its life.
- The strike price is determined at initiation and does not change during the life of the option. The option's premium, also known as the option price, should be equal to the option's value. The option value is positive and an asset for the long option, and negative and a liability for the short option.
- Forward value is a function of the forward price, the time to expiration, the underlying asset price, and the continuously compounded risk-free interest rate. The forward price is a function of the time to expiration, the underlying asset price, and the continuously compounded risk-free interest rate.
- Option value can be estimated using the Black-Scholes model. It is a function of the strike price, the time to expiration, the underlying asset price, the continuously compounded risk-free interest rate, and the underlying asset volatility. A four-step process can be used to calculate option values using the Black-Scholes model.
- The Black-Scholes model makes a number of assumptions, including the key assumptions that the option is European-style; the underlying asset pays no income; there are no "frictions" such as transaction costs or taxes; the risk-free interest rate is known and constant; the underlying asset volatility is known and constant; and returns are normally distributed. All of these assumptions can be problematic. There are many variations and advancements of the Black-Scholes model to allow one to address situations where the assumptions do not hold.
- Through reverse-engineering the Black-Scholes model, we can input the premium and output the underlying asset volatility, known as the "implied volatility." The exact implied volatility can be identified using numerical analysis techniques.
- A volatility term structure is a graph of implied volatility across time to expiration. A "volatility smile" or "volatility skew" is a graph that illustrates implied volatility across strike prices. A "volatility surface" is a three-dimensional graph of implied volatility across both time to expiration and strike prices.

CHAPTER 6

Understanding Pricing and Valuation

INTRODUCTION

In the previous chapter we explored equations through which to calculate forward price, forward value, and option value. In this chapter we will develop an understanding of *why* the equations introduced in the previous chapter represent price and value. The insights provided in this chapter are grounded in the following simple idea: "Value" is the present value of expected future payoff.

After you read this chapter you will be able to

- Understand that forward value and option value are the present value of their expected future payoff at expiration.
- Explain the concepts of risk-aversion, risk-neutrality, and risk-neutral valuation.
- Explain why we use the risk-free rate to form expectations of payoff and to discount.
- Describe equations through which to calculate several key probabilities and expected values.
- Understand why the pricing and valuation equations introduced in the previous chapter represent price and value.

The scope and plan of this chapter

Following the approach used in the previous chapter, we will focus on the following key products:

- Forwards where the underlying asset does not provide income
- European-style call options and put options where the underlying asset does not provide income

TABLE 6.1 Learning objectives of each section of this chapter

Section	Learning objective
Section 6.1	Review of payoff, price, and value equations
Section 6.2	Introduction to the idea that value is the present value of future cash flows
Section 6.3	Introduction to the concepts of "risk-aversion," "risk-neutrality," "risk-neutral valuation," and why we use the risk-free rate
Section 6.4	Exploration of several important probability and expected value concepts
Section 6.5	Understanding the Black-Scholes equation for call value
Section 6.6	Understanding the Black-Scholes equation for put value
Section 6.7	Understanding the equation for forward value
Section 6.8	Understanding the equation for forward price

The insights provided in this chapter are not intended to be comprehensive derivations of the pricing and valuation equations. We will take advantage of certain probability and expected value concepts and will not derive these concepts.

Please note as well that there are a number of perspectives through which one can understand price and value equations. This chapter focuses on a perspective that is straightforward and understandable even for those without significant quantitative backgrounds: value as the present value of expected payoff. This chapter will allow for a meaningful understanding of price and value and can be a foundation for further exploration of quantitative pricing and valuation techniques.

Each stage of the learning that will take place in this chapter builds on the previous learning. The learning objectives of each section of this chapter are outlined in Table 6.1.

6.1 REVIEW OF PAYOFF, PRICE, AND VALUE EQUATIONS

In this chapter we will relate price and value to expected payoffs. Table 6.2 summarizes the equations through which one can calculate payoff, value, and price. Strike prices do not require calculations, as the two counterparties can choose any strike price that they wish.

TABLE 6.2 Review of payoff, price, and value equations

Position	Payoff	Value	Forward/ strike price
Long forward	$S_T - F$	$f_t = S_t - F \cdot e^{-r_t \cdot (T-t)}$	$F = S_0 \cdot e^{r_0 \cdot (T-t_0)}$
Short forward	$F - S_T$	$-f_t$	
Long call	$\max(S_T - K, 0)$	$c_t = S_t \cdot \mathrm{N}(d_1) - K \cdot e^{-r_t \cdot (T-t)} \cdot \mathrm{N}(d_2)$	Any strike price can be used.
Short call	$\min(K - S_T, 0)$	$-c_t$	
Long put	$\max(K - S_T, 0)$	$p_t = K \cdot e^{-r_t \cdot (T-t)} \cdot \mathrm{N}(-d_2) - S_t \cdot \mathrm{N}(-d_1)$	
Short put	$\min(S_T - K, 0)$	$-p_t$	

The notation in Table 6.2 is defined as follows:

f_t = Long forward value
c_t = Long call value
p_t = Long put value
K = Strike price
F = Forward price
t_0 = Initiation date
t = Valuation date
T = Expiration date
$T - t$ = Years between the valuation date and the expiration date
$T - t_0$ = Years between the initiation date and the expiration date
S_t = Underlying asset price on the valuation date
S_0 = Underlying asset price on the initiation date
r_t = Continuously compounded risk-free interest rate on the valuation date
r_0 = Continuously compounded risk-free interest rate on the initiation date
σ_t = Underlying asset volatility on the valuation date
$\mathrm{N}(\ )$ = The standard normal cumulative distribution function

$$d_1 = \frac{\ln\left(\frac{S_t}{K}\right) + \left(r_t + \frac{\sigma_t^2}{2}\right) \cdot (T-t)}{\sigma_t \cdot \sqrt{T-t}}$$

$$d_2 = d_1 - \sigma_t \cdot \sqrt{T-t}$$

6.2 VALUE AS THE PRESENT VALUE OF EXPECTED PAYOFF

The value of any financial security is the present value of its expected cash flows. For example:

- The value of a bond is the present value of its expected future coupons and face value.
- The value of a stock is the present value of its expected future dividends.

Forward and option values are *also* the present value of their expected future payoffs at expiration.

An option provides the long position a right and not an obligation; hence, an option's payoff at expiration is only non-zero when the option ends up in-the-money (ITM). This means that option value is the present value of the probability of the option ending up ITM multiplied by the expected payoff at expiration should the option end up ITM. We can, therefore, describe the value of an option as follows:

$$\textit{Option value} = PV\begin{pmatrix} \textit{probability of ending up ITM} \times \\ \textit{expected payoff when ITM} \end{pmatrix}$$

Both counterparties to a forward are obligated to transact regardless of the underlying asset price. This means that forward value is simply the present value of the expected payoff at expiration. We can describe the value of a forward as follows:

$$\textit{Forward value} = PV(\textit{expected payoff at expiration})$$

In only a few steps, we can show that the Black-Scholes model and the forward value equation follow directly from these equations. Before we do so, let's explore the following topics:

- What rate should we use to form expectations of payoff and calculate present values?
- How do we calculate the probability that the underlying asset price ends up ITM at expiration?
- What is the expected value of the underlying asset at expiration?

We explore these topics in the next two sections.

Knowledge check

Q 6.1: Describe option value in words.
Q 6.2: Describe forward value in words.

6.3 RISK-NEUTRAL VALUATION

We've seen that forward and option values are the present value of their expected payoffs. We require a rate with which to form expectations of payoff and discount (i.e., calculate present value). What rate should we use?

The rate that we will use is the risk-free rate. To understand why, let's first learn about risk-averse and risk-neutral investors. This will allow us to understand the concept of risk-neutral valuation, which will explain why we use the risk-free rate.

6.3.1 Risk-averse versus risk-neutral investors

Investment opportunities can be categorized as either risk-free or risky:

- Risk-free investment: An investment that provides a future cash flow that investors are completely certain they will receive. For example, many investors perceive an investment in government debt as a risk-free investment, as investors fully expect to receive the promised future cash flow from the government.
- Risky investment: An investment that provides a future cash flow where investors are uncertain about the amount they will receive. For example, options and forwards are risky investments as the amount that the long position will receive from the short position in the future is not certain as it depends on the underlying asset price.

When investing, the rate of return that investors demand depends on whether the future cash flow is either risk-free or risky:

- Investors demand the risk-free rate when investing in a risk-free investment.
- Investors demand a rate of return that is greater than the risk-free rate when investing in a risky investment to compensate for taking risk.

Consider the following example. An investor has two investment opportunities. The first investment is risk-free. The second investment is risky. The risk-free rate is 5%. The investor will demand the risk-free rate of 5% when investing in the risk-free investment and will demand a rate of return that is greater than 5% when investing in the risky investment.

The idea that an investor in a risky investment demands a rate of return that is greater than the risk-free rate is straightforward. After all, a typical investor prefers not to take risks! This characteristic of a typical investor is described as "risk-averse." Clearly, the vast majority of investors are risk-averse, though some investors are more risk-averse than others.

TABLE 6.3 Interest rate demanded as a function of the investor type and investment opportunity

	Rate of return demanded	
Investment type	**Risk-averse investor**	**Risk-neutral investor**
Risk-free investment	Risk-free rate	Risk-free rate
Risky investment	Rate of return greater than the risk-free rate	Risk-free rate

Let's imagine another type of investor. This hypothetical investor is not risk-averse. Instead, this hypothetical investor is "risk-neutral." In other words, this investor does *not* demand compensation for accepting risk. Instead, it only demands the risk-free rate despite taking risk.

Table 6.3 summarizes the rate of return demanded by investors as a function of the investor type and investment opportunity.

The vast majority of investors are risk-averse. Indeed, it is hard to imagine why *any* investor would be risk-neutral, as not receiving compensation for accepting risk is completely illogical! Forward and option valuation models do not assume investors are risk-neutral. This may sound like an obvious point now, but it will be crucial shortly.

6.3.2 Implications for valuation

We calculate forward and option value through forming expectations of payoffs and discounting using the risk-free rate. The use of the risk-free rate is surprising. Forwards and options are clearly not risk-free investments. After all:

- Forward payoff can be large or small. Clearly, a forward is a risky investment.
- An option may end up ITM or OTM. If OTM, the payoff is zero. If ITM, the payoff can be large or small. Clearly, an option is a risky investment.

Forwards and options are risky. Further, a typical investor is risk-averse. Shouldn't we use a rate that is greater than the risk-free rate?

The explanation is as follows: One can demonstrate that forward and option payoffs can be synthetically replicated using a portfolio consisting of the underlying asset and a bond, where the proportion of each in the portfolio is continuously rebalanced. This is referred to as "dynamic replication." Since payoff can be synthetically replicated, the cost of a traded position must be the same as the cost of the synthetic position. If so, everyone must end up with the same value. After all:

- If a traded position's cost falls below the synthetic position's cost, investors will buy the traded position and sell an equivalent synthetic position. The demand to buy the traded position will lead its cost to increase until it is equal to the synthetic position's cost.
- If a traded position's cost rises above the synthetic position's cost, investors will sell the traded position and buy an equivalent synthetic position. The supply of traded positions available for sale will lead its cost to decrease until it is equal to the synthetic position's cost.

We see that any deviation between a traded and synthetic position will be exploited until it no longer exists. Because of this, everyone values forwards and options the same. "Everyone" means every investor regardless of his or her attitude towards risk. Hence, a risk-averse investor's valuation will be identical to a risk-neutral investor's valuation. But if everyone's valuation is the same regardless of risk characteristics, we can value positions as if we are in a risk-neutral world where we form expectations and discount using the risk-free rate. After all, whatever value is calculated in a risk-neutral world will be the same as the value that a risk-averse investor will calculate.

This approach is referred to as "risk-neutral valuation." Note that we do not assume that investors are risk-neutral. Instead, we take advantage of the fact that a risk-neutral world's valuation is identical to the real-world valuation, and therefore we can identify value through taking a risk-neutral world's perspective.

Knowledge check

Q 6.3: What is a risk-free investment?

Q 6.4: What is a risky investment?

Q 6.5: What is a risk-averse investor?

Q 6.6: What is a risk-neutral investor?

Q 6.7: What rate of return does a risk-averse investor demand when investing in a risk-free investment?

Q 6.8: What rate of return does a risk-neutral investor demand when investing in a risk-free investment?

Q 6.9: What rate of return does a risk-averse investor demand when investing in a risky investment?

Q 6.10: What rate of return does a risk-neutral investor demand when investing in a risky investment?

Q 6.11: Why does a risk-averse investor demand a rate of return greater than the risk-free rate when investing in a risky investment?

Q 6.12: Why doesn't a risk-neutral investor demand a rate of return greater than the risk-free rate when investing in a risky investment?
Q 6.13: Is a typical investor risk-averse or risk-neutral?
Q 6.14: What is dynamic replication?
Q 6.15: Why will the cost of a traded option be equal to the cost of a synthetic option?
Q 6.16: Why do we form expectations and discount using the risk-free rate?
Q 6.17: Do our valuation models assume that investors are risk-neutral?
Q 6.18: What is risk-neutral valuation?

6.4 PROBABILITY AND EXPECTED VALUE CONCEPTS

To develop a deep understanding of valuation it is useful to be familiar with several probability and expected value concepts. Let's explore following five questions, all from the perspective of a risk-neutral world that both forms expectations and discounts using the risk-free rate:

- Question 1: What is the probability that the underlying asset price will be greater than a given strike price at expiration in a risk-neutral world?
- Question 2: What is the probability that the underlying asset price will be less than a given strike price at expiration in a risk-neutral world?
- Question 3: What is the expected underlying asset price at expiration in a risk-neutral world?
- Question 4: If the underlying asset price will be greater than the strike price when the option expires, what is the expected underlying asset price in a risk-neutral world?
- Question 5: If the underlying asset price will be less than the strike price when the option expires, what is the expected underlying asset price in a risk-neutral world?

Table 6.4 provides the answer to each of these questions. Let's explore each question and answer in-depth.

Question 1: What is the probability that the underlying asset price will be greater than a given strike price at expiration in a risk-neutral world?

The probability that the underlying asset price will be greater than a given strike price in a risk-neutral world is:

$$\text{prob}(S_T > K) = N(d_2)$$

TABLE 6.4 Probability and expected value concepts

Question	Answer
Q1: What is the probability that the underlying asset price will be greater than a given strike price at expiration in a risk-neutral world?	$\text{prob}(S_T > K) = \text{N}(d_2)$
Q2: What is the probability that the underlying asset price will be less than a given strike price at expiration in a risk-neutral world?	$\text{prob}(S_T < K) = \text{N}(-d_2)$
Q3: What is the expected underlying asset price at expiration in a risk-neutral world?	$\text{E}[S_T] = S_t \cdot e^{r_t \cdot (T-t)}$
Q4: If the underlying asset price will be greater than the strike price when the option expires, what is the expected underlying asset price in a risk-neutral world?	$E[\,S_T \vert S_T > K] = S_t \cdot e^{r_t \cdot (T-t)} \cdot \dfrac{\text{N}(d_1)}{\text{N}(d_2)}$
Q5: If the underlying asset price will be less than the strike price when the option expires, what is the expected underlying asset price in a risk-neutral world?	$E[\,S_T \vert S_T < K] = S_t \cdot e^{r_t \cdot (T-t)} \cdot \dfrac{\text{N}(-d_1)}{\text{N}(-d_2)}$

Consider the following example. The underlying asset price is \$24 and the strike price is \$20. Further, the risk-free interest rate is 3%, and the underlying asset volatility is 25%. The probability that the underlying asset price will be greater than the strike price in three years is:

$$
\begin{aligned}
d_1 &= \frac{\ln\left(\dfrac{S_t}{K}\right) + \left(r_t + \dfrac{\sigma_t^2}{2}\right) \cdot (T-t)}{\sigma_t \cdot \sqrt{T-t}} \\
&= \frac{\ln\left(\dfrac{\$24}{\$20}\right) + \left(3\% + \dfrac{25\%^2}{2}\right) \cdot 3}{25\% \cdot \sqrt{3}} \\
&= 0.8454
\end{aligned}
$$

$$
\begin{aligned}
d_2 &= d_1 - \sigma_t \cdot \sqrt{T-t} \\
&= 0.8454 - 25\% \cdot \sqrt{3} \\
&= 0.4214
\end{aligned}
$$

$$
\begin{aligned}
\text{prob}(S_T > K) &= \text{N}(d_2) \\
&= \text{N}(0.4214) \\
&= 66.00\%
\end{aligned}
$$

Question 2: What is the probability that the underlying asset price will be less than a given strike price at expiration in a risk-neutral world?

The probability that the underlying asset price will be less than a given strike price at expiration in a risk-neutral world is:

$$\text{prob}(S_T < K) = \text{N}(-d_2)$$

This is unsurprising. After all, prob($S_T > K$) is equal to N(d_2). Since probabilities always sum to one it makes sense that:

$$\text{prob}(S_T < K) = 1 - \text{N}(d_2) = \text{N}(-d_2)$$

For example, consider a situation where the underlying asset price is \$31 and the strike price is \$25. Further, the risk-free interest rate is equal to 3%, and the underlying asset volatility is 25%. The probability that the underlying asset price will be less than the strike price in three years is:

$$
\begin{aligned}
d_1 &= \frac{\ln\left(\frac{S_t}{K}\right) + \left(r_t + \frac{\sigma_t^2}{2}\right) \cdot (T-t)}{\sigma_t \cdot \sqrt{T-t}} \\
&= \frac{\ln\left(\frac{\$31}{\$25}\right) + \left(3\% + \frac{25\%^2}{2}\right) \cdot 3}{25\% \cdot \sqrt{3}} \\
&= 0.9211
\end{aligned}
$$

$$
\begin{aligned}
d_2 &= d_1 - \sigma_t \cdot \sqrt{T-t} \\
&= 0.4881 - 25\% \cdot \sqrt{3} \\
&= 0.4881
\end{aligned}
$$

$$
\begin{aligned}
\text{prob}(S_T < K) &= \text{N}(-d_2) \\
&= \text{N}(-0.4881) \\
&= 31.27\%
\end{aligned}
$$

Question 3: What is the expected underlying asset price at expiration in a risk-neutral world?

The expected underlying asset price at expiration in a risk-neutral world is:

$$E[S_T] = S_t \cdot e^{r_t \cdot (T-t)}$$

For example, consider a situation where the underlying asset price is \$1.6, and the risk-free interest rate is 2%. The expected underlying asset price in two years is:

$$\begin{aligned} E[S_T] &= S_t \cdot e^{r_t \cdot (T-t)} \\ &= \$1.6 \cdot e^{2\% \cdot 2} \\ &= \$1.67 \end{aligned}$$

Question 4: If the underlying asset price will be greater than the strike price when the option expires, what is the expected underlying asset price in a risk-neutral world?

Let's explore this question to make sure we understand it. This question is not asking "what is the expected underlying asset price when the option expires?" Instead, this question is asking: What is the expected underlying asset price in a risk-neutral world, conditional on it being greater than the strike price? This value is notated as $E[\, S_T | S_T > K\,]$. The vertical line (i.e., "|") is "conditional on." The answer is:

$$E[S_T | S_T > K] = S_t \cdot e^{r_t \cdot (T-t)} \cdot \frac{N(d_1)}{N(d_2)}$$

For example, consider a situation where the underlying asset price is \$31 and the strike price is \$25. Further, the risk-free interest rate is 3% and the underlying asset volatility is 25%. The expected underlying asset price in three years conditional on the market price being greater than the strike price is:

$$\begin{aligned} d_1 &= \frac{\ln\left(\frac{S_t}{K}\right) + \left(r_t + \frac{\sigma_t^2}{2}\right) \cdot (T-t)}{\sigma_t \cdot \sqrt{T-t}} \\ &= \frac{\ln\left(\frac{\$31}{\$25}\right) + \left(3\% + \frac{25\%^2}{2}\right) \cdot 3}{25\% \cdot \sqrt{3}} \\ &= 0.9211 \end{aligned}$$

$$d_2 = d_1 - \sigma_t \cdot \sqrt{T-t}$$
$$= 0.4881 - 25\% \cdot \sqrt{3}$$
$$= 0.4881$$
$$\mathrm{N}(d_1) = \mathrm{N}(0.9211)$$
$$= 0.8215$$
$$\mathrm{N}(d_2) = \mathrm{N}(0.4881)$$
$$= 0.6873$$
$$E[S_T|S_T > K] = S_t \cdot e^{r_t \cdot (T-t)} \cdot \frac{\mathrm{N}(d_1)}{\mathrm{N}(d_2)}$$
$$= \$31 \cdot e^{3\% \cdot 3} \cdot \frac{0.8215}{0.6873}$$
$$= \$40.54$$

Question 5: If the underlying asset price will be less than the strike price when the option expires, what is the expected underlying asset price in a risk-neutral world?

Let's explore this question to make sure it is understandable. This question is asking: What is the expected underlying asset price in a risk-neutral world, conditional on it being less than the strike price? This value is notated as $E[S_T|S_T < K]$. The answer is:

$$E[S_T|S_T < K] = S_t \cdot e^{r_t \cdot (T-t)} \cdot \frac{\mathrm{N}(-d_1)}{\mathrm{N}(-d_2)}$$

For example, consider a situation where the underlying asset price is \$75 and the strike price is \$93. Further, the risk-free interest rate is 3% and the underlying asset volatility is 25%. The expected underlying asset price in three years conditional on the market price being less than the strike price is:

$$d_1 = \frac{\ln\left(\frac{S_t}{K}\right) + \left(r_t + \frac{\sigma_t^2}{2}\right) \cdot (T-t)}{\sigma_t \cdot \sqrt{T-t}}$$
$$= \frac{\ln\left(\frac{\$75}{\$93}\right) + \left(3\% + \frac{25\%^2}{2}\right) \cdot 3}{25\% \cdot \sqrt{3}}$$
$$= -0.0724$$

$$\begin{aligned} d_2 &= d_1 - \sigma_t \cdot \sqrt{T-t} \\ &= -0.0724 - 25\% \cdot \sqrt{3} \\ &= -0.5054 \end{aligned}$$

$$\begin{aligned} \mathrm{N}(-d_1) &= \mathrm{N}(-(-0.0724)) \\ &= 0.5289 \end{aligned}$$

$$\begin{aligned} \mathrm{N}(-d_2) &= \mathrm{N}(-(-0.5054)) \\ &= 0.6934 \end{aligned}$$

$$\begin{aligned} E[S_T|S_T < K] &= S_t \cdot e^{r_t \cdot (T-t)} \cdot \frac{\mathrm{N}(-d_1)}{\mathrm{N}(-d_2)} \\ &= \$75 \cdot e^{3\% \cdot 3} \cdot \frac{0.5289}{0.6934} \\ &= \$62.59 \end{aligned}$$

Knowledge check

Q 6.19: What is the probability that the underlying asset price will be greater than a given strike price at expiration in a risk-neutral world?

Q 6.20: What is the probability that the underlying asset price will be less than a given strike price at expiration in a risk-neutral world?

Q 6.21: What is the expected underlying asset price at expiration in a risk-neutral world?

Q 6.22: If the underlying asset price will be greater than the strike price when the option expires, what is the expected underlying asset price in a risk-neutral world?

Q 6.23: If the underlying asset price will be less than the strike price when the option expires, what is the expected underlying asset price?

6.5 UNDERSTANDING THE BLACK-SCHOLES EQUATION FOR CALL VALUE

The Black-Scholes equation for long call value is:

$$c_t = S_t \cdot \mathrm{N}(d_1) - K \cdot e^{-r_t \cdot (T-t)} \cdot \mathrm{N}(d_2)$$

The value of a long call is the present value of the probability of the call option ending up ITM at expiration multiplied by the expected long call payoff when ITM:

$$c_t = PV\left(\begin{array}{l} probability\ of\ call\ ending\ up\ ITM \times \\ expected\ long\ call\ payoff\ when\ ITM \end{array}\right)$$

Note the following:

- A call option ends up ITM when $S_T > K$.
- The probability of a call option ending up ITM is written as $\text{prob}(S_T > K)$.
- The expected long call payoff when $S_T > K$ is written as $\text{E}[S_T - K|S_T > K]$.

We can, therefore, restate the long call's value as:

$$c_t = \text{PV}(\text{prob}(S_T > K) \cdot \text{E}[S_T - K|S_T > K])$$

The strike price, K, does not change, hence:

$$\text{E}[S_T - K|S_T > K] = \text{E}[S_T|S_T > K] - K$$

We can, therefore, restate the option's value as:

$$c_t = \text{PV}(\text{prob}(S_T > K) \cdot (\text{E}[S_T|S_T > K] - K))$$

Further, we know from Section 6.4 that in a risk-neutral world:

$$\text{prob}(S_T > K) = \text{N}(d_2)$$

and

$$\text{E}[S_T|S_T > K] = S_t \cdot e^{r_t \cdot (T-t)} \cdot \frac{\text{N}(d_1)}{\text{N}(d_2)}$$

We can, therefore, restate the long call value as:

$$c_t = \text{PV}\left(\text{N}(d_2) \cdot \left(S_T \cdot e^{r_t \cdot (T-t)} \cdot \frac{\text{N}(d_1)}{\text{N}(d_2)} - K\right)\right)$$

Further, we know that in a risk-neutral world present value is calculated through multiplying the expected payoff by $e^{-r_t \cdot (T-t)}$. We can, therefore, restate the previous equation as:

$$c_t = e^{-r_t \cdot (T-t)} \cdot \text{N}(d_2) \cdot \left(S_T \cdot e^{r_t \cdot (T-t)} \cdot \frac{\text{N}(d_1)}{\text{N}(d_2)} - K\right)$$

TABLE 6.5 Interpretation of long call value

Long call value	=	*Present value*	×	*Probability of the call ending up ITM*	×	*Expected long call payoff when ITM*
c_t	=	$e^{-r_t \cdot (T-t)}$	×	$N(d_2)$	×	$S_t \cdot e^{r_t \cdot (T-t)} \cdot \frac{N(d_1)}{N(d_2)} - K$

We see from this analysis that a long call position is calculated through multiplying three elements:

- $e^{-r_t \cdot (T-t)}$
- $N(d_2)$
- $S_t \cdot e^{r_t \cdot (T-t)} \cdot \frac{N(d_1)}{N(d_2)} - K$

Table 6.5 interprets each element of the equation for long call value.

We see that the value of a long call is simply the present value of the probability of ending up ITM multiplied by the expected payoff when ITM. The value of a short call is the negative of the value of the long call.

The Black-Scholes equation for a call option's value is typically written as:

$$c_t = S_t \cdot N(d_1) - K \cdot e^{-r_t \cdot (T-t)} \cdot N(d_2)$$

This is simply a "cleaned-up" version of our equation, as the following steps demonstrate:

$$c_t = e^{-r_t \cdot (T-t)} \cdot N(d_2) \cdot \left(S_t \cdot e^{r_t \cdot (T-t)} \cdot \frac{N(d_1)}{N(d_2)} - K \right)$$

$$= e^{-r_t \cdot (T-t)} \cdot N(d_2) \cdot S_t \cdot e^{r_t \cdot (T-t)} \cdot \frac{N(d_1)}{N(d_2)} - K \cdot e^{-r_t \cdot (T-t)} \cdot N(d_2)$$

and since $e^{-r_t \cdot (T-t)} \cdot e^{r_t \cdot (T-t)} = 1$ and $\frac{N(d_2)}{N(d_2)} = 1$, it follows:

$$c_t = S_t \cdot N(d_1) - K \cdot e^{-r_t \cdot (T-t)} \cdot N(d_2)$$

Knowledge check

Q 6.24: Explain how to obtain the Black-Scholes equation for long call value.

Q 6.25: Interpret the Black-Scholes equation for long call value.

6.6 UNDERSTANDING THE BLACK-SCHOLES EQUATION FOR PUT VALUE

The Black-Scholes equation for long put value is:

$$p_t = K \cdot e^{-r_t \cdot (T-t)} \cdot \mathrm{N}(-d_2) - S_t \cdot \mathrm{N}(-d_1)$$

The value of a long put is the present value of the probability of the put option ending up ITM multiplied by the expected long put payoff when ITM:

$$p_t = PV \begin{pmatrix} \textit{probability of put ending up ITM} \times \\ \textit{expected long put payoff when ITM} \end{pmatrix}$$

Note the following:

- A put option ends up ITM when $S_T < K$.
- The probability of a put option ending up ITM is written as prob $(S_T < K)$.
- The expected long put payoff when $S_T < K$ is written as $\mathrm{E}[K - S_T | S_T < K]$.

We can, therefore, restate the long put's value as:

$$p_t = \mathrm{PV}(\mathrm{prob}(S_T < K) \cdot \mathrm{E}[K - S_T | S_T < K])$$

The strike price, K, does not change, hence:

$$\mathrm{E}[K - S_T | S_T < K] = K - \mathrm{E}[S_T | S_T < K]$$

We can, therefore, restate the option's value:

$$p_t = \mathrm{PV}(\mathrm{prob}(S_T < K) \cdot (K - \mathrm{E}[S_T | S_T < K]))$$

Further, we know from Section 6.4 that in a risk-neutral world:

$$\mathrm{prob}(S_T < K) = \mathrm{N}(-d_2)$$

and

$$\mathrm{E}[S_T | S_T < K] = S_t \cdot e^{r_t \cdot (T-t)} \cdot \frac{\mathrm{N}(-d_1)}{\mathrm{N}(-d_2)}$$

We can, therefore, restate the long put value as:

$$p_t = \mathrm{PV}\left(\mathrm{N}(-d_2)\cdot\left(K - S_t \cdot e^{r_t\cdot(T-t)}\cdot\frac{\mathrm{N}(-d_1)}{\mathrm{N}(-d_2)}\right)\right)$$

$$= e^{-r_t\cdot(T-t)}\cdot\mathrm{N}(-d_2)\cdot\left(K - S_t \cdot e^{r_t\cdot(T-t)}\cdot\frac{\mathrm{N}(-d_1)}{\mathrm{N}(-d_2)}\right)$$

We see from this analysis that a long put position is calculated through multiplying three elements:

- $e^{-r_t\cdot(T-t)}$
- $\mathrm{N}(-d_2)$
- $K - S_t \cdot e^{r_t\cdot(T-t)}\cdot\frac{\mathrm{N}(-d_1)}{\mathrm{N}(-d_2)}$

Table 6.6 interprets each element of the equation.

We see that the value of a put option is simply the present value of the probability of ending up ITM multiplied by the expected payoff when ITM. The value of a short put is the negative of the value of the long put.

The Black-Scholes equation for a put option's value is typically written as:

$$p_t = K\cdot e^{-r_t\cdot(T-t)}\cdot N(-d_2) - S_t\cdot N(-d_1)$$

This is simply a "cleaned-up" version of our equation, as the following steps demonstrate:

$$p_t = e^{-r_t\cdot(T-t)}\cdot\mathrm{N}(-d_2)\cdot\left(K - S_t \cdot e^{r_t\cdot(T-t)}\cdot\frac{\mathrm{N}(-d_1)}{\mathrm{N}(-d_2)}\right)$$

$$= K\cdot e^{-r_t\cdot(T-t)}\cdot\mathrm{N}(-d_2) - e^{-r_t\cdot(T-t)}\cdot\mathrm{N}(-d_2)\cdot S_T\cdot e^{r_t\cdot(T-t)}\cdot\frac{\mathrm{N}(-d_1)}{\mathrm{N}(-d_2)}$$

$$= K\cdot e^{-r_t\cdot(T-t)}\cdot\mathrm{N}(-d_2) - S_t\cdot\mathrm{N}(-d_1)$$

TABLE 6.6 Interpretation of long put value

Long put value	=	*Present value*	×	*Probability of the put ending up ITM*	×	*Expected long put payoff when ITM*
p_t	=	$e^{-r_t\cdot(T-t)}$	×	$\mathrm{N}(-d_2)$	×	$K - S_t\cdot e^{r_t\cdot(T-t)}\cdot\frac{\mathrm{N}(-d_1)}{\mathrm{N}(-d_2)}$

Knowledge check

Q 6.26: Explain how to obtain the Black-Scholes equation for long put value.

Q 6.27: Interpret the Black-Scholes equation for long put value.

6.7 UNDERSTANDING THE EQUATION FOR FORWARD VALUE

The equation through which we calculate the value of a long forward is:

$$f_t = S_t - F \cdot e^{-r_t \cdot (T-t)}$$

The value of a long forward is the present value of its expected payoff at expiration:

$$f_t = \text{PV}(\textit{expected long forward payoff})$$

The payoff to the long forward at expiration is $S_T - F$. We can, therefore, rewrite the forward value equation as:

$$f_t = \text{PV}(E[S_T - F])$$

The forward price, F, is fixed at initiation and does not change. Hence:

$$E[S_T - F] = E[S_T] - F$$

We can therefore restate the forward's value as:

$$f_t = \text{PV}(E[S_T] - F)$$

Further, we know from Section 6.4 that in a risk-neutral world:

$$\text{E}[S_T] = S_t \cdot e^{r_t \cdot (T-t)}$$

We can, therefore, restate the long forward value as:

$$\begin{aligned} f_t &= \text{PV}(S_t \cdot e^{r_t \cdot (T-t)} - F) \\ &= e^{-r_t \cdot (T-t)} \cdot (S_t \cdot e^{r_t \cdot (T-t)} - F) \end{aligned}$$

TABLE 6.7 Interpretation of long forward value

Long forward value	=	*Present value*	×	*Expected long forward payoff*
f_t	=	$e^{-r_t \cdot (T-t)}$	×	$S_t \cdot e^{r_t \cdot (T-t)} - F$

The long forward value equation is created through multiplying two elements:

- $e^{-r_t \cdot (T-t)}$
- $S_t \cdot e^{r_t \cdot (T-t)} - F$

Table 6.7 interprets each element of the equation for long forward value. We see that the value of a forward is simply the present value of the expected payoff.

The long forward value equation is typically written as

$$f_t = S_t - F \cdot e^{-r_t \cdot (T-t)}$$

This is simply a "cleaned-up" version of our equation, as the following steps demonstrate:

$$\begin{aligned} f_t &= e^{-r_t \cdot (T-t)} \cdot (S_t \cdot e^{r_t \cdot (T-t)} - F) \\ &= S_t \cdot e^{r_t \cdot (T-t)} \cdot e^{-r_t \cdot (T-t)} - F \cdot e^{-r_t \cdot (T-t)} \\ &= S_t - F \cdot e^{-r_t \cdot (T-t)} \end{aligned}$$

Knowledge check

Q 6.28: Explain how to obtain the equation for long forward value.
Q 6.29: Interpret the equation for long forward value.

6.8 UNDERSTANDING THE EQUATION FOR FORWARD PRICE

The equation through which we calculate the forward price is:

$$F = S_0 \cdot e^{r_0 \cdot (T-t_0)}$$

To understand the forward price equation, recall that at initiation the value of a forward is zero. We can, therefore, easily solve for F. Since:

$$f_0 = S_0 - F \cdot e^{-r_0 \cdot (T - t_0)} = 0$$

it follows:

$$F = \frac{S_0}{e^{-r_0 \cdot (T - t_0)}}.$$

And since $\frac{1}{e^A} = e^{-A}$, it follows:

$$F = S_0 \cdot e^{r_0 \cdot (T - t_0)}$$

This is the expression for the forward price. The forward price is determined at initiation and is fixed for the remainder of the forward's life.

Knowledge check

Q 6.30: Explain how we obtain the equation for forward price.

KEY POINTS

- Forward and option values are the present value of their expected future payoffs at expiration.
- Risk-averse investors demand an interest rate that is greater than the risk-free interest rate to compensate for risk. Risk-neutral investors demand the risk-free interest rate despite taking risk. The vast majority of investors are risk-averse and not risk-neutral.
- Since the payoff associated with a forward and option can be synthetically replicated, the price of a traded position is the same as the price of the synthetic position. Therefore, everyone will value options and forwards the same. While we do not assume that investors are risk-neutral, we can value a position from the perspective of a risk-neutral world and form expectations of payoff and discount using the risk-free rate.
- We can identify equations through which to address, from the perspective of a risk-neutral world, the probability of the underlying asset price

at expiration falling above or below the strike, the expected underlying asset price at expiration, and the expected underlying asset price at expiration conditional on the option ending up ITM.

- Option value is the present value of the probability of the option ending up ITM multiplied by the expected payoff when the option is ITM.
- Forward value is the present value of the expected payoff at expiration.
- Forward price can be obtained through solving for the forward price that ensures that the forward value is zero at initiation.

CHAPTER 7

The Binomial Option Pricing Model

INTRODUCTION

This chapter explores the binomial option pricing model, an alternative to the Black-Scholes model. The binomial option pricing model is relatively simple to understand and can be a powerful tool through which to value both European-style and American-style options.

After you read this chapter you will be able to

- Explain how discrete points in time are modeled in the binomial option pricing model.
- Value European-style options using the one-period binomial option pricing model.
- Value both European-style and American-style options using the two-period binomial option pricing model.
- Understand how the binomial option pricing model can be extended to multiple periods.

7.1 MODELING DISCRETE POINTS IN TIME

The binomial option pricing model provides a simple yet powerful method through which to value options. The academics that initially proposed the model are John Cox, Stephen Ross, and Mark Rubenstein.[1] Therefore, the binomial option pricing model is also known as the Cox-Ross-Rubenstein model.

---

[1]Please see J. C. Cox, S. A. Ross, and M. Rubinstein, "Option Pricing: A Simplified Approach," *Journal of Financial Economics* 7, no. 3 (1979): 229–263.

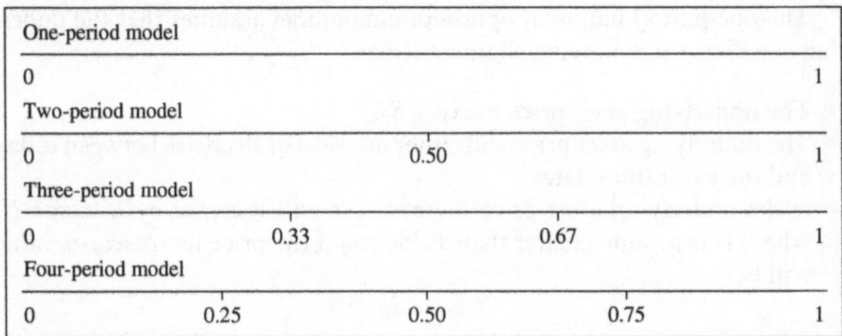

FIGURE 7.1 Discrete points in time in one-, two-, three-, and four-period models

A key characteristic of the binomial option pricing model is that it models the life of the option as a number of discrete points in time. For example, for an option that expires in one year:

- In a one-period model, there are only two points in time: 0 and 1 year.
- In a two-period model, there are three points in time: 0, 0.5 years, and 1 year.
- In a three-period model, there are four points in time: 0, 0.33 years, 0.67 years, and 1 year.
- In a four-period model, there are five points in time: 0, 0.25 years, 0.5 years, 0.75 years, and 1 year.

Figure 7.1 illustrates the discrete points in time that are modeled in one-, two-, three-, and four-period models.

In the next section we will explore the one-period binomial option pricing model.

Knowledge check

Q 7.1: How is time modeled in the binomial option pricing model?

7.2 INTRODUCTION TO THE ONE-PERIOD BINOMIAL OPTION PRICING MODEL

The one-period binomial option pricing model values options using a simplistic model where there are two discrete points in time:

- The valuation date, time 0
- The expiration date, *T* years in the future

The one-period binomial option pricing model assumes that the underlying asset has the following characteristics:

- The underlying asset price today is S_0.
- The underlying asset price will either increase or decrease between today and the expiration date.
- If the underlying asset price increases, it will increase by a factor U, where U is a value greater than 1. Hence, if the price increases, its value will be:

$$S_U = S_0 \cdot U$$

- If the underlying asset price decreases, it will decrease by a factor D, where D is a value less than 1. Hence, if the price decreases, its value will be:

$$S_D = S_0 \cdot D$$

- U and D are the inverse of each other. Hence:

$$D = \frac{1}{U}$$

The characteristics of the underlying asset are illustrated in Figure 7.2.

For example, consider an underlying asset with the following characteristics:

$$S_0 = \$50$$

$$U = 1.1$$

$$D = 1/1.1$$

$$S_U = \$50 \cdot 1.1 = \$55$$

$$S_D = \$50 \cdot \frac{1}{1.1} = \$45.45$$

This example is illustrated in Figure 7.3.

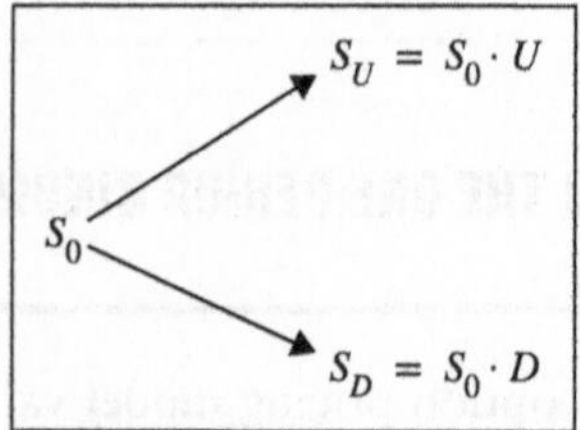

FIGURE 7.2
Characteristics of the underlying asset, one-period binomial model

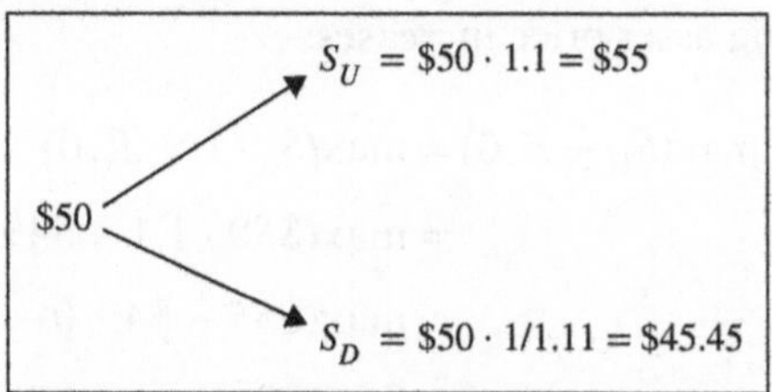

FIGURE 7.3 Underlying asset example, one-period binomial model

Next, consider a call option that has strike price K that expires in T years. The long call pays the short call a premium, c, at initiation, and receives one of the following payoffs at expiration:

- If the underlying asset price increases:

$$\max(S_U - K, 0) = \max(S_0 \cdot U - K, 0)$$

- If the underlying asset price decreases:

$$\max(S_D - K, 0) = \max(S_0 \cdot D - K, 0)$$

The characteristics of the call option are illustrated in Figure 7.4.

Since the one-period binomial option pricing model only models initiation and expiration, there is no opportunity for early exercise. Therefore, the option must be European-style and cannot be American-style.

Continuing the previous example, if the strike price is $49, the long call receives one of the following payoffs:

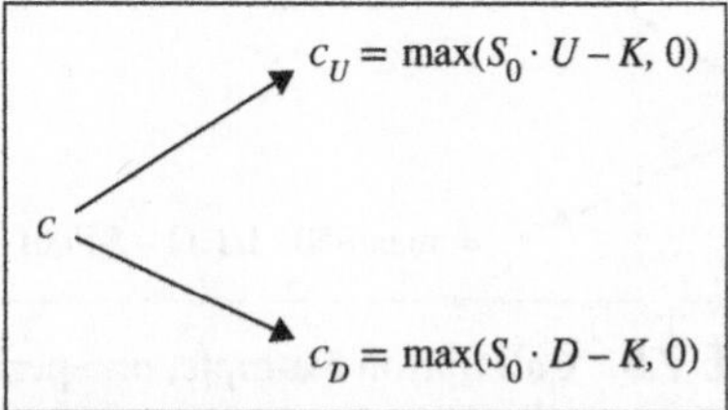

FIGURE 7.4 Characteristics of a call option, one-period binomial model

- If the underlying asset price increases:

$$\begin{aligned}\max(S_U - K, 0) &= \max(S_0 \cdot U - K, 0)\\ &= \max(\$50 \cdot 1.1 - \$49, 0)\\ &= \max(\$55 - \$49, 0)\\ &= \$6\end{aligned}$$

- If the underlying asset price decreases:

$$\begin{aligned}\max(S_D - K, 0) &= \max(S_0 \cdot D - K, 0)\\ &= \max(\$50 \cdot 1/1.1 - \$49, 0)\\ &= \max(\$45.45 - \$49, 0)\\ &= \$0\end{aligned}$$

The characteristics of this call option are illustrated in Figure 7.5.

Knowledge check

Q 7.2: What are the underlying asset's characteristics in a one-period binomial option pricing model?
Q 7.3: What are U and D?
Q 7.4: What is the relationship between U and D?
Q 7.5: What are the call option's characteristics in a one-period binomial option pricing model?
Q 7.6: Why is it impossible to model an American-style option using a one-period binomial option pricing model?

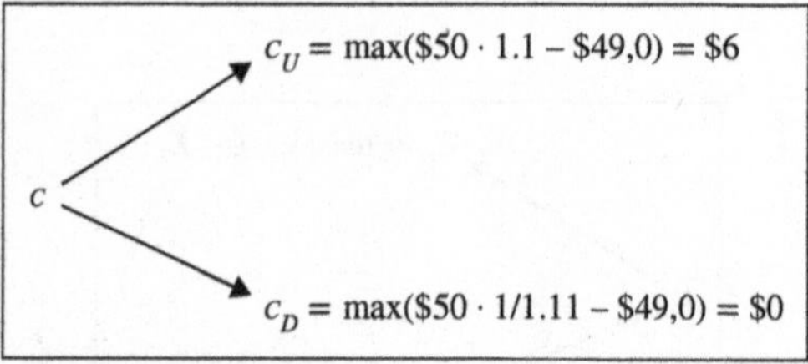

FIGURE 7.5 Call option example, one-period binomial model

7.3 OPTION VALUATION, ONE-PERIOD BINOMIAL OPTION PRICING MODEL

The purpose of the binomial option pricing model is to solve for the option value at initiation. Let's explore call option value in the context of the one-period model.

To obtain an equation for call value we form a portfolio consisting of the following two positions:

- A portion of the underlying asset
- A short call

We form this portfolio, as through doing so it will be possible to structure the portfolio so that it has the same payoff whether the underlying asset price increases or decreases. If the portfolio has identical payoffs in both scenarios it is a risk-free investment as its future payoff is known with certainty. If the payoff is risk-free, we can discount it to the present using the risk-free interest rate. Once we do so, we can solve for the option's value. To summarize, the steps through which we will identify the option value are as follows:

- Step 1: Structure a portfolio so that it has the same payoff whether the underlying asset price increases or decreases.
- Step 2: Discount the portfolio's payoff to the present using the risk-free rate.
- Step 3: Solve for the option value.

Let's explore each of these steps.

Step 1: Structure a portfolio so that it has the same payoff whether the underlying asset price increases or decreases.

The cost at initiation and payoff at expiration associated with a portfolio consisting of some portion α of the underlying asset and a short position in the call is illustrated in Figure 7.6.

We identify the value of α for which the two payoffs are equal as follows:

$$\alpha \cdot S_0 \cdot U - \max(S_0 \cdot U - K, 0) = \alpha \cdot S_0 \cdot D - \max(S_0 \cdot D - K, 0)$$

Solving, we find:

$$\alpha = \frac{\max(S_0 \cdot U - K, 0) - \max(S_0 \cdot D - K, 0)}{S_0 \cdot (U - D)}$$

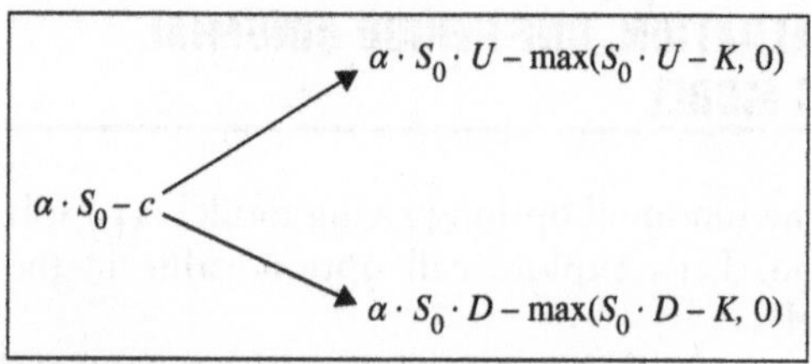

FIGURE 7.6 Cost and payoffs associated with a portfolio consisting of α of the underlying asset and a short call

Step 2: Discount the portfolio's payoff to the present using the risk-free rate.

Since both payoffs are identical, the portfolio is risk-free and we can discount it to the present using the risk-free rate. Let's discount the payoff when the underlying asset price increases:[2]

$$Present\ value = (\alpha \cdot S_0 \cdot U - \max(S_0 \cdot U - K, 0)) \cdot e^{-r \cdot \frac{T}{n}}$$

where:

r = the continuously compounded risk-free interest rate
n = the number of periods associated with the given model. Our model is a one-period model; hence, $n = 1$.

Step 3: Solve for the option value.

We know that the cost of the portfolio consisting of α of the underlying asset and a short position in the call is:

$$Portfolio\ cost = \alpha \cdot S_0 - c$$

In words, this indicates that the portfolio cost is equal to the cost associated with acquiring portion α of the underlying asset minus the revenue received through writing the short call. We also know that the present value of its payoff is:

$$Present\ value = (\alpha \cdot S_0 \cdot U - \max(S_0 \cdot U - K, 0)) \cdot e^{-r \cdot \frac{T}{n}}$$

[2]Discounting the payoff when the underlying asset price decreases will lead to the same result, as both payoffs are identical.

Since the portfolio value should be equal to the present value of its payoff, it follows:

$$\alpha \cdot S_0 - c = (\alpha \cdot S_0 \cdot U - \max(S_0 \cdot U - K, 0)) \cdot e^{-r \cdot \frac{T}{n}}$$

Rearranging this equation we obtain *c*:

$$c = \alpha \cdot S_0 - (\alpha \cdot S_0 \cdot U - \max(S_0 \cdot U - K, 0)) \cdot e^{-r \cdot \frac{T}{n}}$$

With reorganization, one can show that this expression is equivalent to the following:

$$c = \begin{pmatrix} \max(S_0 \cdot U - K, 0) \cdot \omega \\ +\max(S_0 \cdot D - K, 0) \cdot (1 - \omega) \end{pmatrix} \cdot e^{-r \cdot T/n}$$

where:

$$\omega = \frac{e^{r \cdot T/n} - D}{U - D}$$

Let's explore this approach using the example introduced earlier, where:

$S_0 = \$50$
$U = 1.1$
$D = 1/1.1$
$K = \$49$
$T = 1$ year
$n = 1$-period
$r = 5\%$

In this example:

$$\alpha = \frac{\max(\$55 - \$49, 0) - \max(\$45.45 - \$49, 0)}{\$55 - \$45.45}$$
$$= 0.6286$$

As illustrated in Figure 7.7 the payoff is $28.57 in both scenarios.

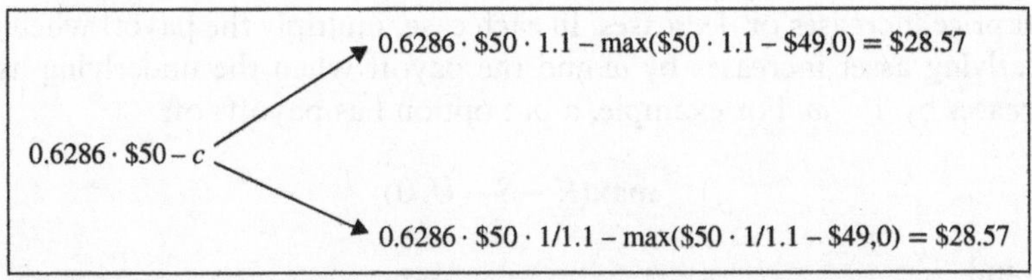

FIGURE 7.7 Cost and payoffs example associated with a portfolio consisting of α of the underlying asset and a short call

The value of ω is:

$$\begin{aligned}\omega &= \frac{e^{r\cdot T/n} - D}{U - D}\\ &= \frac{e^{5\%\cdot 1/1} - 1/1.1}{1.1 - 1/1.1}\\ &= 0.7448\end{aligned}$$

The value of this call is:

$$\begin{aligned}c &= \begin{pmatrix} \max(S_0 \cdot U - K, 0)\cdot \omega \\ +\max(S_0 \cdot D - K, 0)\cdot (1-\omega)\end{pmatrix}\cdot e^{-r\cdot 1/1}\\ &= \begin{pmatrix} \max(\$50 \cdot 1.1 - \$49.0)\cdot 0.7448 \\ +\max\left(\$50 \cdot \frac{1}{1.11} - \$49, 0\right)\cdot (1-0.7448)\end{pmatrix}\cdot e^{-5\%\cdot 1/1}\\ &= \$4.25\end{aligned}$$

This analysis uses as inputs the factors U and D, where U is the factor by which the underlying asset increases and D, which is equal to $1/U$, is the factor by which the underlying asset decreases. U can be identified as follows, where σ = underlying asset volatility:

$$U = e^{\sigma\cdot\sqrt{T/n}}$$

In our example, the value for U was given as 1.1. This value for U is due to the fact that the underlying asset volatility is 9.531%, as the following demonstrates:

$$\begin{aligned}U &= e^{\sigma\cdot\sqrt{1/1}}\\ &= e^{9.531\%\cdot\sqrt{1/1}}\\ &= 1.1\end{aligned}$$

The methodology through which we price a call can be used to price any position that has payoffs that are a function of whether the underlying asset price increases or decreases. In each case, multiply the payoff when the underlying asset increases by ω and the payoff when the underlying asset decreases by $1-\omega$. For example, a put option has payoffs of:

$$\max(K - S_0 \cdot U, 0)$$

and

$$\max(K - S_0 \cdot D, 0)$$

when the underlying asset prices increase or decrease, respectively. The expression for a put's value is therefore:

$$p = \begin{pmatrix} \max(K - S_0 \cdot U, 0) \cdot \omega \\ + \max(K - S_0 \cdot D, 0) \cdot (1 - \omega) \end{pmatrix} \cdot e^{-r \cdot \frac{T}{n}}$$

Knowledge check

Q 7.7: What are the steps through which we obtain an equation for call value?

Q 7.8: Why do we form a portfolio of a portion of the underlying asset and a short call?

Q 7.9: Why do we structure a portfolio so that it has the same payoff whether the underlying price increases or decreases?

Q 7.10: What is the expression for call value in the one-period binomial option pricing model?

Q 7.11: What is the relationship between *U* and volatility?

Q 7.12: What is the expression for put value in the one-period binomial option pricing model?

7.4 TWO-PERIOD BINOMIAL OPTION PRICING MODEL, EUROPEAN-STYLE OPTION

The one-period binomial option pricing model only allows for two points in time, initiation and expiration. Therefore, it is impossible to model an American-style option in the context of the one-period model as early exercise is impossible. A two-period model allows us to explore the distinction between American-style and European-style options as a two-period model allows for three points in time:

- Initiation
- The midpoint between initiation and expiration
- Expiration

An American-style option allows the long position to exercise at the midpoint between initiation and expiration, while a European-style option does not. In this section we explore European-style options in the context of the two-period model, and in the next section we explore American-style options.

To value an option using the two-period model, we implement the following steps:

- Step 1: Build the two-period binomial "tree."
- Step 2: Identify the potential payoffs at expiration.
- Step 3: Calculate the midpoint node values.
- Step 4: Calculate option value at initiation.

Let's explore each step. We will do so in the context of an example of the pricing of a European-style put option, where:

$S_0 = \$25$
$K = \$26$
$r = 4\%$
$\sigma = 6.9\%$
$T = 1$
$n = 2$
$U = e^{6.9\% \cdot \sqrt{1/2}} = 1.05$
$D = 1/1.05$
$\omega = \frac{e^{4\% \cdot 1/2} - 1/1.05}{1.05 - 1/1.05} = 0.6947$

Step 1: Build the two-period binomial "tree."
In our first step we build the two-period binomial "tree" to identify the potential underlying asset prices at expiration. Characteristics of the tree are as follows:

- In each of the periods the underlying asset either increases by a factor of U or decreases by a factor of D.
- The length of each period is T/n years.
- Each point on the tree is referred to as a "node."
- The "tree" is also referred to as a "lattice."

Figure 7.8 illustrates the binomial tree in this example.

Step 2: Identify the potential payoffs at expiration.
In step 2, we identify the payoff of the position in each of these scenarios, as illustrated in Figure 7.9.

Step 3: Calculate the midpoint node values.
We calculate the value of the position at each of the two midpoint nodes. We do so through recognizing that from the perspective of each of the midpoint nodes there are two potential payoffs in the subsequent period. Therefore, we can use the one-period model to identify the value at each of the midpoint nodes, as illustrated in Figure 7.10.

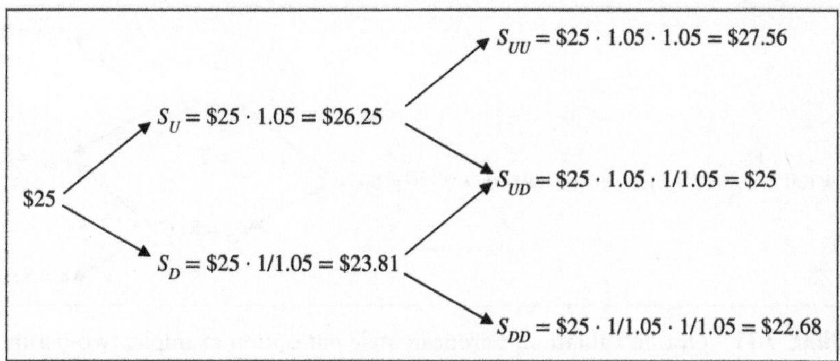

FIGURE 7.8 Underlying asset example, two-period binomial model

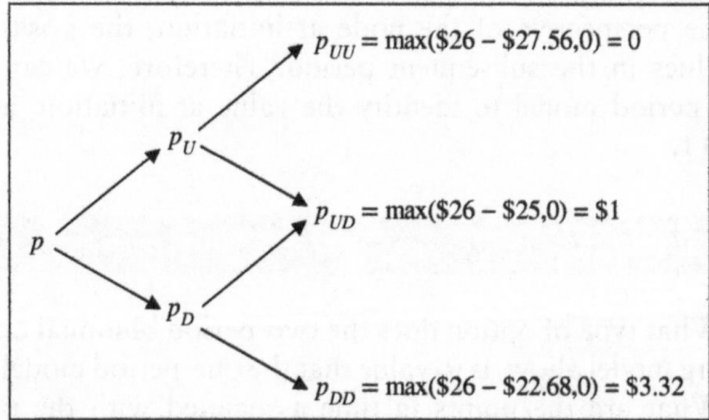

FIGURE 7.9 European-style put option example, two-period binomial model

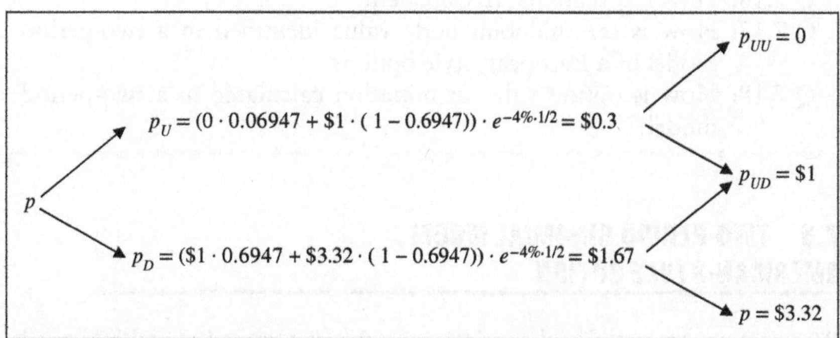

FIGURE 7.10 Midpoint node valuation, European-style put option example, two-period binomial model

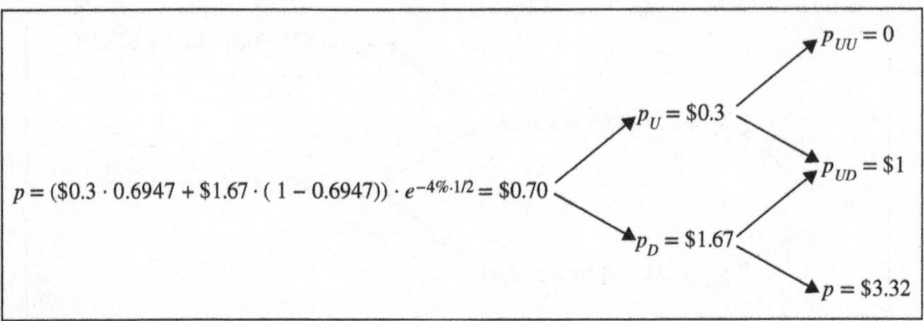

FIGURE 7.11 Option valuation, European-style put option example, two-period binomial model

Step 4: Calculate option value at initiation

From the perspective of the node at initiation, the position has two potential values in the subsequent period. Therefore, we can once again use the one-period model to identify the value at initiation, as illustrated in Figure 7.11.

Knowledge check

Q 7.13: What type of option does the two-period binomial option pricing model allow us to value that the one-period model does not?

Q 7.14: What are the points in time associated with the two-period model?

Q 7.15: What are the steps through which we value an option using the two-period model?

Q 7.16: How is a binomial tree created?

Q 7.17: How is the midpoint node value identified in a two-period model of a European-style option?

Q 7.18: How is option value at initiation calculated in a two-period model?

7.5 TWO-PERIOD BINOMIAL MODEL, AMERICAN-STYLE OPTION

We value an American-style option using the two-period model in a similar fashion to the method through which we valued a European-style option in the previous section. The only difference is that in an American-style option early exercise is permitted and the model allows for this possibility.

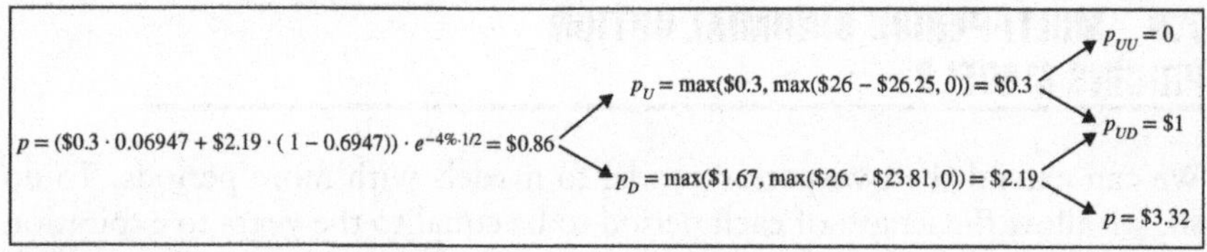

FIGURE 7.12 Option valuation, American-style put option example, two-period binomial model

This is implemented as follows: When calculating the midpoint node values we identify *both* of the following:

- The payoff if exercised early (i.e., early payoff).
- The value of holding the option: The value of holding the option is the value of the two potential payoffs at expiration. To identify the value of holding the option, we value the midpoint nodes as we did for the European-style option.

The value recorded for each of the midpoint nodes is as follows:

- Early payoff is greater than the value of holding the option: The early payoff is recorded as the node value as the option will be exercised early.
- Early payoff is less than the value of holding the option: The value of holding the option is recorded as the node value as the option will not be exercised early.

Consider an American-style put option that is identical to the European-style put option explored in the previous section, other than its American-style characteristic. Figure 7.12 illustrates the valuation of this put option.

The payoffs at expiration are identical to those for the European-style option. The midpoint node values are the greater of either the node values calculated for the European-style option or the payoffs if the option is exercised early. The American-style put option is valued at $0.86, which is $0.16 greater than the value of the European-style option.

Knowledge check

Q 7.19: How is valuation of an American-style option using the two-period binomial option pricing model different than valuation of a European-style option?

Q 7.20: What do we identify as the midpoint node values of an American-style option?

7.6 MULTI-PERIOD BINOMIAL OPTION PRICING MODELS

We can extend the two-period model to models with more periods. To do so, we allow the length of each period to be equal to the years to expiration divided by the number of periods, or T/n. We then implement the methodologies detailed in this chapter to value the option. It is common to use 20 or more periods when implementing the binomial model, to allow for more realistic ranges of potential payoffs at expiration. As the number of periods increases, the value identified using the binomial option pricing model for European-style options converges to the value one identifies using the Black-Scholes model.

Knowledge check

Q 7.21: What is the length of each period in a multi-period binomial option pricing model?

Q 7.22: To what does European-style option value using a multi-period binomial option pricing model converge as the number of periods increase?

KEY POINTS

- The binomial option pricing model, otherwise known as the Cox-Ross-Rubenstein model, provides a simple yet powerful method through which to value options. The model analyzes the time between option initiation and expiration as a number of discrete points in time.
- The one-period binomial option pricing model assumes that the underlying asset price will either increase or decrease by specified factors. Based on this, an option's payoffs at expiration can be identified.
- An investment in a portion of the underlying asset and an option position can be structured such that payoffs are identical whether the underlying increases or decreases. This allows for discounting of the cash flow at the risk-free rate, which allows for solving for option value.
- Since the one-period binomial option pricing model only models initiation and expiration it cannot be used to value an American-style option. A multi-period binomial option pricing model can be used to value both European-style and American-style options.

- To value a European-style option using a multi-period model, we build the multi-period binomial "tree," identify the potential payoffs at expiration, calculate the value of the position at the midpoint "nodes," and calculate the value of the position at initiation.
- To value an American-style option using a multi-period model, we proceed similarly to the valuation of a European-style option except early exercise is permitted. At each midpoint node the value of holding the option and the payoff if exercised early is identified. If the payoff if exercised early is greater than the value of holding the option the early payoff is recorded as the node value. Otherwise, the value of holding the option is recorded as the node value.
- It is common to use 20 or more periods when implementing the binomial model to allow for more realistic ranges of potential payoffs at expiration. As the number of periods increases, the value identified using the binomial option pricing model for European-style options converges to the value one identifies using the Black-Scholes model.

PART Three

The Greeks

CHAPTER 8

Introduction to the Greeks

INTRODUCTION

The "Greeks" is the name given to various measures of position sensitivity to changes in the underlying asset price and volatility, the risk-free interest rate, and the time to expiration. This chapter focuses on defining, calculating, and interpreting the Greeks. The subsequent chapters will focus on *why* each position has its sensitivities.

After you read this chapter you will be able to

- Define each of the Greeks.
- Understand the characteristics of the Greeks.
- Calculate the Greeks.
- Interpret the Greeks.
- Compare the estimates provided through the Greeks to changes in value estimated using the Black-Scholes model.

Scope of this chapter

This chapter will focus on the following products:

- Forwards where the underlying asset does not provide income
- European-style call options and put options where the underlying asset does not provide income

While limited to these products, this chapter will provide insights that are broadly applicable to other forwards, futures, and option products.

8.1 DEFINITIONS OF THE GREEKS

The measures of forward and option sensitivity that we will explore are:

- Delta
- Gamma
- Vega
- Rho
- Theta

These measures of sensitivities are referred to as the "Greeks" as most of their names are Greek letters (the exception being Vega, which is not a Greek letter). Here is a definition of each:

- Delta: The estimated dollar change in position value per one dollar increase in the underlying asset price
- Gamma: The estimated change in position Delta per one dollar increase in the underlying asset price
- Vega: The estimated dollar change in position value per one percent increase in the underlying asset volatility
- Rho: The estimated dollar change in position value per one percent increase in the risk-free interest rate
- Theta: The estimated dollar change in position value per one day decrease in the time to expiration

Knowledge check

Q 8.1: What are the Greeks?
Q 8.2: Why are they called the "Greeks"?
Q 8.3: What is Delta?
Q 8.4: What is Gamma?
Q 8.5: What is Vega?
Q 8.6: What is Rho?
Q 8.7: What is Theta?

8.2 CHARACTERISTICS OF THE GREEKS

Characteristics of the Greeks are as follows:

The Greeks measure sensitivity. Each of the Greeks measures a different type of sensitivity. For each we can identify the sensitivity being measured and the source of the sensitivity, as summarized in Table 8.1.

TABLE 8.1 The Greeks as measures of sensitivity

Greek	What sensitivity is being measured?	Source of sensitivity
Delta	Value	Underlying asset price
Gamma	Delta	Underlying asset price
Vega	Value	Underlying asset volatility
Rho	Value	Risk-free interest rate
Theta	Value	Time to expiration

TABLE 8.2 Source of sensitivity for each of the Greeks

Greek	Underlying asset price	Underlying asset volatility	Risk-free interest rates	Time to expiration
Delta	Increase by $1	No change	No change	No change
Gamma	Increase by $1	No change	No change	No change
Vega	No change	Increase by 1%	No change	No change
Rho	No change	No change	Increase by 1%	No change
Theta	No change	No change	No change	Decrease by 1 day

There are no Greeks for changes in forward price or strike price. There is no Greek that measures sensitivity to changes in the strike price or forward price, as the strike price and forward price do not change during the life of the position.

The Greeks assume "holding everything else equal." All of the Greeks measure sensitivity "holding everything else equal." Hence for each of the Greeks the given source of sensitivity is assumed to change and other potential sources of sensitivity are assumed to not change, as summarized in Table 8.2.

Almost all of the Greeks measure sensitivity per-unit of increase. With one exception, all of the Greeks measure sensitivity per-unit of *increase* of the given source of sensitivity. The exception is Theta, which measures sensitivity to a *decrease* in time to expiration.

The Greeks measure per-unit sensitivity. The Greeks measure sensitivity per-unit change in the source of sensitivity. For a multiple-unit change in the source of sensitivity, the given Greek should be multiplied by the given multiple-unit change. For example:

Delta = 0.43. This is per $1 increase in the underlying asset price. Hence, the estimated change in position value as the underlying asset price decreases by $2 is:

$$0.43 \times -\$2 = -\$0.86$$

Gamma = −0.02. This is per $1 increase in the underlying asset price. Hence, the estimated change in Delta as the underlying asset price increase by $10 is:

$$-0.02 \times \$10 = -0.20$$

Theta = 0.13. This is per one-day decrease in the time to expiration. Hence, the estimated change in position value as the time to expiration decreases by three days is:

$$0.13 \times 3 = \$0.39$$

Percentage change is above *the current level, not* of *the current level.* Vega and Rho measure sensitivity to 1% increases in volatility and the risk-free interest rate, respectively. This refers to increases of 1% *above* the current level (e.g., from 25% to 26%) and not *of* the current level (e.g., from 25% to 25.25%).

Delta is often presented without the decimal. The decimal is often excluded when referring to Delta. For example, Delta of 0.35 can also be referred to as "35 Delta" and Delta of 0.73 can also be referred to as "73 Delta."

The equations for the Greeks are obtained using calculus. The field of calculus informs us that one can identify the change in a function as a variable changes through the use of the first derivative of the function with respect to the given variable. The equations for the Greeks are obtained using calculus derivatives and are presented in the next section.

The Greeks are estimates and are not perfectly accurate. The fact that the Greeks are identified using calculus is crucial: In calculus, a first derivative provides an *estimate* of change in value that is often not completely accurate.[1]

Knowing how to interpret the Greeks is more important than knowing how to calculate the Greeks. In practice, data providers will typically provide the values of the Greeks. Hence, for most practitioners the ability to *calculate* the Greeks is not of primary importance. Instead, *interpreting* and

[1]Technically, the first derivative provides a linear estimate of a function. If the underlying function is not linear, the first derivative will misestimate the change in value.

understanding the Greeks are of primary importance. While the equations for the Greeks are presented in the next section, our main focus is on interpreting and intuitively understanding the Greeks.

Knowledge check

Q 8.8: Which of the Greeks measure sensitivity of value?
Q 8.9: Which of the Greeks measure sensitivity of Delta?
Q 8.10: What is Delta's source of sensitivity?
Q 8.11: What is Gamma's source of sensitivity?
Q 8.12: What is Vega's source of sensitivity?
Q 8.13: What is Rho's source of sensitivity?
Q 8.14: What is Theta's source of sensitivity?
Q 8.15: Why is there no sensitivity measure for changes in forward price or strike price?
Q 8.16: Does Delta measure sensitivity to increase or decrease in its source of sensitivity?
Q 8.17: Does Gamma measure sensitivity to increase or decrease of its source of sensitivity?
Q 8.18: Does Vega measure sensitivity to increase or decrease of its source of sensitivity?
Q 8.19: Does Rho measure sensitivity to increase or decrease of its source of sensitivity?
Q 8.20: Does Theta measure sensitivity to increase or decrease of its source of sensitivity?
Q 8.21: How can the sensitivity to a multiple-unit change in a source of sensitivity be measured using the Greeks?
Q 8.22: In the definitions of Vega and Rho, does percentage change refer to percentage change *above* or *of* the current level?
Q 8.23: How are the equations for the Greeks obtained?
Q 8.24: Why are the Greeks estimates of sensitivity and not perfectly accurate?

8.3 EQUATIONS FOR THE GREEKS

In this section we explore the equations through which one can estimate the Greeks. As noted in the previous section, knowing how to calculate the Greeks is less important than knowing how to interpret the Greeks. The equations for the Greeks for long positions in a forward, call, and put are detailed in Table 8.3.

TABLE 8.3 Equations for the Greeks

	Long Forward	Long Call	Long Put
Delta	1	$N(d_1)$	$-N(-d_1)$
Gamma	0	$\frac{N'(d_1)}{S_t \cdot \sigma_t \cdot \sqrt{T-t}}$	$\frac{N'(d_1)}{S_t \cdot \sigma_t \cdot \sqrt{T-t}}$
Vega	0	$\frac{S_t \cdot \sqrt{T-t} \cdot N'(d_1)}{100}$	$\frac{S_t \cdot \sqrt{T-t} \cdot N'(d_1)}{100}$
Rho	$\frac{F \cdot (T-t) \cdot e^{(-r_t \cdot (T-t))}}{100}$	$\frac{K \cdot (T-t) \cdot e^{(-r_t \cdot (T-t))} \cdot N(d_2)}{100}$	$\frac{-K \cdot (T-t) \cdot e^{(-r_t \cdot (T-t))} \cdot N(-d_2)}{100}$
Theta	$\frac{-F \cdot r_t \cdot e^{(-r_t \cdot (T-t))}}{365}$	$\frac{\left(\begin{array}{c} -S_t \cdot \sigma_t \cdot \frac{N'(d_1)}{2 \cdot \sqrt{T-t}} \\ -K \cdot r_t \cdot e^{(-r_t \cdot (T-t))} \cdot N(d_2) \end{array}\right)}{365}$	$\frac{\left(\begin{array}{c} -S_t \cdot \sigma_t \cdot \frac{N'(d_1)}{2 \cdot \sqrt{T-t}} \\ +K \cdot r_t \cdot e^{(-r_t \cdot (T-t))} \cdot N(-d_2) \end{array}\right)}{365}$

The notation in Table 8.3 is defined as follows:

K = Strike price
F = Forward price
t = Greek calculation date
T = Expiration date
$T - t$ = Years between the calculation date and the expiration date
S_t = Underlying asset price on the calculation date
r_t = Continuously compounded risk-free interest rate on the calculation date
σ_t = Underlying asset volatility on the calculation date
$N(\,)$ = The standard normal cumulative distribution function

$$d_1 = \frac{\ln\left(\frac{S_t}{K}\right) + \left(r_t + \frac{\sigma_t^2}{2}\right) \cdot (T-t)}{\sigma_t \cdot \sqrt{T-t}}$$

$$d_2 = d_1 - \sigma_t \cdot \sqrt{T-t}$$

$$N'(d_1) = e^{-\frac{d_1^2}{2}} / \sqrt{2 \cdot \pi}$$

The value of the Greek for a short position in a given position is always the negative of the value of the Greek for the corresponding long position. This is because forwards, calls, and puts are zero-sum games: Any change that benefits one of the counterparties harms the other counterparty in the exactly opposite fashion and *vice versa.*

Knowledge check

Q 8.25: What is the equation for long forward Delta?
Q 8.26: What is the equation for long forward Gamma?
Q 8.27: What is the equation for long forward Vega?
Q 8.28: What is the equation for long forward Rho?
Q 8.29: What is the equation for long forward Theta?
Q 8.30: What is the equation for long call Delta?
Q 8.31: What is the equation for long call Gamma?
Q 8.32: What is the equation for long call Vega?
Q 8.33: What is the equation for long call Rho?
Q 8.34: What is the equation for long call Theta?
Q 8.35: What is the equation for long put Delta?
Q 8.36: What is the equation for long put Gamma?
Q 8.37: What is the equation for long put Vega?
Q 8.38: What is the equation for long put Rho?
Q 8.39: What is the equation for long put Theta?
Q 8.40: To what is $N'(d_1)$ equal?
Q 8.41: To what are the Greeks of short positions equal?

8.4 CALCULATING THE GREEKS

Let's explore the calculation of the Greeks through the following detailed example: Consider a long call. The inputs are:

- Underlying asset price = \$45.56
- Strike price = \$45
- Years to expiration = 1 year
- Underlying asset volatility = 56.25%
- Risk-free interest rate = 2%

Calculations of the long call value and its Greeks are detailed in Table 8.4.

Table 8.5 summarizes the long call position's value and Greeks.

TABLE 8.4 Calculations of position value and the Greeks, long call example

Calculations

$$d_1 = \frac{\ln\left(\frac{S_t}{K}\right) + \left(r_t + \frac{\sigma_t^2}{2}\right)\cdot(T-t)}{\sigma_t \cdot \sqrt{T-t}} = \frac{\ln\left(\frac{\$45.56}{\$45}\right) + \left(2\% + \frac{56.25\%^2}{2}\right)\cdot 1}{56.25\% \cdot \sqrt{1}} = 0.3388$$

$$d_2 = d_1 - \sigma_t \cdot \sqrt{T-t} = 0.3388 - 56.25\% \cdot \sqrt{1} = -0.2237$$

$$N(d_1) = N(0.3388) = 0.6326$$

$$N(d_2) = N(-0.2237) = 0.4115$$

$$N'(d_1) = e^{-\frac{d_1{}^2}{2}} / \sqrt{2\cdot\pi} = e^{-\frac{0.6326^2}{2}} / \sqrt{2\cdot\pi} = 0.3767$$

$$c_t = S_t \cdot N(d_1) - K \cdot e^{-r_t\cdot(T-t)} \cdot N(d_2) = \$45.56 \cdot 0.6326 - \$45 \cdot e^{-2\%\cdot 1} \cdot 0.4115 = \$10.6715$$

$$\textit{Long Call Delta} = N(d_1) = N(0.3388) = 0.6326$$

$$\textit{Long Call Gamma} = \frac{N'(d_1)}{S_t \cdot \sigma_t \cdot \sqrt{T-t}} = \frac{0.3767}{\$45.56 \cdot 56.25\% \cdot \sqrt{1}} = 0.0147$$

$$\textit{Long Call Vega} = \frac{S_t \cdot \sqrt{T-t} \cdot N'(d_1)}{100} = \frac{\$45.56 \cdot \sqrt{1} \cdot 0.3767}{100} = 0.1716$$

$$\textit{Long Call Rho} = \frac{K \cdot (T-t) \cdot e^{(-r_t\cdot(T-t))} \cdot N(d_2)}{100} = \frac{\$45 \cdot 1 \cdot e^{(-2\%\cdot 1)} \cdot 0.4115}{100} = 0.1815$$

$$\textit{Long Call Theta} = \frac{\begin{pmatrix} -S_t \cdot \sigma_t \cdot \dfrac{N'(d_1)}{2\cdot\sqrt{T-t}} \\ -K \cdot r_t \cdot e^{(-r_t\cdot(T-t))} \cdot N(d_2) \end{pmatrix}}{365} = \frac{\begin{pmatrix} -\$45.56 \cdot 56.25\% \cdot \dfrac{0.3767}{2\cdot\sqrt{1}} \\ -\$45 \cdot 2\% \cdot e^{(-2\%\cdot 1)} \cdot 0.4115 \end{pmatrix}}{365} = -0.0142$$

TABLE 8.5 Summary of position value and Greeks, long call example

Long call	
Call value	\$10.6715
Delta	0.6326
Gamma	0.0147
Vega	0.1716
Rho	0.1815
Theta	−0.0142

8.5 INTERPRETING THE GREEKS

Let's interpret each of the Greeks calculated in the previous section.

8.5.1 Interpretation of Delta

Delta is the estimated dollar change in position value per one dollar increase in the underlying asset price. In other words, Delta answers the following question: Holding everything else equal, as the underlying asset price increases by one dollar, by how many dollars will the position change in value?

In our example:

- The underlying asset price is $45.56.
- The long call value is $10.6715.
- The long call Delta is 0.6326.

The Delta of 0.6326 is interpreted as follows: As the underlying asset price increases by one dollar, from $45.56 to $46.56, the long call is estimated to increase in value by $0.6326, from $10.6715 to $11.3042.

8.5.2 Interpretation of Gamma

Gamma is estimated change in position Delta per one dollar increase in the underlying asset price. Gamma is useful as it measures the stability of Delta through answering the following question: Holding everything else equal, as the underlying asset price increases by one dollar, by how much will Delta change in value? We can contrast Delta and Gamma as follows:

- Delta measures the sensitivity of value to changes in the underlying asset price.
- Gamma measures the sensitivity of Delta to changes in the underlying asset price.

In our example:

- The underlying asset price is $45.56.
- The long call Delta is 0.6326.
- The long call Gamma is 0.0147.

The Gamma of 0.0147 is interpreted as follows: Holding everything else equal, as the underlying asset price increases by one dollar, from $45.56 to $46.56, the Delta of the long call is estimated to increase in value by 0.0147, from 0.6326 to 0.6473.

8.5.3 Interpretation of Vega

Vega is the estimated dollar change in position value per 1% increase in the underlying asset volatility. In other words, Vega answers the following question: Holding everything else equal, as the underlying asset volatility increases by 1% above its current volatility, by how many dollars will the position change in value?

In our example:

- The underlying asset volatility is 56.25%.
- The long call value is $10.6715.
- The long call Vega is 0.1716.

The Vega of 0.1716 is interpreted as follows: As the underlying asset volatility increases by 1%, from 56.25% to 57.25%, the long call is estimated to increase in value by $0.1716, from $10.6715 to $10.8432.

8.5.4 Interpretation of Rho

Rho is the estimated dollar change in position value per 1% increase in the risk-free interest rate. In other words, Rho answers the following question: Holding everything else equal, as the risk-free interest rate increases by 1% above the current risk-free interest rate, by how many dollars will the position change in value?

In our example:

- The risk-free interest rate is 2%.
- The long call value is $10.6715.
- The long call Rho is 0.1815.

The Rho of 0.1815 is interpreted as follows: As the risk-free interest rate increases by 1%, from 2% to 3%, the long call is estimated to increase in value by $0.1815, from $10.6715 to $10.8530.

8.5.5 Interpretation of Theta

Theta is the estimated dollar change in position value per one day decrease in the time to expiration. In other words, Theta answers the following question: Holding everything else equal, as the time to expiration decreases by one day, by how many dollars will the position change in value? Two notes:

- Theta measures the change in value as the time to expiration *decreases*.
- Typically, Theta assumes 365 days in a year.

TABLE 8.6 Comparison of the Greeks to Black-Scholes model estimated changes

Greek	What is being measured?	Initial level	Greek-estimated change	Greek-estimated new level	Black-Scholes estimated change	Black-Scholes estimated new level
Delta	Change in value following $1 increase in underlying asset price	$10.67153	$0.63262	$11.30415	$0.63988	$11.31141
Gamma	Change in Delta following $1 increase in underlying asset price	0.63262	0.01470	0.647316	0.01444	0.64706
Vega	Change in value following 1% increase in the underlying asset volatility	$10.67153	$0.17162	$10.84315	$0.17150	$10.84304
Rho	Change in value following 1% increase in the risk-free interest rate	$10.67153	$0.18150	$10.85304	$0.16746	$10.83900
Theta	Change in value following 1 day decrease in time to expiration	$10.67153	–$0.01422	$10.65731	–$0.01423	$10.65730

In our example:

- The time to expiration is one year, or 365 days.
- The long call value is $10.6715.
- The long call Theta is –0.0142.

The Theta of –0.0142 is interpreted as follows: As the time to expiration decreases by one day, from 365 days to 364 days, the long call is estimated to decrease in value by $0.0142, from $10.6715 to $10.6573.

Knowledge check

Q 8.42: What question does Delta answer?
Q 8.43: What question does Gamma answer?
Q 8.44: What question does Vega answer?
Q 8.45: What question does Rho answer?
Q 8.46: What question does Theta answer?

8.6 THE ACCURACY OF THE GREEKS

The Greeks are estimates that are typically not completely accurate. To demonstrate, in Table 8.6 the Greek-based estimates are compared to estimated changes using the Black-Scholes model.

KEY POINTS

- The "Greeks" is the name given to various measures of position sensitivity.
- Delta is the estimated dollar change in position value per one dollar increase in the underlying asset price.
- Gamma is the estimated change in position Delta per one dollar increase in the underlying asset price.
- Vega is the estimated dollar change in position value per one percent increase in the underlying asset volatility.
- Rho is the estimated dollar change in position value per one percent increase in the risk-free interest rate.
- Theta is the estimated dollar change in position value per one day decrease in the time to expiration.

- The Greeks measure per-unit sensitivity, holding everything else equal, to either an increase or decrease in the source of sensitivity. There is no sensitivity measure for changes in forward price or strike price.
- The Greeks can be calculated using equations. The equations for the Greeks are identified using calculus. Because of this, the Greeks are estimates and are not perfectly accurate. For most practitioners, knowing how to interpret the Greeks is more important than knowing how to calculate the Greeks.

CHAPTER 9

Understanding Delta and Gamma

INTRODUCTION

In the previous chapter we defined the Greeks and learned how to calculate and interpret them. In this and the subsequent chapter we will learn how the Greeks can be used to understand and describe sensitivity. This chapter explores the use of Delta and Gamma as sensitivity measures. The subsequent chapter will explore Vega, Rho, and Theta.

After you read this chapter you will be able to

- Understand that Delta and Gamma are measures of sensitivity.
- Describe each position's sensitivity using Delta and Gamma.
- Understand the Delta and Gamma characteristics of each position.
- Explain why the levels of Delta and Gamma can differ across underlying asset prices.

9.1 DESCRIBING SENSITIVITY USING DELTA AND GAMMA

Table 9.1 details the types of sensitivities that positive, negative, and zero values of Delta and Gamma represent. The expressions "long," "short," and "neutral" are used to refer to whether a given Greek is positive, negative, or zero. For example, a position that is "long Delta" has positive Delta and changes in the position's value are positively related to changes in the underlying asset price.

While "sensitivity" may be superficially perceived as interchangeable with "risk," the two concepts are distinct. "Sensitivity" measures what happens to one variable as another variable changes; "risk" indicates that there is uncertainty about whether the change will take place and the magnitude of the change. The source of sensitivity for both Delta and Gamma is the underlying asset price, which can increase or decrease by varying amounts. Hence, it is legitimate to perceive Delta and Gamma as measures of risk.

TABLE 9.1 Describing sensitivity using Delta and Gamma

Description of sensitivity	Delta and Gamma: Positive, negative, or zero	Delta and Gamma: Long, short, or neutral
Changes in the position's value are positively related to changes in the underlying asset price.	Positive Delta	Long Delta
Changes in the position's value are negatively related to changes in the underlying asset price.	Negative Delta	Short Delta
The position's value does not change as the underlying asset price changes.	Zero Delta	Delta Neutral
Changes in the position's Delta are positively related to changes in the underlying asset price.	Positive Gamma	Long Gamma
Changes in the position's Delta are negatively related to changes in the underlying asset price.	Negative Gamma	Short Gamma
The position's Delta does not change as the underlying asset price changes.	Zero Gamma	Gamma Neutral

TABLE 9.2 Delta and Gamma of forwards and options

Greek	Long forward	Short forward	Long call	Short call	Long put	Short put
Delta	Long	Short	Long	Short	Short	Long
Gamma	Neutral	Neutral	Long	Short	Long	Short

Table 9.2 presents whether each position is long, short, or neutral Delta and Gamma.

To illustrate, let's calculate Delta and Gamma for six scenarios: long and short positions in a forward, call, and put. Assume the call and put are European-style, the underlying asset pays no income, and the inputs through which we will calculate Delta and Gamma are:

- Underlying asset price = $100
- Strike price/forward price = $102
- Time to expiration = 1 year
- Underlying asset volatility = 25%
- Risk-free interest rate = 3%

TABLE 9.3 Example of Delta and Gamma for long and short forward and option positions

Greek	Long forward	Short forward	Long call	Short call	Long put	Short put
Delta	1	−1	0.5658	−0.5658	−0.4342	0.4342
Gamma	0	0	0.0157	−0.0157	0.0157	−0.0157

Table 9.3 presents the Delta and Gamma for each position.

The "sign" of a number refers to whether it is positive, negative, or zero. The signs of Delta and Gamma in the example presented in Table 9.3 correspond to whether the given position is characterized as having long, short, or neutral values for Delta and Gamma.

In the next sections we will explore the following questions for both Delta and Gamma for each position: *Why* is it long, short, or neutral?

Knowledge check

Q 9.1: What do the expressions "long," "short," and "neutral" refer to in the context of the Greeks?
Q 9.2: If a position is long Delta, what is the nature of its sensitivity?
Q 9.3: If a position is short Delta, what is the nature of its sensitivity?
Q 9.4: If a position is Delta neutral, what is the nature of its sensitivity?
Q 9.5: If a position is long Gamma, what is the nature of its sensitivity?
Q 9.6: If a position is short Gamma, what is the nature of its sensitivity?
Q 9.7: If a position is Gamma neutral, what is the nature of its sensitivity?
Q 9.8: How do the concepts of "sensitivity" and "risk" differ?
Q 9.9: Is Delta a measure of risk?
Q 9.10: Is Gamma a measure of risk?
Q 9.11: What are the Delta and Gamma characteristics of a long forward?
Q 9.12: What are the Delta and Gamma characteristics of a short forward?
Q 9.13: What are the Delta and Gamma characteristics of a long call?
Q 9.14: What are the Delta and Gamma characteristics of a short call?
Q 9.15: What are the Delta and Gamma characteristics of a long put?
Q 9.16: What are the Delta and Gamma characteristics of a short put?

9.2 UNDERSTANDING DELTA

Delta measures value sensitivity to change in the underlying asset price. A position that is long Delta has positive sensitivity, a position that is short Delta has negative sensitivity, and a position that is Delta neutral has no sensitivity.

Whether Delta is long or short is determined by whether the given position is the purchasing or selling counterparty to the transaction. The purchasing counterparty is long Delta and the selling counterparty is short Delta. After all, the value of a position is a function of its expected payoff, and changes in the underlying asset price impact the expected payoff in different ways for purchasing and selling counterparties:

- Purchasing entails *receiving* the underlying asset. Therefore, position value is positively sensitive to changes in the underlying asset price. Hence, purchasing counterparties are long Delta.
- Selling entails *delivering* the underlying asset. Therefore, position value is negatively sensitive to changes in the underlying asset price. Hence, selling counterparties are short Delta.

A long forward, long call, and short put are purchasing counterparties, while a short forward, short call, and long put are selling counterparties, as summarized in Table 9.4. Hence long forward, long call, and short put positions are long Delta; and short forward, short call, and long put positions are short Delta.

Knowledge check

Q 9.17: Why are long forwards, long calls, and short puts long Delta?
Q 9.18: Why are short forwards, short calls, and long puts short Delta?

TABLE 9.4 The purchasing and selling counterparties in a forward, call, and put

Position	Long position	Short position
Forward	Obligation to *purchase*	Obligation to *sell*
Call option	Right to *purchase*	Obligation to *sell* if long call exercises
Put option	Right to *sell*	Obligation to *purchase* if long put exercises

9.3 DELTA ACROSS THE UNDERLYING ASSET PRICE

The magnitude of Delta can vary across the underlying asset price. Table 9.5 presents the value of Delta across the underlying asset price for each position.

Some notes in relation to Table 9.5 are as follows:

- Deltas of option positions vary across the underlying asset price, while Deltas of forward positions do not.
- The concept of moneyness does not apply to forwards, as both parties face obligations and neither party gets to choose whether to transact.
- A long call is deep-OTM when the underlying asset price is much lower than the strike price, and deep-ITM when the underlying asset price is much higher than the strike price.
- A long put is deep-OTM when the underlying asset price is much higher than the strike, and deep-ITM when the underlying asset price is much lower than the strike price.
- Technically, option Delta is not exactly equal to 0, 1, and −1, even when deep-ITM or deep-OTM, though the values for Delta approach very close to these values.
- The ranges of values are for forwards and European-style options where the underlying asset pays no income. The ranges for other variations are similar but not identical.

Because long forward Delta never changes, a long forward is known as a "one Delta" or "Delta one" position. It is described this way as its Delta is universally the same number across the underlying asset price.

The diagrams in Figure 9.1 illustrate Delta across underlying asset prices for long and short positions in calls and puts for the following example:

- Strike price = $95
- Time to expiration = 1 year
- Underlying asset volatility = 20%
- Risk-free interest rate = 2%

Why does the Delta of a forward position remain constant, while the Delta of an option position does not? The explanation is provided next.

9.3.1 Why Delta of a forward position is constant

The Delta of a forward position is constant because the counterparties to a forward are both obligated to transact. Since the transaction will

TABLE 9.5 Delta across the underlying asset price

Position	Delta: long or short	Delta range	Delta when deep-OTM	Delta when deep-ITM	Delta when underlying asset price is much lower than the forward price/strike price	Delta when underlying asset price is much higher than the forward price/strike price
Long forward	Long	Always 1	N/A	N/A	1	1
Short forward	Short	Always –1	N/A	N/A	–1	–1
Long call	Long	Between 0 and 1	Approaches 0	Approaches 1	Approaches 0	Approaches 1
Short call	Short	Between –1 and 0	Approaches 0	Approaches -1	Approaches 0	Approaches –1
Long put	Short	Between –1 and 0	Approaches 0	Approaches -1	Approaches –1	Approaches 0
Short put	Long	Between 1 and 0	Approaches 0	Approaches 1	Approaches 1	Approaches 0

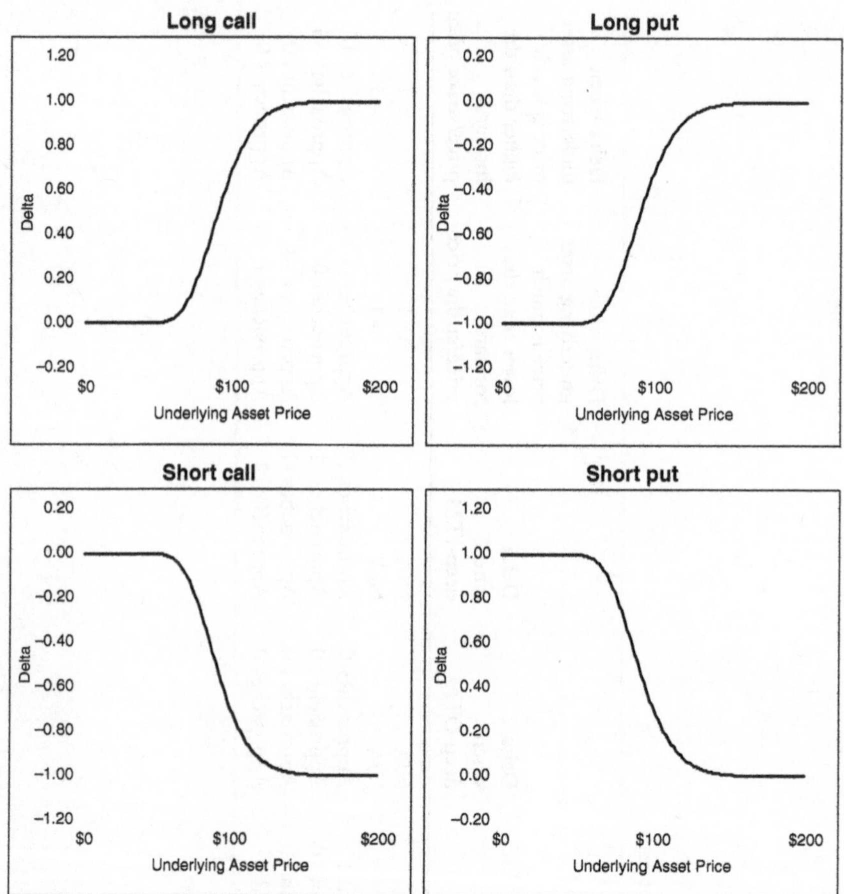

FIGURE 9.1 Delta across the underlying asset price for long and short calls and puts

certainly take place, the counterparties fully experience gains or losses as the underlying asset price changes. After all, the long forward will, with certainty, eventually receive the asset while the short forward will, with certainty, eventually deliver the asset. Hence, each position is fully sensitive to the change in the underlying asset price. Therefore, the long forward Delta is 1 and the short forward Delta is –1.

9.3.2 Why Delta of an option position varies across the underlying asset price

The Delta of an option position varies across the underlying asset price as the long position to an option is not obligated to transact. Therefore:

- When the option is deep-OTM, it doesn't matter very much that the underlying asset price has changed, as there is low likelihood the transaction will occur. Hence, there is little value sensitivity and Delta is negligible.
- When the option is deep-ITM, changes in the underlying asset price impact the counterparties, as there is high likelihood that the transaction will occur. The option positions are fully sensitive and Delta is 1 for the purchasing counterparty and −1 for the selling counterparty.
- When the option is near-the-money, changes in the underlying asset price are somewhat impactful, as there is some likelihood that the transaction will occur. The option positions are therefore somewhat sensitive, and Delta will be between 0 and 1 for the purchasing counterparty and between 0 and −1 for the selling counterparty.

To illustrate, consider a call option that has a strike price of $100. Delta across the underlying asset price is as follows:

- When the underlying asset price is $20, this option is deep-OTM. It is highly unlikely that this option will be exercised. After all, the long call will not rationally exercise its right to purchase the underlying asset for $100 when the asset is worth only $20. Should the underlying asset price increase to $21, it is not impactful: Just as the long call will not exercise its right to purchase for $100 when the underlying asset price is $20, so too the long call will not exercise when the underlying asset price is $21. Hence, both the long and short calls' Deltas are negligible.
- When the underlying asset price is $150, this option is deep-ITM. It is highly likely that this option will be exercised. Should the underlying asset price then increase to $151, it is very impactful: Since the long call will almost certainly exercise, the long call benefits fully from the increase in the underlying asset price. Hence, Delta will approach 1 for the long position and −1 for the short call.
- When the underlying asset price is $100, this option is ATM. There is some likelihood of it being exercised. Therefore, should the underlying asset price increase to $101, it is somewhat impactful. Hence, Delta will be between 0 and 1 for the long call and between 0 and −1 for the short call.

We see that Delta close to 0 indicates that the option will very likely not be exercised, while a Delta of close to either 1 or −1 indicates that the option will very likely be exercised.

The absolute value of Delta approaches 1 when an option is deep-ITM and approaches 0 when deep-OTM. Hence the absolute value of Delta can be perceived as a measure of moneyness. When perceiving Delta from this perspective, Delta is presented in absolute terms and without the use of a decimal. For example, an absolute Delta of 75 indicates that the position is ITM, while an absolute Delta of 25 indicates that the position is OTM.

Knowledge check

Q 9.19: For which positions does Delta not vary across the underlying asset price?
Q 9.20: How does long call Delta vary across the underlying asset price?
Q 9.21: How does short call Delta vary across the underlying asset price?
Q 9.22: How does long put Delta vary across the underlying asset price?
Q 9.23: How does short put Delta vary across the underlying asset price?
Q 9.24: What is a "one Delta" position?
Q 9.25: Why are forward positions one Delta?
Q 9.26: Why does the Delta of an option position vary across the underlying asset price?

9.4 UNDERSTANDING GAMMA

Gamma measures Delta sensitivity to change in the underlying asset price. A position that is long Gamma has positive sensitivity, a position that is short Gamma has negative sensitivity, and a position that is Gamma neutral has no sensitivity. Whether a position's Gamma is long, short, or neutral is determined by whether the position's Delta varies across the underlying asset price, as follows:

- When Delta is constant across the underlying asset price, the position is Gamma neutral.
- When Delta is positively sensitive to changes in the underlying asset price, the position is long Gamma.
- When Delta is negatively sensitive to changes in the underlying asset price, the position is short Gamma.

TABLE 9.6 Why Gamma is long, short, or neutral for each position

Position	Gamma: long, short, or neutral	Why Gamma is long, short, or neutral
Long forward	Neutral	Because Delta is always 1
Short forward	Neutral	Because Delta is always −1
Long call	Long	Because Delta increases from 0 to 1 as the underlying asset price increases
Short call	Short	Because Delta decreases from 0 to −1 as the underlying asset price increases
Long put	Long	Because Delta increases from −1 to 0 as the underlying asset price increases
Short put	Short	Because Delta decreases from 1 to 0 as the underlying asset price increases

Table 9.6 details whether Gamma is long, short, or neutral for each positon and explains why.

Knowledge check

- Q 9.27: What determines whether a position's Gamma is long, short, or neutral?
- Q 9.28: Why is a long forward Gamma neutral?
- Q 9.29: Why is a short forward Gamma neutral?
- Q 9.30: Why is a long call long Gamma?
- Q 9.31: Why is a short call short Gamma?
- Q 9.32: Why is a long put long Gamma?
- Q 9.33: Why is a short put short Gamma?

9.5 GAMMA ACROSS THE UNDERLYING ASSET PRICE

The magnitude of Gamma can vary across underlying asset prices. The magnitude of Gamma depends on the moneyness of the option, as detailed in Table 9.7.

Note that the concept of moneyness does not apply to forwards as both counterparties are obligated to transact. Note as well that while technically option Gamma is not exactly zero even when deep-ITM or deep-OTM, the values for Gamma approach very close to zero.

TABLE 9.7 Gamma across underlying asset prices

Position	Gamma: long, short, or neutral	Gamma when deep-OTM	Gamma when near-the-money	Gamma when deep-ITM
Long forward	Neutral	N/A	N/A	N/A
Short forward	Neutral	N/A	N/A	N/A
Long call	Long	Approaches zero	Highest	Approaches zero
Short call	Short	Approaches zero	Lowest	Approaches zero
Long put	Long	Approaches zero	Highest	Approaches zero
Short put	Short	Approaches zero	Lowest	Approaches zero

The diagrams in Figure 9.2 illustrate Gamma across the underlying asset price for long and short positions in calls and puts for the same example that is presented in Figure 9.2.

Observe the following from Figure 9.2:

- Gamma approaches zero when the options are either deep-OTM or deep-ITM.
- The magnitude of an option's Gamma is largest near-the-money.
- Call and put Gamma are identical to each other.

Let's explore each of these observations in detail.

Why does Gamma approach zero when the options are either deep-OTM or deep-ITM?

Gamma approaches zero when Delta is not sensitive to changes in the underlying asset price, which occurs when deep-OTM and deep-ITM, for the following reasons:

- A deep-OTM option is unlikely to be exercised. Hence, change in the underlying asset price barely impacts option value. Therefore, Delta is stable at close to zero, and Gamma approaches zero.
- A deep-ITM option is likely to be exercised, and change in the underlying asset price barely changes this likelihood. Hence, Delta is stable at close to 1 or −1, and Gamma approaches zero.

Why is the magnitude of an option's Gamma largest near-the-money?

Delta is quite sensitive to changes in the underlying asset price when near-the-money. After all, when near-the-money, a change in the underlying asset price can significantly change the likelihood of the option being exercised and, as a result, the value of the option. Therefore, Delta is very sensitive to changes in the underlying asset price, and the magnitude of Gamma is relatively large.

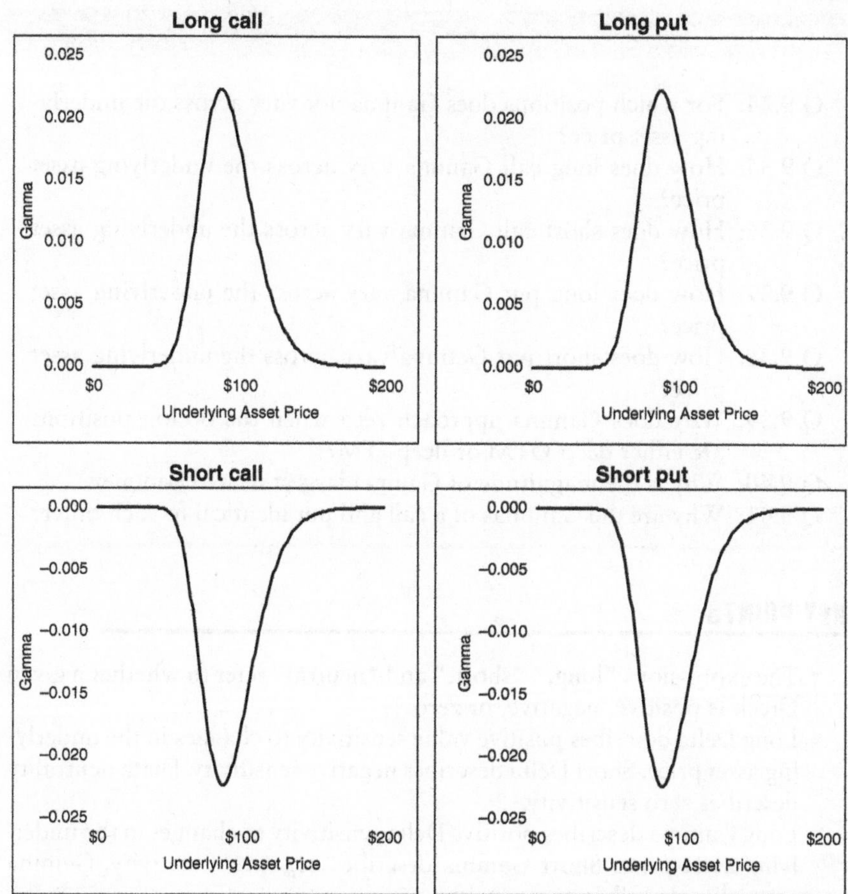

FIGURE 9.2 Gamma across the underlying asset price for long and short calls and puts

Why are the Gammas of a call and put identical to each other?

Long call Gamma is identical to long put Gamma. This is despite the fact that a long call is always long Delta and a long put is always short Delta. The Gammas are identical because both long call and long put Delta increase in identical fashion as the underlying asset price increases, as illustrated in Figure 9.1:

- The long call Delta increases from 0 to 1.
- The long put Delta increases from −1 to 0.

Similarly, short call Gamma is identical to short put Gamma, as the Delta of both decreases in an identical fashion as the underlying asset price increases, as illustrated in Figure 9.1.

Knowledge check

Q 9.34: For which positions does Gamma not vary across the underlying asset price?
Q 9.35: How does long call Gamma vary across the underlying asset price?
Q 9.36: How does short call Gamma vary across the underlying asset price?
Q 9.37: How does long put Gamma vary across the underlying asset price?
Q 9.38: How does short put Gamma vary across the underlying asset price?
Q 9.39: Why does Gamma approach zero when the option positions are either deep-OTM or deep-ITM?
Q 9.40: Why is the magnitude of Gamma largest near-the-money?
Q 9.41: Why are the Gammas of a call and put identical to each other?

KEY POINTS

- The expressions "long," "short," and "neutral" refer to whether a given Greek is positive, negative, or zero.
- Long Delta describes positive value sensitivity to changes in the underlying asset price. Short Delta describes negative sensitivity. Delta neutrality describes zero sensitivity.
- Long Gamma describes positive Delta sensitivity to changes in the underlying asset price. Short Gamma describes negative sensitivity. Gamma neutrality describes zero sensitivity.
- A long forward is long Delta and Gamma neutral. A long call is long Delta and long Gamma. A long put is short Delta and long Gamma. Short positions have the opposite characteristic to their corresponding long positions due to the zero-sum nature of forwards and options.
- A purchasing counterparty is long Delta and a selling counterparty is short Delta.
- Option Delta varies across the underlying asset price and forward Delta does not. The Delta of a forward position is constant because its counterparties are both obligated to transact. The Delta of an option is sensitive to the underlying asset price as its long position is not obligated to transact.
- An option's Gamma varies across the underlying asset price and a forward's Gamma is always zero.

CHAPTER 10

Understanding Vega, Rho, and Theta

INTRODUCTION

In the previous chapter we learned about position sensitivity as measured by Delta and Gamma. This chapter explores the use of Vega, Rho, and Theta to understand and describe position sensitivity.

After you read this chapter, you will be able to

- Understand that Vega, Rho, and Theta are measures of sensitivity.
- Describe each position's sensitivity using Vega, Rho, and Theta.
- Understand the Vega, Rho, and Theta characteristics of each position.
- Understand the symmetrical sensitivity of forwards and the asymmetric sensitivity of options.
- Explain when positions are long Theta and when they are short Theta.

10.1 DESCRIBING SENSITIVITY USING VEGA, RHO, AND THETA

Table 10.1 details the types of sensitivities that positive, negative, and zero values of Vega, Rho, and Theta represent. The expressions "long," "short," and "neutral" are used to refer to whether the given Greek is positive, negative, or zero.

The sources of sensitivity for Vega and Rho are the underlying asset volatility and the risk-free interest rate. These sources of sensitivity can increase or decrease by varying amounts. Hence, it is legitimate to perceive Vega and Rho as measures of risk. The source of sensitivity for Theta is time to expiration. The passage of one day is never a surprise. It is, therefore, inappropriate to refer to Theta as a measure of risk. Instead, the sensitivity captured by Theta communicates a characteristic of the position.

TABLE 10.1 Describing sensitivity using Vega, Rho, and Theta

Description of sensitivity	Vega, Rho, and Theta: Positive, negative, or zero	Vega, Rho, and Theta: Long, short, or neutral
Changes in the position's value are positively related to changes in the underlying asset volatility.	Positive Vega	Long Vega
Changes in the position's value are negatively related to changes in the underlying asset volatility.	Negative Vega	Short Vega
The position's value does not change as the underlying asset volatility changes.	Zero Vega	Vega Neutral
Changes in the position's value are positively related to changes in the risk-free interest rate.	Positive Rho	Long Rho
Changes in the position's value are negatively related to changes in the risk-free interest rate.	Negative Rho	Short Rho
The position's value does not change as the risk-free interest rate changes.	Zero Rho	Rho Neutral
The position's value will increase as time to expiration decreases.	Positive Theta	Long Theta
The position's value will decrease as time to expiration decreases.	Negative Theta	Short Theta
The position's value will not change as time to expiration decreases.	Zero Theta	Theta Neutral

Table 10.2 presents whether each position is long, short, or neutral for each of the Greeks.

Table 9.2 of Chapter 9 presented an example of the values of Delta and Gamma for long and short forwards, calls, and puts. Table 10.3 expands Table 9.2 through including all of the Greeks for each position. In this example the call and put are European-style, the underlying asset pays no income, and the inputs through which the Greeks are calculated are:

- Underlying asset price = $100
- Strike price/forward price = $102
- Time to expiration = 1 year
- Underlying asset volatility = 25%
- Risk-free interest rate = 3%

The sign of each of the Greeks presented in Table 10.3 corresponds to whether the given position is characterized as having long, short, or neutral

TABLE 10.2 The Greeks of forwards and options

Greek	Long Forward	Short Forward	Long Call	Short Call	Long Put	Short Put
Delta	Long	Short	Long	Short	Short	Long
Gamma	Neutral	Neutral	Long	Short	Long	Short
Vega	Neutral	Neutral	Long	Short	Long	Short
Rho	Long	Short	Long	Short	Short	Long
Theta	Short	Long	Short	Long	Long or Short	Long or Short

TABLE 10.3 Example of the Greeks for long and short forward and option positions

Greek	Long Forward	Short Forward	Long Call	Short Call	Long Put	Short Put
Delta	1	−1	0.5658	−0.5658	−0.4342	0.4342
Gamma	0	0	0.0157	−0.0157	0.0157	−0.0157
Vega	0	0	0.3935	−0.3935	0.3935	−0.3935
Rho	0.9899	−0.9899	0.4617	−0.4617	−0.5281	0.5281
Theta	−0.0081	0.0081	−0.0173	0.0173	−0.0091	0.0091

values for the given Greek. While long and short puts can be either long or short Theta, in this example the long put is short Theta and the short put is long Theta.

In the previous chapter we explored Delta and Gamma for each position. In the next sections of this chapter we will explore the following questions for the Vega, Rho, and Theta for each position: *Why* is it long, short, or neutral?

Knowledge check

Q 10.1: If a position is long Vega, what is the nature of its sensitivity?
Q 10.2: If a position is short Vega, what is the nature of its sensitivity?
Q 10.3: If a position is Vega neutral, what is the nature of its sensitivity?
Q 10.4: If a position is long Rho, what is the nature of its sensitivity?
Q 10.5: If a position is short Rho, what is the nature of its sensitivity?
Q 10.6: If a position is Rho neutral, what is the nature of its sensitivity?
Q 10.7: If a position is long Theta, what is the nature of its sensitivity?
Q 10.8: If a position is short Theta, what is the nature of its sensitivity?

Q 10.9: If a position is Theta neutral, what is the nature of its sensitivity?
Q 10.10: Is Vega a measure of risk?
Q 10.11: Is Rho a measure of risk?
Q 10.12: Is Theta a measure of risk?
Q 10.13: What are the Vega, Rho, and Theta characteristics of a long forward?
Q 10.14: What are the Vega, Rho, and Theta characteristics of a short forward?
Q 10.15: What are the Vega, Rho, and Theta characteristics of a long call?
Q 10.16: What are the Vega, Rho, and Theta characteristics of a short call?
Q 10.17: What are the Vega, Rho, and Theta characteristics of a long put?
Q 10.18: What are the Vega, Rho, and Theta characteristics of a short put?

10.2 UNDERSTANDING VEGA

Vega measures value sensitivity to changes in the underlying asset volatility. A position that is long Vega has positive sensitivity, a position that is short Vega has negative sensitivity, and a position that is Vega neutral has no sensitivity.

Volatility is the degree to which asset returns are dispersed over time. Increases in volatility mean that returns will be more widely dispersed than previously expected, while decreases in volatility mean that returns will be less widely dispersed. Hence, sensitivity to volatility measures sensitivity to changes in the dispersion of the underlying asset returns.

Let's explore the following:

- Why are forward positions Vega neutral?
- Why are long calls and puts long Vega?
- Why are short calls and puts short Vega?

10.2.1 Why forward positions are Vega neutral

Forward positions are Vega neutral as their payoffs are symmetrical: Change in volatility can lead to offsetting benefit and harm. The diagrams in Figure 10.1 illustrate the symmetrical nature of forward positions. For both long and short positions, increases in volatility increase potential positive

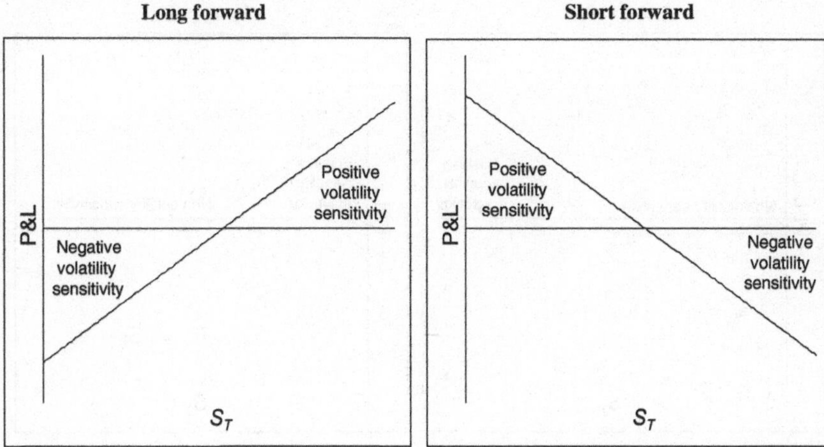

FIGURE 10.1 The symmetrical sensitivity of forward positions

payoff but also increase potential negative payoff. Conversely, decreases in volatility reduce potential positive payoff but also reduce potential negative payoff. Due to this symmetry both long and short forward positions are Vega neutral.

10.2.2 Why long calls and puts are long Vega

Long calls and puts are long Vega as their payoffs are asymmetrical: Wider dispersion of the underlying asset returns caused by increased volatility is very beneficial as there is potential for larger positive payoff, while the limited downside of long calls and puts means that increased volatility has no potential for harm. The diagrams in Figure 10.2 illustrate the asymmetrical nature of the sensitivity of long call and long put positions. Since increased volatility is beneficial and not harmful, both long calls and long puts are positively sensitive to changes in volatility.

10.2.3 Why short calls and puts are short Vega

Short calls and puts are short Vega, as their payoffs are asymmetrical: Wider dispersion of the underlying asset returns caused by increased volatility is very harmful as there is potential for larger negative payoff, while the limited upside of short calls and puts means that the increased volatility has no potential for benefit. The diagrams in Figure 10.3 illustrate the asymmetrical nature of the sensitivity of short call and short put positions. Since increased volatility can be harmful and is not beneficial, both long calls and long puts are negatively sensitive to changes in volatility.

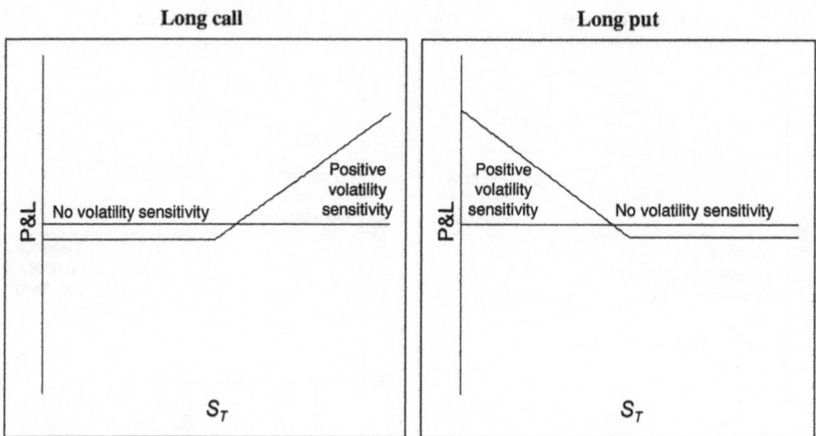

FIGURE 10.2 The asymmetrical sensitivity of long calls and puts

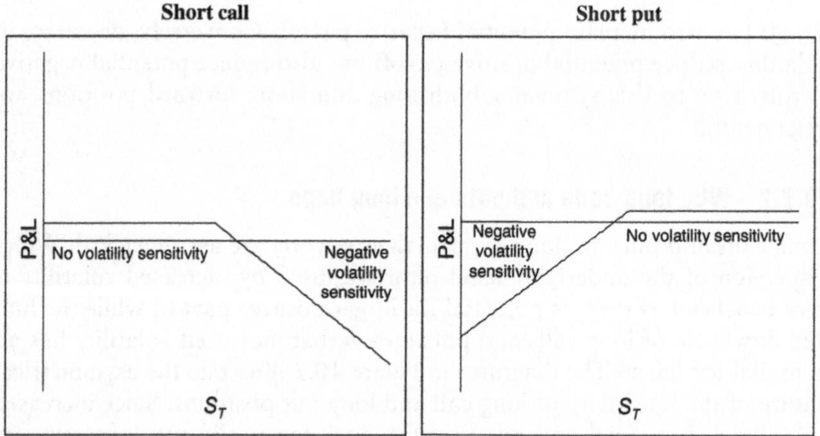

FIGURE 10.3 The asymmetrical sensitivity of short calls and puts

10.2.4 Vega across the underlying asset price

The magnitude of Vega is largest for near-the-money options and smallest for deep-OTM and deep-ITM positions. This is because the asymmetry that drives volatility sensitivity is the most acute near-the-money, where a change in price in one direction has no impact and a change in price in the other direction has a large impact. Conversely, deep-OTM positions have little to gain or lose from changes in price in either direction, while deep-ITM positions gain and lose in symmetrical fashion. Therefore, there is little net impact from a change in volatility for deep-OTM and deep-ITM positions.

Knowledge check

Q 10.19: Are long forward payoffs symmetrical or asymmetrical?
Q 10.20: Are short forward payoffs symmetrical or asymmetrical?
Q 10.21: Are long call payoffs symmetrical or asymmetrical?
Q 10.22: Are short call payoffs symmetrical or asymmetrical?
Q 10.23: Are long put payoffs symmetrical or asymmetrical?
Q 10.24: Are short put payoffs symmetrical or asymmetrical?
Q 10.25: Why are forward positions Vega neutral?
Q 10.26: Why are long calls and puts long Vega?
Q 10.27: Why are short calls and puts short Vega?
Q 10.28: Why is the magnitude of Vega largest for near-the-money options?

10.3 UNDERSTANDING RHO

Rho measures value sensitivity to changes in the risk-free interest rate. A position that is long Rho has positive sensitivity, a position that is short Rho has negative sensitivity, and a position that is Rho neutral has no sensitivity.

To understand why a given position is long or short Rho, we first have to understand that when the risk-free interest rate increases, the present value of the forward price/strike price decreases. To demonstrate, consider the following example:

- Forward price/strike price = \$20
- Time to expiration = 90 days (assuming 365 days in a year)
- Risk-free interest rate = 7%

The present value of the forward price/strike price is:

$$\$20 \times e^{-7\% \times \frac{90}{365}} = \$19.66$$

If the interest rate increases to 8%, the present value of the forward price/strike price is:

$$\$20 \times e^{-8\% \times \frac{90}{365}} = \$19.61$$

This shows a decrease of five cents. We see that as the risk-free interest increases, the present value of the forward/strike price decreases.

This observation can help us understand the sensitivity of a position's value to the risk-free interest rate. The sensitivity will depend on whether the position is purchasing or selling:

- Purchasing counterparties *pay* the forward price/strike price. The present value of the forward price/strike price decreases as the risk-free interest rate increases. Hence, the purchasing counterparty effectively pays less. Therefore, the purchasing counterparty's value is positively sensitive to the risk-free interest rate, and their position is long Rho.
- Selling counterparties *receive* the forward price/strike price. The present value of the forward price/strike price decreases as the risk-free interest rate increases. Hence, the selling counterparty effectively receives less. Therefore, selling counterparty value is negatively sensitive to the risk-free interest rate, and their position is short Rho.

Long forward, long call, and short put positions are purchasing counterparties. Hence, they are long Rho. Short forward, short call, and long put positions are selling counterparties. Hence, they are short Rho.

Knowledge check

Q 10.29: What impact does an increase in the risk-free interest rate have on the present value of the forward price/strike price?
Q 10.30: Why are long forwards, long calls, and short puts long Rho?
Q 10.31: Why are short forwards, short calls, and long puts short Rho?

10.4 UNDERSTANDING THETA

Theta measures value sensitivity as time to expiration decreases. The passage of one day is never a surprise; and, therefore, the sensitivity captured by Theta communicates a characteristic of the position and is not a measure of risk.

There are two ways that a decrease in the time to expiration can impact the value of a position:

- The present value effect: As time to expiration decreases, the present value of the forward price/strike increases.
- The optionality value effect: As time to expiration decreases, optionality value erodes.

Let's explore each of these effects in detail.

10.4.1 The present value effect

As the time to expiration decreases, the present value of the forward price/strike price will increase. To demonstrate, consider the following example:

- Forward price/strike price = \$500
- Time to expiration = 30 days (assuming 365 days in a year)
- Risk-free interest rate = 5%

The present value of the forward price/strike price is:

$$\$500 \times e^{-5\% \times \frac{30}{365}} = \$497.95$$

If the time to expiration decreases to 29 days rather than 30 days, the present value of the forward price/strike price is:

$$\$500 \times e^{-5\% \times \frac{29}{365}} = \$498.02$$

This shows an increase of seven cents. We see that as the time to expiration decreases, the present value of the forward price/strike price decreases.

This observation can help us understand the sensitivity of a position's value to decreases in the time to expiration. The sensitivity will depend on whether the position is purchasing or selling:

- Purchasing counterparties *pay* the forward price/strike price. The present value of the forward price/strike that is paid increases as time to expiration decreases. Hence, the purchasing counterparty effectively pays more. Therefore, the purchasing counterparty's value is negatively sensitive to decreases in the time to expiration.
- The selling counterparty *receives* the forward price/strike price. The present value of the forward price/strike received increases as time to

expiration decreases. Hence, the selling counterparty effectively receives more. Therefore, the selling counterparty value is positively sensitive to decreases in the time to expiration.

This suggests that purchasing counterparties (long forward, long call, and short put positions) should be short Theta, and selling counterparties (short forward, short call, and long put positions) should be long Theta. However, the present value effect is not the only effect. Let's next explore the optionality value effect.

10.4.2 The optionality value effect

Optionality value is the value of having the right to decide whether to exercise or not. Optionality is valuable, as the investor can exercise if it is beneficial and otherwise not exercise. Options, which provide their long positions rights, are characterized by optionality value. Forward positions have obligations, not rights, and are therefore not characterized by optionality value. Optionality is a valuable asset for long call and long put positions, as they have the right to exercise. Optionality is a liability for short call and short put position, as they provide their counterparties the right to exercise.

As time to expiration decreases, optionality value erodes as with less time to expiration there is less time to decide whether to exercise or not.

To illustrate, consider a call option that provides the right purchase a given underlying asset:

- With one year to expiration optionality is quite valuable. For an entire year the long position can benefit if the underlying asset price increases. Should the underlying asset price decrease, the long position can choose not to exercise.
- With one day to expiration optionality is not valuable. While the long position has the right to exercise, that right is provided for only one day. After one day the right is lost.

Whether the erosion of optionality increases or decreases value depends on whether the position has the right to exercise or provides the right to exercise:

- For a long position that has the right to exercise, the erosion of optionality value has a negative impact on its value.
- For a short position that provides the right to exercise, the erosion of optionality value decreases the size of its liability and, therefore, has a positive impact on its value.

This suggests that long calls and puts should be short Theta, and short calls and puts should be long Theta. However, we must take into account the present value effect as well. Let's next explore the net impact of decreases in time to expiration.

10.4.3 The net impact of a decrease in the time to expiration

Whether a position is long or short Theta will depend on both the present value effect and the optionality value effect. Table 10.4 presents the characteristics of each position and how these characteristics influence whether the given position is long or short Theta.

As Table 10.4 shows, long forwards and calls are always short Theta and short forwards and calls are always long Theta. Interestingly, put positions can be either long or short Theta depending on whether the present value effect or optionality value effect is more impactful.

Generally, we observe that the optionality value effect is most acute when the option has significant optionality value. Near-the-money options have significant optionality value, while deep-ITM options do not, for the following reasons:

- Optionality is very valuable when the option is near-the-money, as there are significant likelihoods that underlying asset price changes will result in the option ending up either ITM or OTM at expiration.
- Optionality is not particularly valuable when deep-ITM, as there is not much of a choice to make: If deep-in-the-money, a long option position will almost certainly exercise. The value of a deep-ITM option is therefore primarily driven by its intrinsic value (the difference between underlying asset price and the strike price) and not optionality value.

Further, the present value effect is most acute when interest rates are high, as present values are more sensitive to decreases in time when interest rates are high.

The implication is as follows: Typically, long puts are short Theta, and short puts are long Theta. However, when interest rates are very high and/or when the put option is deep-ITM, it is possible to observe long puts that are long Theta, and short puts that are short Theta.[1]

---

[1]The value of a deep-OTM option, while quite low, is exclusively driven by optionality value; and, therefore, erosion of optionality value drives erosion of value.

TABLE 10.4 The net impact of decreases in time to expiration

Position	How position value is impacted by the present value effect	How position value is impacted by optionality value effect	The net impact as time to expiration decreases	Theta: long or short
Long forward	Value decreases as time to expiration decreases, because the present value of the forward price to be paid increases.	Value is not impacted as forwards do not have optionality value.	Value decreases	Short
Short forward	Value increases as time to expiration decreases, because the present value of the forward price to be received increases.	Value is not impacted as forwards do not have optionality value.	Value increases	Long
Long call	Value decreases as time to expiration decreases, because the present value of the strike price to be paid increases.	Value decreases as time to expiration decreases, because the value of the optionality that the long call holds decreases.	Value decreases	Short
Short call	Value increases as time to expiration decreases, because the present value of the strike price to be received increases.	Value increases as time to expiration decreases, because the short call's liability due to providing optionality decreases.	Value increases	Long
Long put	Value increases as time to expiration decreases, because the present value of the strike price to be received increases.	Value decreases as time to expiration decreases, because the value of optionality that the long put holds decreases.	Value increases when the present value effect is larger than the optionality value effect. Value decreases when the optionality value effect is larger than the present value effect.	Long or short
Short put	Value decreases as time to expiration decreases, because the present value of the strike price to be paid increases.	Value increases as time to expiration decreases, because the short put's liability due to providing optionality decreases.	Value decreases when the present value effect is larger than the optionality value effect. Value increases when the optionality value effect is larger than the present value effect.	Long or short

Because long forwards and calls are always short Theta, and long puts are typically short Theta, Theta is referred to as "decay." This name connotes that options "decay" in value as time to expiration decreases, holding everything else equal.

Let's explore an example to illustrate the net impact of the passage of time on options. Throughout, we assume:

- Strike price = \$105
- Underlying asset volatility = 20%
- European-style, underlying asset pays no income

Figure 10.4 presents the value of a long call and put across time to expiration for the following three scenarios:

- Base scenario: Underlying asset price = \$100; risk-free interest rate = 2%.
- Alternative scenario 1: Underlying asset price = \$100; risk-free interest rate = 20%.
- Alternative scenario 2: Underlying asset price = \$50; risk-free interest rate = 2%.

Figure 10.4 illustrates the following:

- Base case: Optionality value is very important, as the option is near-the-money, while the present value effect is small, as interest rates are low. The net effect on the long put is that optionality value effect is more impactful than the present value effect. The long put decreases in value as time to expiration decreases and is short Theta.
- Alternative scenario 1: Optionality value is important as the option is near-the-money. However, due to the high risk-free interest rate of 20%, the present value effect is more impactful than the optionality value effect. The long put increases in value as time to expiration decreases and is long Theta.
- Alternative scenario 2: Optionality value is not very important, as the option is deep ITM. While the risk-free interest rate is low, the present value effect is more impactful than the optionality value effect. The long put increases in value with less time to expiration and is long Theta.
- For all scenarios, both the optionality value effect and the present value effect lead the long call to decrease in value as time to expiration decreases, and the long call is short Theta.

Base scenario: underlying asset price = $100, risk-free interest rate = 2%

Long call **Long put**

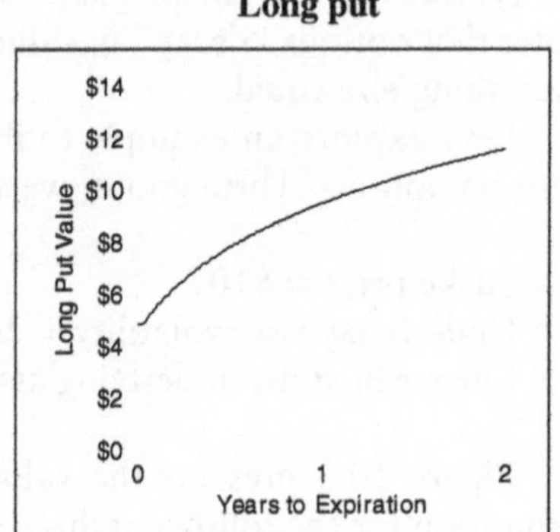

Alternative scenario 1: underlying asset price = $100, risk-free interest rate = 20%

Long call **Long put**

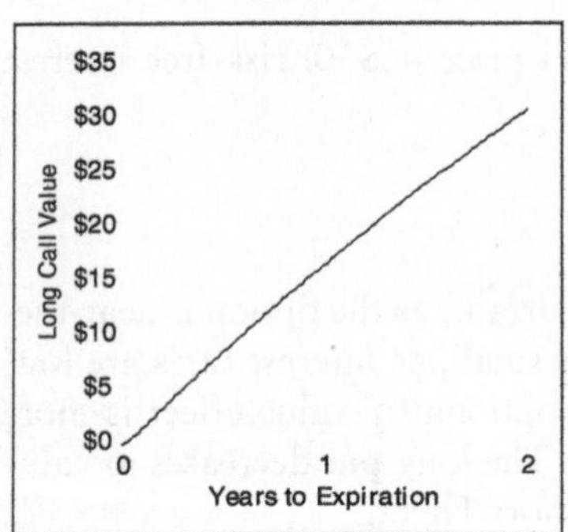

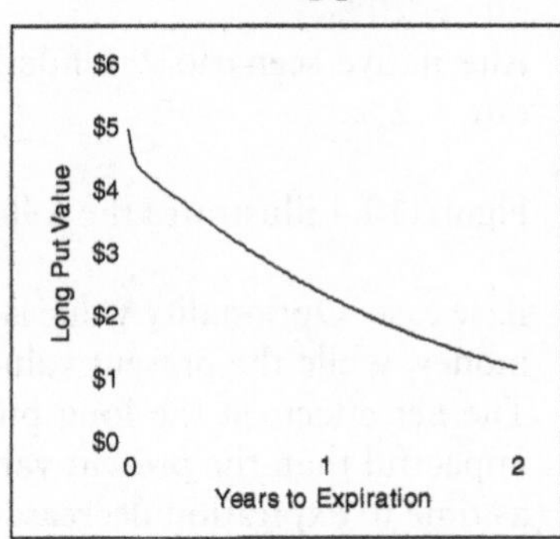

Alternative scenario 2: underlying asset price = $50, risk-free interest rate = 2%

Long call **Long put**

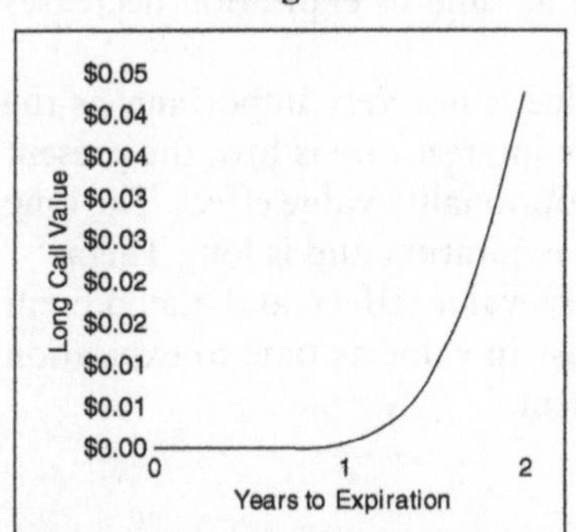

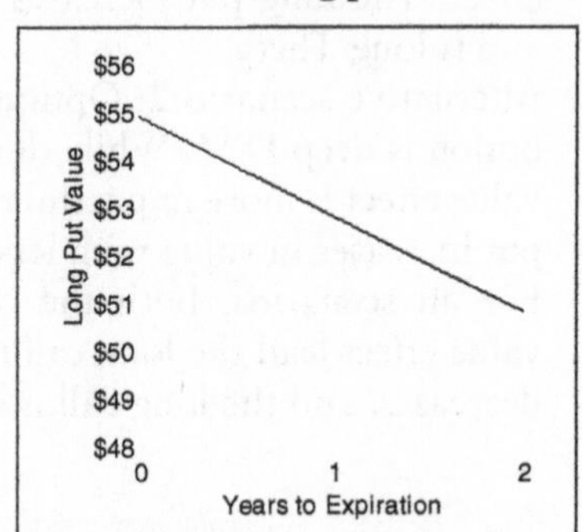

FIGURE 10.4 Examples of long call and put values across time to expiration

Knowledge check

Q 10.32: What is the present value effect of a decrease in time to expiration?
Q 10.33: How does the present value effect impact long forwards, long calls, and short puts?
Q 10.34: How does the present value effect impact short forwards, short calls, and long puts?
Q 10.35: What is the optionality value effect of a decrease in time to expiration?
Q 10.36: How does the optionality value effect impact forward positions?
Q 10.37: How does the optionality value effect impact long calls and puts?
Q 10.38: How does the optionality value effect impact short calls and puts?
Q 10.39: Why are long forwards short Theta?
Q 10.40: Why are short forwards long Theta?
Q 10.41: Why are long calls short Theta?
Q 10.42: Why are short calls long Theta?
Q 10.43: Why are long puts either long or short Theta?
Q 10.44: Why are short puts either long or short Theta?

KEY POINTS

- Long Vega and long Rho describe positive value sensitivity to changes in the underlying asset volatility and the risk-free interest rate, respectively. Short Vega and short Rho describe negative sensitivity and Vega neutrality, and Rho neutrality describes no sensitivity.
- Long Theta describes positive value sensitivity to decreases in the time to expiration. Short Theta describes negative sensitivity, and Theta neutrality describes no sensitivity.
- Vega and Rho are measures of risk. Theta communicates a characteristic of a position, described as "decay," and not risk.
- Forward positions are Vega neutral as their payoffs are symmetrical. Long calls and puts are long Vega as their payoffs are asymmetrical: They can benefit from increased volatility and not be harmed. Short calls and puts are short Vega as their payoffs are asymmetrical: They can be harmed by increased volatility and cannot benefit.
- Purchasing counterparties are long Rho, as the present value of the forward price/strike price paid decreases as the risk-free interest rate

increases. Selling counterparties are short Rho, as the present value of the forward price/strike price received decreases as the risk-free interest rate increases.

- The impact on a position of a decrease in the time to expiration is twofold. First, as time to expiration decreases, the present value of the forward price/strike increases. Second, as time to expiration decreases, optionality value erodes. Whether a given position is long or short Theta depends on the net impact of these two effects. Long forwards and long calls are short Theta; short forwards and short calls are long Theta; and long and short put options can be either long or short Theta, depending on the relative impact of the present value effect versus the optionality value effect.

PART Four

Trading Strategies

CHAPTER 11

Price and Volatility Trading Strategies

INTRODUCTION

In this and the subsequent two chapters we will explore a variety of trading strategies. In this chapter we will explore price and volatility trading strategies. We will learn about price and volatility views, relate them to Delta and Vega, and learn how one can use positions in forwards and options to monetize combinations of price and volatility views. We will also learn about volatility trading strategies known as "straddles" and "strangles."

After you read this chapter, you will be able to

- Describe price and volatility views.
- Relate price and volatility views to sensitivity and Delta and Vega.
- Explain how forward and option trading strategies can be used to monetize combinations of price and volatility views.
- Describe how to form straddles and strangles.
- Explain the Delta and Vega characteristics of straddles and strangles.
- Identify the at-the-money Delta-neutral straddle (ATM DNS) strike price.
- Contrast the ATM DNS strike price with the at-the-money (ATM) strike price.
- Describe the P&L diagrams for straddles and strangles.
- Identify the breakeven points for straddles and strangles.

11.1 PRICE AND VOLATILITY VIEWS

A core purpose of forwards, calls, and puts is to allow an investor to turn a view about the future into profits. Investors have many views. The two key types of views are price views and volatility views. Let's explore both in detail.

11.1.1 Price views

A price view is a view about whether the underlying asset price will increase or decrease in the future. Price views can be one of the following:

- Price bullish: The view that the underlying asset price will increase
- Price bearish: The view that the underlying asset price will decrease
- Price neutral: Neither price bullish nor price bearish

Here are some examples:

- A stock price is $600. An investor believes that the stock price will decrease to $400. The investor is price bearish.
- A municipal bond is trading at 97.50. An investor believes that the bond will increase in value to 102.25. The investor is price bullish.
- An ounce of gold is trading at $900. An investor is unsure as to whether the price of gold will increase or decrease. The investor is price neutral.

11.1.2 Volatility views

A volatility view is a view about whether the underlying asset volatility will increase or decrease in the future. Volatility views can be one of the following:

- Volatility bullish: The view that the underlying asset volatility will increase
- Volatility bearish: The view that the underlying asset volatility will decrease
- Volatility neutral: Neither volatility bullish nor volatility bearish

Some examples:

- A stock's current volatility is 25%. An investor believes that the stock's volatility will increase to 26%. The investor is volatility bullish.
- A Treasury bond's current volatility is 10%. An investor is unsure as to whether the bond's volatility will increase or decrease. The investor is volatility neutral.
- Gold's current volatility is 80%. An investor believes that gold's volatility will decrease to 65%. The investor is volatility bearish.

Knowledge check

Q 11.1: What is a price view?
Q 11.2: What is a volatility view?

11.2 RELATING PRICE AND VOLATILITY VIEWS TO DELTA AND VEGA

An investor can hold views regarding both price and volatility. To identify a trading strategy for each combination of views we can take advantage of our understanding of position sensitivity as explored in Chapters 9 and 10, where we learned that each position can be characterized by its Greeks. Two of the Greeks are Delta and Vega, which measure value sensitivity to changes in underlying asset price and volatility, respectively. Table 11.1 details the sensitivities and Greek positions that allow an investor to monetize price and volatility views.

An investor can form combinations of bullish, bearish, or neutral views regarding both price and volatility. Hence, we can classify views as one of 3 × 3 = 9 combinations. For each combination we can identify the Greek position that monetizes the combination of views as presented in Table 11.2.

In the next sections we will identify a trading strategy for each of the view combinations presented in Table 11.2. The trading strategy for one of these combinations, price neutral and volatility neutral, is very simple: Don't trade. If an investor is both price neutral and volatility neutral, the investor shouldn't expose himself or herself to price or volatility sensitivity.

TABLE 11.1 Sensitivities and Greek positions that monetize price and volatility views

View	Sensitivity that monetizes the view	Greek position that monetizes the view
Price bullish	Positive value sensitivity to underlying asset price change	Long Delta
Price bearish	Negative value sensitivity to underlying asset price change	Short Delta
Price neutral	No value sensitivity to underlying asset price change	Neutral Delta
Volatility bullish	Positive value sensitivity to underlying asset volatility change	Long Vega
Volatility bearish	Negative value sensitivity to underlying asset volatility change	Short Vega
Volatility neutral	No value sensitivity to underlying asset volatility change	Neutral Vega

TABLE 11.2 Targeted Greek positions as function of price and volatility view combination

Combination of views	Greek positions that monetize the view
Price bullish and volatility bullish	Long Delta and Long Vega
Price bullish and volatility bearish	Long Delta and Short Vega
Price bullish and volatility neutral	Long Delta and Vega Neutral
Price bearish and volatility bullish	Short Delta and Long Vega
Price bearish and volatility bearish	Short Delta and Short Vega
Price bearish and volatility neutral	Short Delta and Vega Neutral
Price neutral and volatility bullish	Delta Neutral and Long Vega
Price neutral and volatility bearish	Delta Neutral and Short Vega
Price neutral and volatility neutral	Delta Neutral and Vega Neutral

Knowledge check

Q 11.3: What type of sensitivity monetizes a price bullish view?
Q 11.4: What type of sensitivity monetizes a price bearish view?
Q 11.5: What type of sensitivity monetizes a volatility bullish view?
Q 11.6: What type of sensitivity monetizes a volatility bearish view?
Q 11.7: What Greek positions monetize a price bullish and volatility bullish view?
Q 11.8: What Greek positions monetize a price bullish and volatility bearish view?
Q 11.9: What Greek positions monetize a price bullish and volatility neutral view?
Q 11.10: What Greek positions monetize a price bearish and volatility bullish view?
Q 11.11: What Greek positions monetize a price bearish and volatility bearish view?
Q 11.12: What Greek positions monetize a price bearish and volatility neutral view?
Q 11.13: What Greek positions monetize a price neutral and volatility bullish view?
Q 11.14: What Greek positions monetize a price neutral and volatility bearish view?
Q 11.15: What trading strategy should a price neutral and volatility neutral investor enter into?

11.3 USING FORWARDS, CALLS, AND PUTS TO MONETIZE VIEWS

The Delta and Vega characteristics of forwards and options are as detailed in Table 11.3.[1]

Since each position provides the investor with a combination of sensitivities to the underlying asset price and volatility, each can be used to monetize one of the view combinations shown in Table 11.4.

Table 11.4 is missing recommendations through which the following view combinations can be monetized:

- Price neutral and volatility bullish
- Price neutral and volatility bearish

In the next two sections we will explore strategies through which an investor can monetize a volatility view while maintaining price neutrality. The strategies we will explore are called "straddles" and "strangles."

TABLE 11.3 Delta and Vega of forwards and options

Greek	Long forward	Short forward	Long call	Short call	Long put	Short put
Delta	Long	Short	Long	Short	Short	Long
Vega	Neutral	Neutral	Long	Short	Long	Short

TABLE 11.4 Forward and option positions that monetize price and volatility view combinations

		Price view		
		Bullish	Neutral	Bearish
Volatility view	Bullish	Long call		Long put
	Neutral	Long forward	No position	Short forward
	Bearish	Short put		Short call

[1]The Delta and Vega characteristics of forwards and options are discussed in Chapters 9 and 10.

Knowledge check

Q 11.16: What trading strategy should a price bullish and volatility bullish investor enter into?
Q 11.17: What trading strategy should a price bullish and volatility bearish investor enter into?
Q 11.18: What trading strategy should a price bullish and volatility neutral investor enter into?
Q 11.19: What trading strategy should a price bearish and volatility bullish investor enter into?
Q 11.20: What trading strategy should a price bearish and volatility bearish investor enter into?
Q 11.21: What trading strategy should a price bearish and volatility neutral investor enter into?
Q 11.22: Which view combinations cannot be monetized with a single long or short position in a forward, call, or put?

11.4 INTRODUCTION TO STRADDLES

Straddles are trading strategies through which price neutral and volatility bullish or bearish views can be monetized. A long straddle is a trading strategy in which an investor holds both a long call and a long put with identical strike prices. A short straddle is the mirror image of a long straddle: It is a trading strategy in which an investor holds both a short call and a short put with identical strike prices. Since a long straddle consists of long positions and a short straddle consists of short positions, the long straddle pays premiums and the short straddle receives premiums at initiation.

In the next sections we will explore Delta and Vega characteristics of long and short straddles, their P&L diagrams, and their breakeven points.

Knowledge check

Q 11.23: How is a long straddle formed?
Q 11.24: How is a short straddle formed?
Q 11.25: Which straddle position pays and which receives premiums at initiation?

11.5 DELTA AND VEGA CHARACTERISTICS OF LONG AND SHORT STRADDLES

The Delta and Vega characteristics of long and short straddles are reflective of the Delta and Vega characteristics of the underlying positions, as Table 11.5 illustrates. We see the following:

- A straddle's call and put positions have opposite Delta exposures that broadly offset each other, and the long straddle is broadly Delta neutral.
- A long straddle is long Vega, as both its long call and long put are long Vega.
- A short straddle is short Vega, as both its short call and short put are short Vega.

Straddles are "broadly" Delta neutral, as the magnitude of the call Delta and put Delta may not be identical. To ensure exact Delta neutrality, the positive Delta must exactly offset the negative Delta. In the next subsection we will explore how to identify strike prices that allow the straddle to be exactly Delta neutral. Note, that even when a straddle is structured with exact *Delta* neutrality, the straddle will not be exactly neutral to *underlying asset price change*. The reason for this is that the Greeks, including Delta, are estimates and are not perfectly accurate, as discussed in Section 8.2 of Chapter 8.

Knowledge check

Q 11.26: What are the Delta characteristics of a long straddle?
Q 11.27: What are the Delta characteristics of a short straddle?
Q 11.28: What are the Vega characteristics of a long straddle?
Q 11.29: What are the Vega characteristics of a short straddle?
Q 11.30: Why isn't a straddle always exactly Delta neutral?
Q 11.31: Why won't a straddle that is exactly Delta neutral be exactly neutral to underlying asset price change?

TABLE 11.5 The Delta and Vega characteristics of long and short straddles

Strategy	Call Position	Put Position	Call Delta	Put Delta	Straddle Delta	Call Vega	Put Vega	Straddle Vega
Long straddle	Long	Long	Long	Short	Broadly neutral	Long	Long	Long
Short straddle	Short	Short	Short	Long	Broadly neutral	Short	Short	Short

11.6 THE ATM DNS STRIKE PRICE

When do call and put Delta exactly offset each other? To answer this question, recall that long call Delta is equal to $N(d_1)$ and long put Delta is equal to $-N(-d_1)$.[2] Hence a straddle will be Delta neutral when:

$$N(d_1) - N(-d_1) = 0$$

And since $N(-d_1) = 1 - N(d_1)$, it follows:

$$N(d_1) - (1 - N(d_1)) = 0$$

Solving for $N(d_1)$, we find that this occurs when $N(d_1) = 0.5$. Hence call and put Delta will exactly offset each other when absolute Delta is 0.5. One can show that this occurs when the strike price is related to the underlying asset price as follows:

$$K = S_t \cdot e^{\left(r_t + \frac{\sigma_t^2}{2}\right) \cdot (T-t)}$$

An option with this strike price is referred to as being "ATM DNS." This is an acronym for "at-the-money Delta-neutral-straddle" and reflects the fact that a straddle that consists of options with these strike prices will be Delta neutral.

This discussion indicates that we have two ways to conceptualize moneyness:[3]

- ATM
- ATM DNS

Table 11.6 summarizes the relationship between the strike price and the underlying asset price for each of these moneyness concepts as well as the relevance of each.

Note that:

ATM DNS strike price > ATM strike price

After all:

$$S_t \cdot e^{\left(r_t + \frac{\sigma_t^2}{2}\right) \cdot (T-t)} > S_t$$

---

[2]The equations for Delta are explored in Section 8.3 of Chapter 8. They assume a European-style option, where the underlying asset pays no income.

[3]ATM is discussed in Sections 2.9 and 3.9 of Chapters 2 and 3. In Section 12.3 of Chapter 12 we will learn about a third way to conceptualize moneyness known as at-the-money forward (ATMF).

TABLE 11.6 ATM and ATM DNS

Type of moneyness	Relationship between strike price and underlying asset price	Relevance of moneyness concept
ATM	$K = S_t$	Long position is indifferent about exercising or not.
ATM DNS	$K = S_t \cdot e^{\left(r_t + \frac{\sigma_t^2}{2}\right) \cdot (T-t)}$	Call absolute Delta is equal to put absolute Delta.

Knowledge check

Q 11.32: What is "ATM DNS"?

Q 11.33: What strike price should be used to create an exactly Delta neutral straddle?

Q 11.34: What will the absolute Delta of the call and put be when a straddle is Delta neutral?

Q 11.35: Is the ATM DNS strike price larger or smaller than the ATM strike price?

11.7 STRADDLE: NUMERICAL EXAMPLE

Let's consider an example through which to explore the Delta and Vega characteristics of a straddle. An investor holds a long straddle with the following characteristics:

- Underlying asset price = $75
- Time to expiration = 0.5 years
- Underlying asset volatility = 35%
- Risk-free interest rate = 1.5%
- Strike price = ATM DNS strike price

The ATM DNS strike price is identified as follows:

$$K = S_t \cdot e^{\left(r_t + \frac{\sigma_t^2}{2}\right) \cdot (T-t)}$$

$$= \$75 \cdot e^{\left(1.5\% + \frac{35\%^2}{2}\right) \cdot 0.5}$$

$$= \$77.91$$

TABLE 11.7 Example of long straddle premiums, Delta and Vega

Strategy	Premium paid	Delta	Vega
Long call	$6.3918	0.5	0.2116
Long put	$8.7242	−0.5	0.2116
Long straddle	$15.1161	0	0.4231

Hence, the long straddle consists of a long call and a long put with strike price of $77.91. The premiums and the Delta and Vega for the long call, the long put, and the long straddle are detailed in Table 11.7.

Table 11.8 explores what happens to the value of this straddle in two separate scenarios:

- Scenario 1: The underlying asset volatility increases by 1%, from 35% to 36%.
- Scenario 2: The underlying asset price increases by $1, from $75 to $76.

We learn the following from Table 11.8:

- Scenario 1: As the underlying asset volatility increased by 1%, the long straddle increased in value by $0.4231. Clearly, the long straddle has positive sensitivity to volatility.
- Scenario 2: As the underlying asset price increased by $1, the long straddle increased in value by $0.0214. While broadly indicative of neutrality to the underlying asset price, this small change in value takes place despite the long straddle being exactly Delta neutral at initiation. The reason for this small change in value is that the Greeks are estimates and are not perfectly accurate.

TABLE 11.8 Example of long straddle sensitivity

Strategy	Initial premium paid	Scenario 1: Underlying asset volatility increases by 1%		Scenario 2: Underlying asset price increases by $1	
		Premium	Change	Premium	Change
Long call	$6.3918	$6.6034	$0.2116	$6.9025	$0.5107
Long put	$8.7242	$8.9358	$0.2116	$8.2349	−$0.4893
Long straddle	$15.1161	$15.54392	$0.4231	$15.14392	$0.0214

11.8 P&L DIAGRAMS FOR LONG AND SHORT STRADDLES

To explore the P&L diagrams for long and short straddles, let's consider the following example:

- Call: strike price = $75 and premium = $9
- Put: strike price = $75 and premium = $7

Figure 11.1 shows the P&L diagrams for long and short straddles and the call and put positions that form them.

Knowledge check

Q 11.36: What does a long straddle's P&L diagram look like?
Q 11.37: What does a short straddle's P&L diagram look like?

11.9 BREAKEVEN POINTS FOR LONG AND SHORT STRADDLES

The P&L diagrams in Figure 11.1 demonstrate that straddles have two breakeven points where the straddle transitions from profit to loss. The breakeven points are

Lower straddle breakeven point:

Underlying asset price = strike price − call premium − put premium

Higher long straddle breakeven point:

Underlying asset price = strike price + call premium + put premium

In the example illustrated in Figure 11.1 the strike price is $75 for both the call and the put, the call premium is $9, and the put premium is $7. It follows that the breakeven points are

Lower straddle breakeven point:

$$\begin{aligned} \textit{Underlying asset price} &= \textit{strike price} - \textit{call premium} - \textit{put premium} \\ &= \$75 - \$9 - \$7 \\ &= \$59 \end{aligned}$$

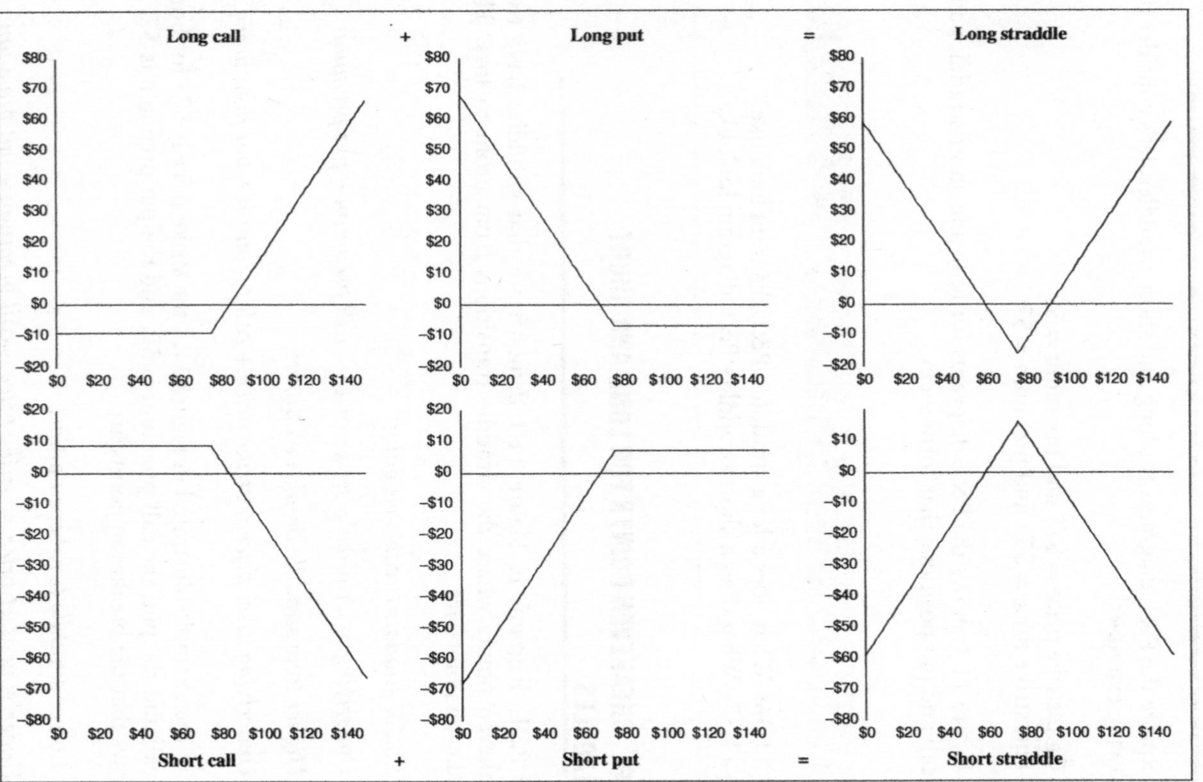

FIGURE 11.1 Long and short straddles' P&L diagrams

Higher long straddle breakeven point:

$$\begin{aligned} \textit{Underlying asset price} &= \textit{strike price} + \textit{call premium} + \textit{put premium} \\ &= \$75 + \$9 + \$7 \\ &= \$91 \end{aligned}$$

Knowledge check

Q 11.38: What is the lower straddle breakeven point?
Q 11.39: What is the higher straddle breakeven point?

11.10 INTRODUCTION TO STRANGLES

A strangle is similar, but not identical, to a straddle. Like a straddle, a long strangle consists of a long call and a long put, while a short strangle consists of a short call and a short put. However, while in a straddle the two positions share an identical strike price, in a strangle the call strike is higher than the put strike.

Other similarities between strangles and straddles are as follows:

- Like straddles, strangles are trading strategies through which price neutral and volatility bullish or bearish views can be monetized.
- Since the long strangle is taking long positions in the call and put and the short strangle is taking short positions, the long strangle pays premiums and the short strangle receives premiums at initiation, similar to the long straddle paying premiums and the short straddle receiving premiums.
- Since a long strangle consists of a long call and a long put it is broadly price neutral and volatility bullish, similar to a long straddle. Similarly, because a short strangle consists of a short call and a short put it is broadly price neutral and volatility bearish, similar to a short straddle.

A strangle will typically consist of a high strike OTM call and a low strike OTM put. Since OTM options are cheaper than ATM options, the long strangle will pay lower premiums than those associated with an otherwise equivalent straddle with ATM strike prices.

In the next sections we will explore P&L diagrams and breakeven points for long and short strangles.

Knowledge check

Q 11.40: How is a long strangle formed?
Q 11.41: How is a short strangle formed?

Q 11.42: Which strangle position pays and which receives premiums at initiation?
Q 11.43: Why will a strangle consisting of OTM options have lower premiums than an otherwise equivalent ATM straddle?
Q 11.44: What are the Delta characteristics of a long strangle?
Q 11.45: What are the Delta characteristics of a short strangle?
Q 11.46: What are the Vega characteristics of a long strangle?
Q 11.47: What are the Vega characteristics of a short strangle?

11.11 P&L DIAGRAMS FOR LONG AND SHORT STRANGLES

To explore the P&L diagrams for long and short strangles, let's consider the following example:

- Call: strike price = \$95, and premium = \$6
- Put: strike price = \$55, and premium = \$3.9

Figure 11.2 shows the P&L diagrams for long and short strangles and the call and put positions that form them.

Knowledge check

Q 11.48: What does a long strangle's P&L diagram look like?
Q 11.49: What does a short strangle's P&L diagram look like?

11.12 BREAKEVEN POINTS FOR LONG AND SHORT STRANGLES

The P&L diagrams in Figure 11.2 demonstrate that the long strangle is profitable as the price of the underlying asset increases or decreases dramatically and suffers a loss otherwise. The two breakeven points are

Lower long strangle breakeven point:

Underlying asset price = put strike − call premium − put premium

Higher long strangle breakeven point:

Underlying asset price = call strike + call premium + put premium

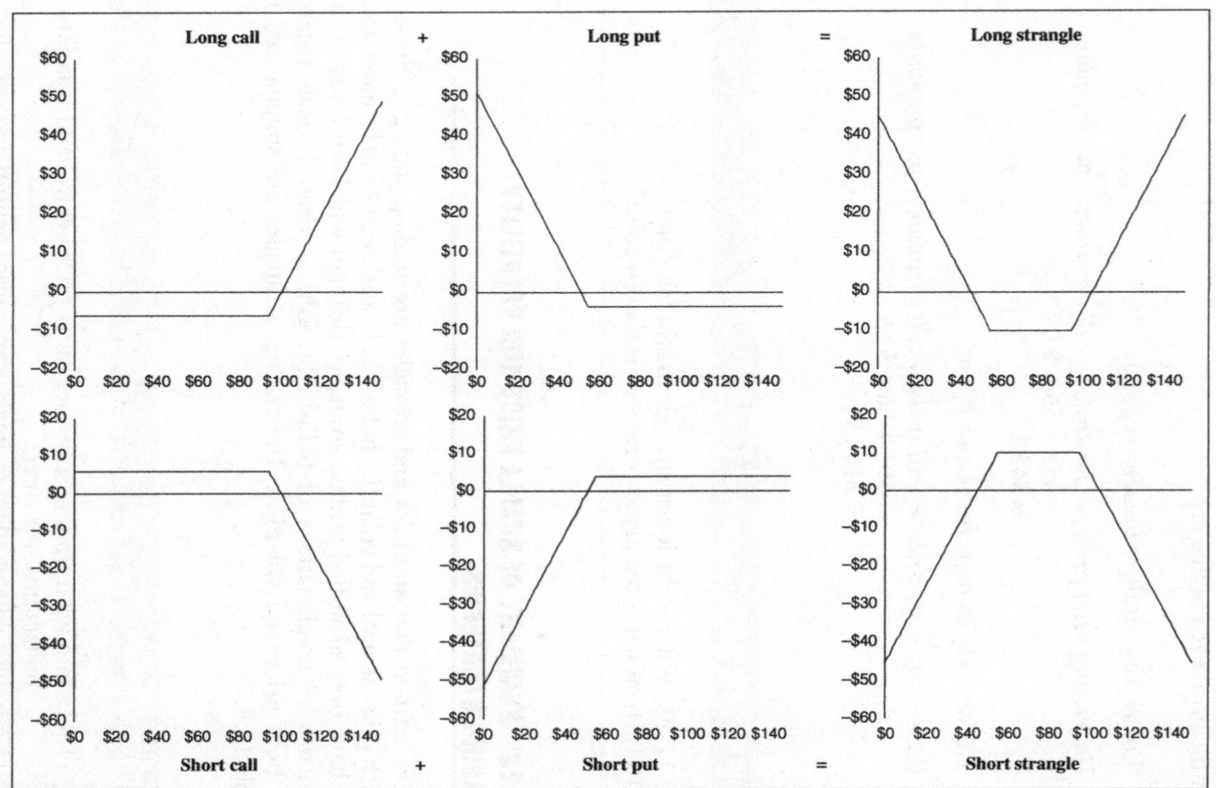

FIGURE 11.2 Long and short strangles' P&L diagrams

In the previous example, the call option strike is \$95, the put option strike is \$55, the call premium is \$6, and the put premium is \$3.9. It follows that the breakeven points are

Lower long strangle breakeven point:

$$\begin{aligned} \textit{Underlying asset price} &= \textit{put strike} - \textit{call premium} - \textit{put premium} \\ &= \$55 - \$6 - \$3.9 \\ &= \$45.1 \end{aligned}$$

Higher long strangle breakeven point:

$$\begin{aligned} \textit{Underlying asset price} &= \textit{call strike} + \textit{call premium} + \textit{put premium} \\ &= \$95 + \$6 + \$3.9 \\ &= \$104.9 \end{aligned}$$

Knowledge check

Q 11.50: What is the lower strangle breakeven point?
Q 11.51: What is the higher strangle breakeven point?

11.13 SUMMARY OF SIMPLE PRICE AND VOLATILITY TRADING STRATEGIES

We've learned that straddles and strangles are trading strategies through which price neutral and volatility bullish or bearish views can be monetized. We have now identified trading strategies through which an investor can monetize all combinations of bullish, bearish, or neutral views regarding both price and volatility. The trading strategies are summarized in Table 11.9.

Knowledge check

Q 11.52: Into what trading strategies can a price neutral and volatility bullish investor enter?
Q 11.53: Into what trading strategies can a price neutral and volatility bearish investor enter?

TABLE 11.9 Trading strategies through which to monetize price and volatility view combinations

		Price view		
		Bullish	Neutral	Bearish
Volatility view	Bullish	Long call	Long straddle or long strangle	Long put
	Neutral	Long forward	No position	Short forward
	Bearish	Short put	Short straddle or short strangle	Short call

KEY POINTS

- An investor can form combinations of bullish, bearish, or neutral price and volatility views. A price view is a view about whether the underlying asset price will increase or decrease in the future. A volatility view is a view about whether the underlying asset volatility will increase or decrease in the future.
- Each price and volatility view combination can be related to sensitivities and Greek positions that can monetize the view combination.
- Forward and option positions can be used by an investor to monetize a number of price and volatility view combinations.
- Investors that are neutral price and bullish volatility can monetize this view through entering into a long straddle or long strangle. Investors that are neutral price and bearish volatility can monetize this view through entering into a short straddle or short strangle.
- A long straddle is a trading strategy in which the investor holds both a long call and long put with identical strike prices. A short straddle is a trading strategy in which the investor holds both a short call and a short put with identical strike prices.
- The at-the-money Delta-neutral strategy (ATM DNS) strike price is the strike price where the absolute Delta of a call and a put are equal to each other. The ATM DNS strike price is distinct from the at-the-money (ATM) strike price, which is equal to the underlying asset price.
- The P&L for straddles and strangles can be described using P&L diagrams. Straddles and strangles each have two breakeven points. The lower straddle breakeven points occur when the underlying asset price is equal to the strike price minus both premiums, and the upper breakeven point is strike price plus both premiums. The lower strangle breakeven points occur when the underlying asset price is equal to the put strike minus both premiums, and the upper breakeven point is equal to the call strike plus both premiums.

CHAPTER 12

Synthetic, Protective, and Yield-Enhancing Trading Strategies

INTRODUCTION

In this chapter we will explore "put-call parity," which is the concept that one can synthetically create a forward or option position through holding other traded positions. We will learn that put-call parity has important implications for the relationship between call and put premiums and can be used to identify trading opportunities. This chapter will also discuss protective puts through which a long position in an asset can be protected using a long put; covered calls through which profit can be enhanced using a short call; and collars in which a covered call finances a protective put.

After you read this chapter, you will be able to

- Understand put-call parity.
- Create synthetic positions in forwards and options.
- Understand the premiums and Greeks of synthetic positions.
- Understand the relationship between call and put premiums.
- Understand the relationship between call and put Greeks.
- Identify the at-the-money forward (ATMF) strike price.
- Contrast the ATMF strike price with the at-the-money (ATM) and at-the-money Delta-neutral-straddle (ATM DNS) strike prices.
- Identify and implement option arbitrage opportunities.
- Describe how to form protective puts, covered calls, and collars.
- Understand the purpose of entering into protective puts, covered calls, and collars.
- Identify the breakeven points for protective puts, covered calls, and collars.

12.1 INTRODUCTION TO PUT-CALL PARITY AND SYNTHETIC POSITIONS

"Put-call parity" is the concept that a forward or option position can be synthetically created through holding combinations of other traded positions, as detailed in Table 12.1. In the next section of this chapter we will explore P&L diagrams that demonstrate that the combinations of traded positions listed in Table 12.1 form the corresponding synthetic positions.

To create a synthetic position, the following must be specified for each of the traded positions that form the synthetic position:

- A forward price/strike price identical to the forward price/strike price of the intended synthetic position.
- An expiration date identical to the expiration date of the intended synthetic position.
- An underlying asset identical to the underlying asset of the intended synthetic position.

For example:

- To create a synthetic long forward with a forward price of $50 and expiration in one year, both the traded long call and short put must have strike prices of $50 and expiration in one year.
- To create a synthetic short put with a strike price of $33 and expiration in three months, the traded long forward must have a forward price of $33 and expiration in three months, and the traded short call must have a strike price of $33 and expiration in three months.

TABLE 12.1 Synthetic positions

Synthetic positions	How formed
Synthetic long forward	Combination of a traded long call and a traded short put
Synthetic short forward	Combination of a traded short call and a traded long put
Synthetic long call	Combination of a traded long forward and a traded long put
Synthetic short call	Combination of a traded short forward and a traded short put
Synthetic long put	Combination of a traded short forward and a traded long call
Synthetic short put	Combination of a traded long forward and a traded short call

Knowledge check

Q 12.1: What is "put-call parity"?
Q 12.2: How is a synthetic long forward formed?
Q 12.3: How is a synthetic short forward formed?
Q 12.4: How is a synthetic long call formed?
Q 12.5: How is a synthetic short call formed?
Q 12.6: How is a synthetic long put formed?
Q 12.7: How is a synthetic short put formed?
Q 12.8: To exactly create a synthetic position, what forward price/strike price is specified for the traded positions that form it?
Q 12.9: To exactly create a synthetic position, what expiration date is specified for the traded positions that form it?

12.2 P&L DIAGRAMS OF SYNTHETIC POSITIONS

Let's explore the P&L diagrams of synthetic positions in more depth. Throughout, we will use the following example:

- Call: strike price = $75 and premium = $9
- Put: strike price = $75 and premium = $9
- Forward: forward price = $75

Figures 12.1, 12.2, and 12.3 illustrate the P&L diagrams for long and short positions in synthetic forwards, calls, and puts.

Knowledge check

Q 12.10: Show that the P&L diagram of a synthetic long forward is the combination of the P&L diagrams of traded positions.
Q 12.11: Show that the P&L diagram of a synthetic short forward is the combination of the P&L diagrams of traded positions.
Q 12.12: Show that the P&L diagram of a synthetic long call is the combination of the P&L diagrams of traded positions.
Q 12.13: Show that the P&L diagram of a synthetic short call is the combination of the P&L diagrams of traded positions.
Q 12.14: Show that the P&L diagram of a synthetic long put is the combination of the P&L diagrams of traded positions.
Q 12.15: Show that the P&L diagram of a synthetic short put is the combination of the P&L diagrams of traded positions.

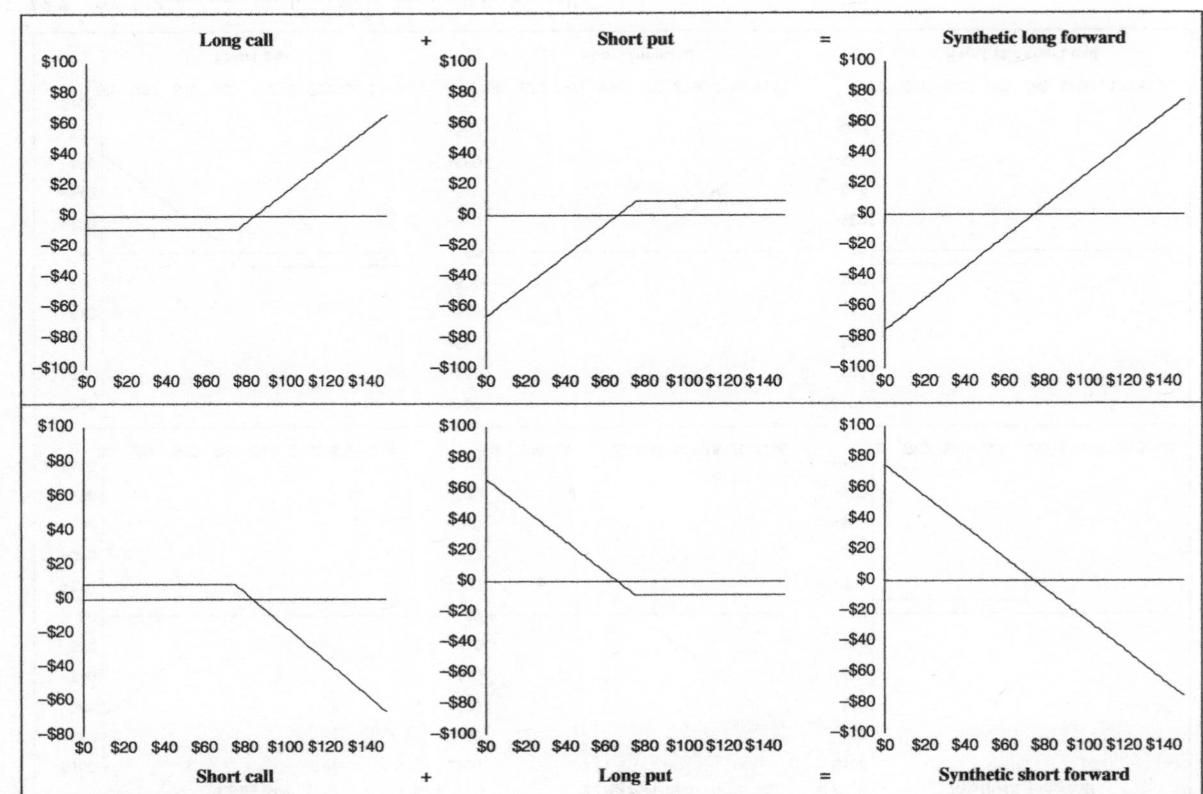

FIGURE 12.1 P&L diagrams for long and short synthetic forwards

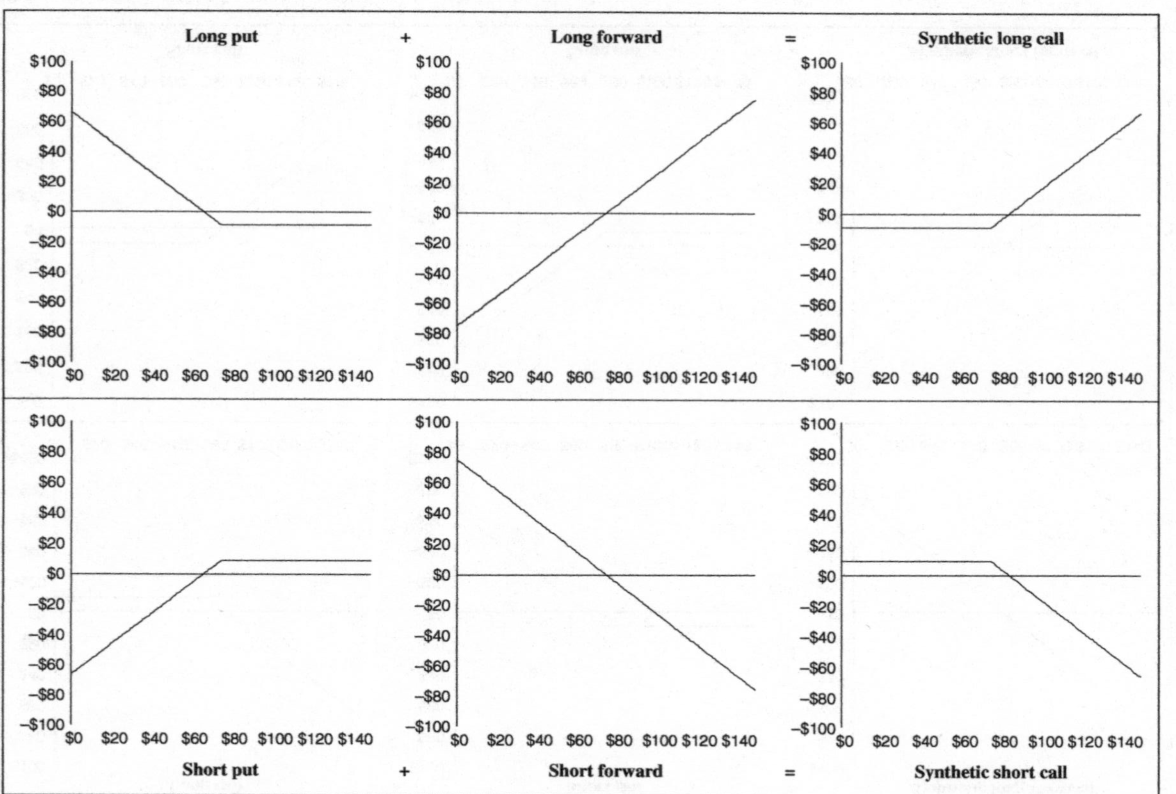

FIGURE 12.2 P&L diagrams for long and short synthetic calls

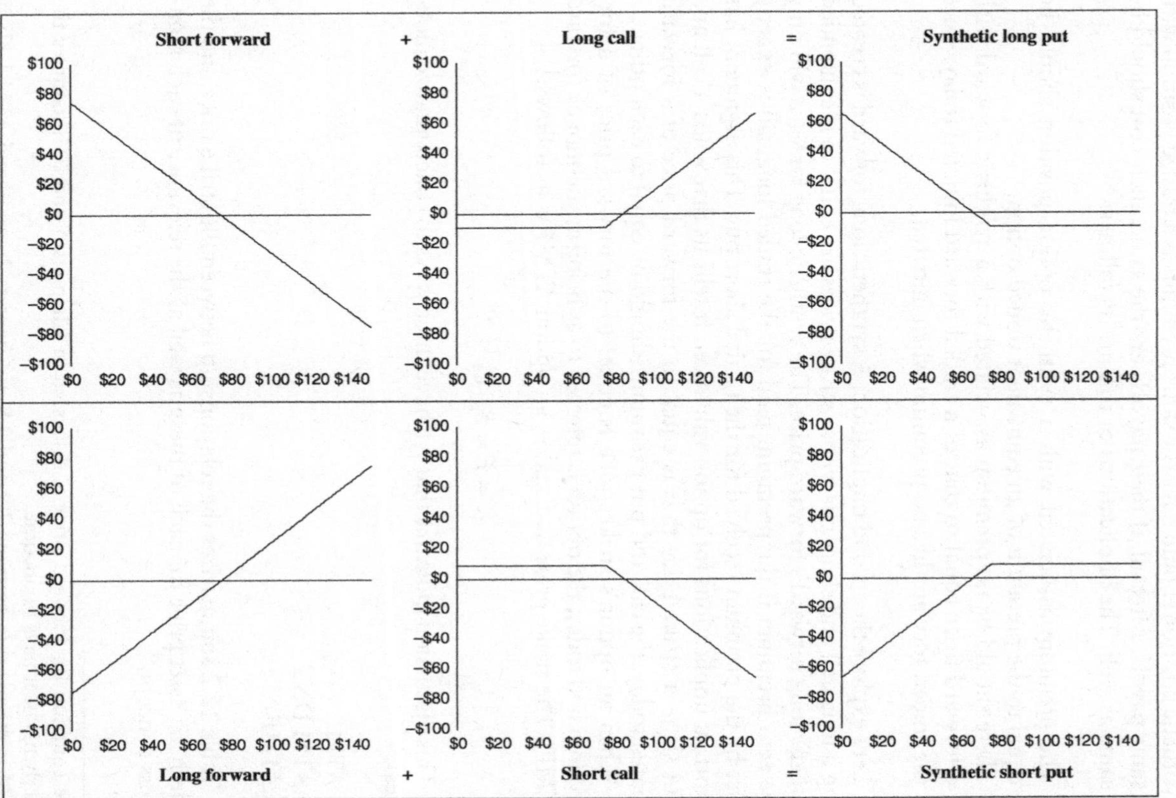

FIGURE 12.3 P&L diagrams for long and short synthetic puts

12.3 SYNTHETIC POSITIONS PREMIUMS AND ATMF

A synthetic position should have the same premium as a traded position with the same payoff. After all, if their payoffs are the same, their cost should be the same as well. The implications of this are as follows:

- The premium associated with a synthetic option position should be equal to the premium of an equivalent traded option.
- There should be no premium associated with a synthetic forward with a forward price equal to that of a traded forward initiated today, since the traded forward has no premium when initiated.

Let's explore the second implication. A synthetic long forward is created using a long call and short put whose strike prices are equal to the intended synthetic long forward's forward price. The synthetic long forward will only have zero premium if the premium paid for the traded long call is exactly offset by the premium received for the traded short put. This argument has important implications for option valuation: It tells us that when a call and a put share a strike price that is equal to the forward price of a forward initiated today, the call and put premiums should be equal to each other.

When an option's strike price is equal to the forward price of a forward initiated today, the option is referred to as being at-the-money forward (ATMF). The strike price that makes an option ATMF is as follows:[1]

$$K = F = S_t \cdot e^{r_t \cdot (T-t)}$$

This discussion indicates that we have three ways to conceptualize moneyness:[2]

- ATM
- ATM DNS
- ATMF

Table 12.2 summarizes the relationship between the strike price and the underlying asset price for each of these as well as the relevance of each moneyness concept.

[1]The equation for forward price is discussed in Chapters 5 and 6. It assumes the underlying asset pays no income.

[2]ATM is discussed in Sections 2.9 and 3.9 of Chapters 2 and 3, and ATM DNS is discussed in Section 11.6 of Chapter 11.

TABLE 12.2 ATM, ATMF, and ATM DNS

Type of moneyness	Relationship between strike price and underlying asset price	Relevance of moneyness concept
ATM	$K = S_t$	Long position is indifferent about exercising or not.
ATMF	$K = F = S_t \cdot e^{r_t \cdot (T-t)}$	Call price is equal to put price.
ATM DNS	$K = S_t \cdot e^{\left(r_t + \frac{\sigma_t^2}{2}\right) \cdot (T-t)}$	Call absolute Delta is equal to put absolute Delta.

Note that:

ATM DNS strike > ATMF strike > ATM strike

After all:

$$S_t \cdot e^{\left(r_t + \frac{\sigma_t^2}{2}\right) \cdot (T-t)} > S_t \cdot e^{r_t \cdot (T-t)} > S_t$$

Knowledge check

Q 12.16: What should be the relationship between the premium of a synthetic position and a traded position with the same payoff?

Q 12.17: What premium should be associated with a synthetic forward?

Q 12.18: What is the relationship between the premiums of calls and puts that share a strike price that is equal to the forward price of a forward initiated today?

Q 12.19: What is "ATMF"?

Q 12.20: For what strike price will call and put premiums be identical?

Q 12.21: What is the relevance of each of the three ways to conceptualize moneyness?

Q 12.22: Is the ATMF strike price larger or smaller than the ATM strike price?

Q 12.23: Is the ATMF strike price larger or smaller than the ATM DNS strike price?

12.4 THE GREEKS OF SYNTHETIC POSITIONS

The Greeks associated with a synthetic position should be identical to the Greeks associated with a traded position with the same payoff. After all, if their payoffs are the same, their sensitivities should be the same as well. This idea allows us to learn interesting insights into the relationship between the Greeks across positions. Let's look at Delta, Gamma, and Vega. This discussion will take place in the context of a European-style option where the underlying asset pays no income, though the ideas are broadly similar for other products as well.

Here are four concepts that were introduced in Chapters 9 and 10:

- The Delta of a long forward is one.
- The Gamma of a long forward is zero.
- The Vega of a long forward is zero.
- The Greek for a short position is the negative of the Greek of the corresponding long position.

The implications of these concepts are as follows: Since a synthetic long forward is formed through combining a long call and short put with identical strike prices, this implies that when strike prices are identical:

$$\textit{Long Call Delta} + \textit{Short Put Delta} = 1$$

$$\textit{Long Call Gamma} + \textit{Short Put Gamma} = 0$$

$$\textit{Long Call Vega} + \textit{Short Put Vega} = 0$$

And since a short put's Greek is the negative of the corresponding long put's Greeks, this implies:

$$\textit{Long Call Delta} - \textit{Long Put Delta} = 1$$

$$\textit{Long Call Gamma} - \textit{Long Put Gamma} = 0$$

$$\textit{Long Call Vega} - \textit{Long Put Vega} = 0$$

And therefore we can conclude:

$$\textit{Long Put Delta} = \textit{Long Call Delta} - 1$$

$$\textit{Long Call Gamma} = \textit{Long Put Gamma}$$

$$\textit{Long Call Vega} = \textit{Long Vega}$$

Knowledge check

Q 12.24: What is the relationship between the Greeks of a synthetic position and a traded position with the same payoff?
Q 12.25: What are Delta, Gamma, and Vega of a synthetic forward?
Q 12.26: What is the relationship between long call Delta and long put Delta when the call and put have the same strike price?
Q 12.27: What is the relationship between long call Gamma and long put Gamma when the call and put have the same strike price?
Q 12.28: What is the relationship between long call Vega and long put Vega when the call and put have the same strike price?

12.5 OPTION ARBITRAGE

We learned in Section 12.3 that a synthetic position should have the same premium as a traded position with the same payoff. Should the cost of entering into a traded position differ from the cost of entering into its synthetic version, an investor will take advantage of the discrepancy through engaging in "option arbitrage." The trades one can enter into should such discrepancies be identified are detailed in Table 12.3.

Throughout, these strategies entail taking a long position in the less costly of either the synthetic or traded position while taking a short position in the other. While six scenarios are provided, the identified discrepancies can lead to one of two trade implementations:

- Long forward, short call, and long put
- Short forward, long call, and short put

All of the above strategies assume that the traded and synthetic positions are identical except for the cost discrepancy. Often, this assumption is violated due to factors such as liquidity differences across markets, differences in trading conventions and margin requirements, or difficulties identifying positions with appropriate prices.

Knowledge check

Q 12.29: What is option arbitrage?
Q 12.30: What trades will be implemented if the synthetic forward cost is greater than the traded forward cost?

Q 12.31: What trades will be implemented if the synthetic forward cost is less than the traded forward cost?

Q 12.32: What trades will be implemented if the synthetic call cost is greater than the traded call cost?

Q 12.33: What trades will be implemented if the synthetic call cost is less than the traded call cost?

Q 12.34: What trades will be implemented if the synthetic put cost is greater than the traded put cost?

Q 12.35: What trades will be implemented if the synthetic put cost is less than the traded put cost?

TABLE 12.3 Option arbitrage

Discrepancy identified	Trading strategy		Trade implementation		
	Long	Short	Forward	Call	Put
Synthetic forward cost greater than traded forward cost	Traded forward	Synthetic forward	Long	Short	Long
Synthetic forward cost less than traded forward cost	Synthetic forward	Traded forward	Short	Long	Short
Synthetic call cost greater than traded call cost	Traded call	Synthetic call	Short	Long	Short
Synthetic call cost less than traded call cost	Synthetic call	Traded call	Long	Short	Long
Synthetic put cost greater than traded put cost	Traded put	Synthetic put	Long	Short	Long
Synthetic put cost less than traded put cost	Synthetic put	Traded put	Short	Long	Short

12.6 PROTECTIVE PUTS

An investor holding an asset, such as a stock or a bond, suffers losses if the asset price decreases. An investor can protect against such losses through entering into a long put position, a strategy referred to as a "protective put." The long put profits when the market price of the asset declines, thereby offsetting the losses that the asset suffers. Typically, the protective put will be OTM, with a strike price below the asset price.

A position in an asset is similar to a long forward position, insofar as it has Delta equal to one and is Vega neutral. Since a position in an asset is similar to a long forward position, a protective put strategy (combination of an asset position and a long put) is similar to a synthetic long call (combination of a long forward and a long put). The P&L diagram for a protective put is similar to the P&L diagram, illustrated in Figure 12.2, for a synthetic long call and the Greeks of a protective put are also similar to the Greeks of a long call.

While an investor benefits from the protection that a protective put strategy provides, a protective put strategy is expensive. After all, to enter into the protective put the investor must pay the premium associated with the long put position.

The breakeven point for a protective put is

Protective put breakeven point:

$$\textit{Asset price} = \textit{asset purchase price} + \textit{put premium}$$

For example, if the asset purchase price is \$80 and the put premium is \$3, it follows:

Protective put breakeven point:

$$\begin{aligned} \textit{Asset price} &= \textit{asset purchase price} + \textit{put premium} \\ &= \$80 + \$3 \\ &= \$83 \end{aligned}$$

The protective put's breakeven point is higher than the breakeven point for a position in only the asset, whose breakeven point is its purchase price.

Knowledge check

Q 12.36: What is a "protective put" strategy?
Q 12.37: What is the purpose of a protective put strategy?

Q 12.38: Are protective puts typically ITM, ATM, or OTM?
Q 12.39: To what option position is a protective put strategy similar?
Q 12.40: Why is a protective put strategy expensive?
Q 12.41: What is a protective put strategy's breakeven point?
Q 12.42: Is a protective put strategy's breakeven point higher or lower than the asset's?

12.7 COVERED CALLS

An investor holding an asset can try to enhance his or her profits through receiving a premium by entering into a short call. The strategy of adding a short call to a portfolio consisting of a position in an asset is referred to as a "covered call" strategy. A covered call is an example of a yield-enhancing trading strategy. Typically, the covered call will be OTM, with a strike price above the asset price.

Since a position in an asset is similar to a long forward, a covered call (combination of an asset and a short call) is similar to a synthetic short put (combination of a long forward and a short call). The P&L diagram for a covered call is similar to the P&L diagram for a synthetic short put, illustrated earlier in Figure 12.3, and the Greeks of a covered call are also similar to the Greeks of a short put.

While an investor benefits from the yield enhancement that a covered call strategy provides, the investor will regret entering into the covered call strategy if the underlying asset price increases. After all, the short call's losses negate the asset's upside.

The breakeven point for a covered call is

Covered call breakeven point:

Asset price = asset purchase price – call premium

For example, if the asset price when purchased is \$72, and the call premium is \$6, it follows:

Covered call breakeven point:

Asset price = *asset purchase price – call premium*
= \$72 – \$6
= \$66

The covered call's breakeven point is lower than the breakeven point for a position in only the asset, whose breakeven point is its purchase price.

Knowledge check

Q 12.43: What is a "covered call" strategy?
Q 12.44: What is the purpose of a covered call strategy?
Q 12.45: Are covered calls typically ITM, ATM, or OTM?
Q 12.46: To what option position is a covered call strategy similar?
Q 12.47: Why may an investor regret entering into a covered call?
Q 12.48: What is a covered call strategy's breakeven point?
Q 12.49: Is a covered call strategy's breakeven point higher or lower than the asset's?

12.8 COLLARS

We learned about a protective put strategy, through which investors can protect against losses if an asset price decreases. We also learned that the protective put strategy is expensive, as the investor must pay the premium associated with the long put.

To offset the expense associated with a protective put, the investor can choose to enter into a covered call as well. The purpose of entering into the covered call is to use the call premium received to pay for the protective put's premium. A strategy consisting of an asset, a protective put, and a covered call is referred to as a "collar" strategy. Typically, both the protective put and covered call will be OTM.

For example, consider the following scenario:

- Asset: purchase price = $65
- Put: strike price = $50 and premium = $7
- Call: strike price = $80 and premium = $7

Figure 12.4 shows the P&L diagram for a collar.

What is the exposure of the collar strategy? To answer this question, note the exposures of the asset, long put, and short call:

- Asset: Positively sensitive to the asset price and volatility neutral
- Long put: Negatively sensitive to the asset price and positively sensitive to asset volatility
- Short call: Negatively sensitive to the asset price and negatively sensitive to asset volatility

A collar is positively sensitive to the asset price and is broadly volatility neutral for the following reasons:

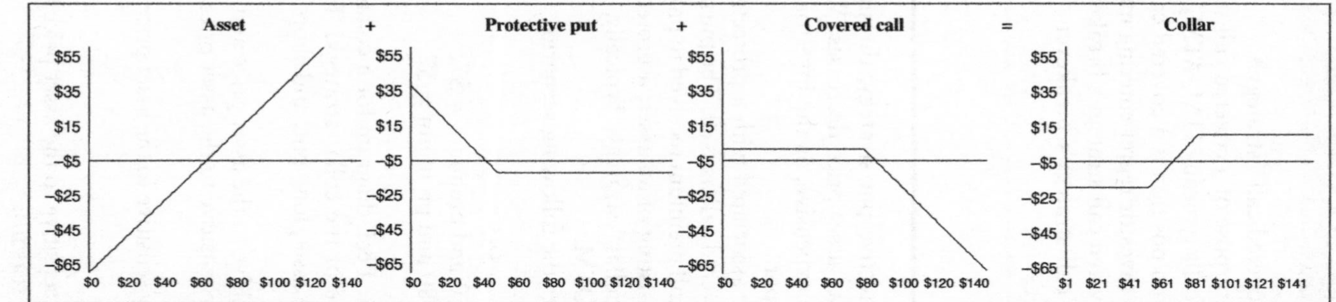

FIGURE 12.4 P&L diagram for a collar

- Positively sensitive to the asset price: While the two option positions are negatively sensitive to the asset price, they only partially offset the positive sensitivity of the asset to its own price. Hence, the collar is positively sensitive to the asset price.
- Volatility neutral: The asset is volatility neutral. Further, the long put and short call volatility exposures broadly offset each other. Hence, the collar is broadly volatility neutral.

The breakeven point for a collar is

Collar breakeven point:

Asset price = asset purchase price + put premium – call premium

If the asset price when purchased is $22, the put premium is $3, and the call premium is $2.5. It follows that the breakeven point is

Collar breakeven point:

Asset price = asset purchase price + put premium – call premium

= $22 + $3 – $2.5

= $22.5

Knowledge check

Q 12.50: What is a "collar" strategy?
Q 12.51: What is the purpose of a collar strategy?
Q 12.52: Are the option positions used in collars typically ITM, ATM, or OTM?
Q 12.53: What does a collar's P&L diagram look like?
Q 12.54: What are the exposures of a collar strategy?
Q 12.55: What is a collar strategy's breakeven point?

KEY POINTS

- "Put-call parity" is the concept that one can synthetically create a forward or option position through holding other traded positions.
- The payoff and premiums associated with a synthetic position are identical to the payoff and premiums associated with the corresponding traded position.

- The forward price/strike price, expiration date, and underlying asset of the traded positions used to create the synthetic position must be equal to those of the intended synthetic position.
- When an option's strike price is equal to the forward price of a forward initiated today, the option is referred to as being at-the-money forward (ATMF). The ATMF strike price is distinct from the at-the-money Delta-neutral straddle (ATM DNS) and at-the-money (ATM) strike prices.
- An implication of put-call parity is that an ATMF call premium and ATMF put premium should be equal to each other. Other implications are that long put Delta is equal to the corresponding long call Delta minus one, and that long call Gamma and Vega are equal to the corresponding long put Gamma and Vega.
- Should the cost associated with entering into a traded position differ from the cost of its synthetic version, an investor will engage in option arbitrage. Identified discrepancies lead to one of two trade implementations: either entering into the combination of a traded long forward, short call, and long put; or entering into the combination of a traded short forward, long call, and short put.
- An investor holding an asset can protect the position through entering into a long put position, known as a "protective put" strategy. Typically, the put will be OTM. A protective put strategy is similar to a synthetic long call.
- An investor holding an asset can try to enhance his or her profits through entering into a short call position, known as a "covered call" strategy. Typically, the call will be OTM. A covered call strategy is similar to a synthetic short put.
- A collar strategy is a strategy consisting of an asset, a protective put, and a covered call. The protective put protects the investor against losses, while the covered call finances the protective put.

CHAPTER 13

Spread Trading Strategies

INTRODUCTION

In this chapter we will explore various spread trading strategies including bull spreads, bear spreads, risk reversals, butterfly spreads, and condor spreads. For each we will learn how to form the strategy and develop insight into its objective. We will also explore the P&L diagrams, sensitivity, and breakeven points for each strategy.

After you read this chapter, you will be able to

- Form bull and bear spreads using either call options or put options.
- Describe the P&L diagram for bull and bear spreads.
- Explain the exposures of bull and bear spreads.
- Identify the breakeven points for bull and bear spreads.
- Form risk reversals, butterfly spreads, and condor spreads.
- Describe the P&L diagram for risk reversals, butterfly spreads, and condor spreads.
- Explain the exposures of risk reversals, butterfly spreads, and condor spreads.
- Identify the breakeven points for risk reversals, butterfly spreads, and condor spreads.

13.1 BULL AND BEAR SPREADS USING CALLS

Bull and bear spreads can be formed using call options, as follows:

- Bull spread: Combination of a lower strike long call and a higher strike short call
- Bear spread: Combination of a lower strike short call and a higher strike long call

Consider the following example:

- Lower strike call: strike price = \$60 and premium = \$12.
- Higher strike call: strike price = \$90 and premium = \$3.

Figure 13.1 shows the P&L diagrams for bull and bear spreads that are formed using calls.

Some observations are as follows:

- We learned in Section 12.8 of Chapter 12 that one can create a collar through entering into a position in an asset, a protective put, and a covered call. A bull spread provides similar exposure to a collar, while a bear spread provides opposite exposure.
- Lower strike call options have higher premiums than higher strike call options, as they have greater moneyness. Hence, a higher strike call premium received will not fully offset a lower strike call premium paid. Because of this, a bull spread using calls will require a net payment of premium, while a bear spread using calls will provide a net reception of premium.

The exposures of bull and bear spreads using calls are as follows:

- A bull spread using calls is long Delta. This is because the lower strike long call Delta is positive and, due to its greater moneyness, of greater magnitude than the higher strike short call's negative Delta.[1]
- A bull spread using calls is broadly Vega neutral. This is because the long call is long Vega, and the short call is short Vega.
- Because options are zero-sum games, a bear spread using calls has the opposite exposure of a bull spread using calls: It is short Delta and broadly Vega neutral.

The breakeven point for bull and bear spreads using calls is

Bull and bear spreads using calls breakeven point:

Asset price = lower strike price

+ lower strike call premium − higher strike call premium

[1]The relationship between moneyness and the magnitude of Delta is discussed in Section 9.3 of Chapter 9.

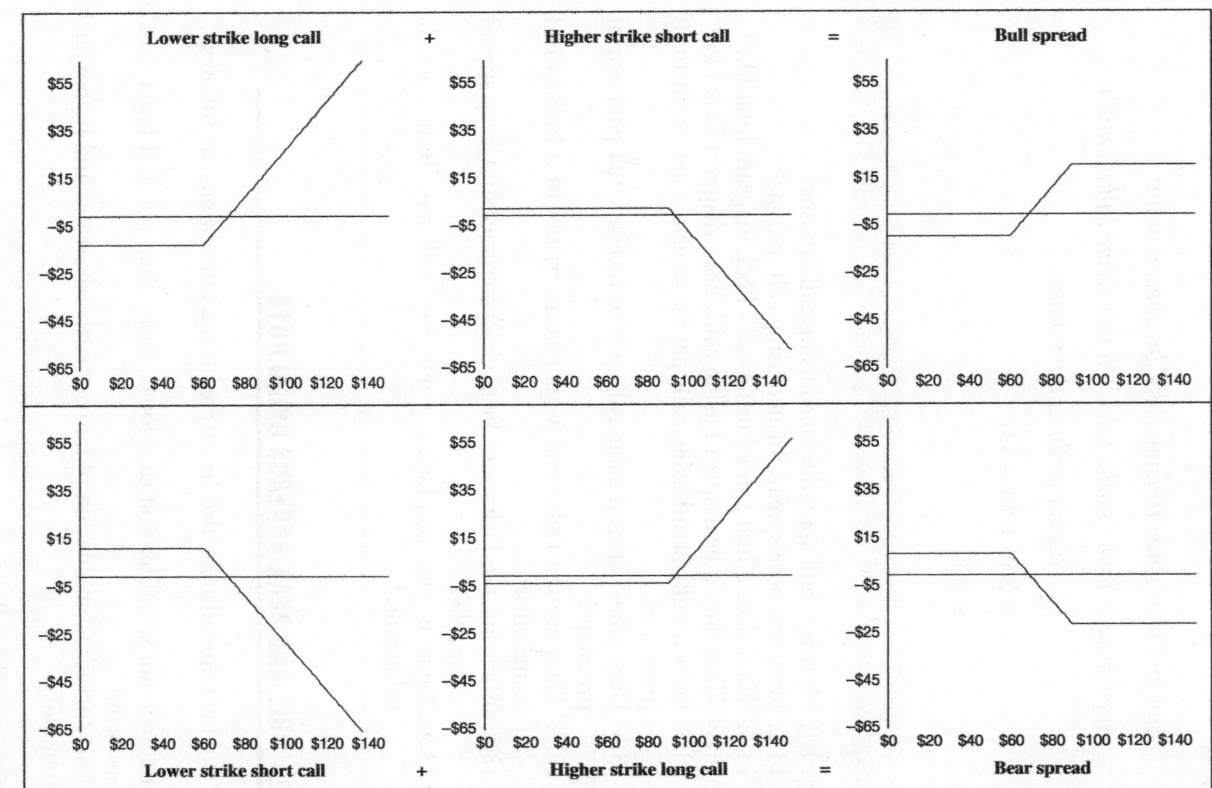

FIGURE 13.1 P&L diagrams for bull and bear spreads using calls

For example, if the lower strike is \$30, the lower strike call premium is \$4, and the higher strike call premium is \$2, it follows that the breakeven point is

Bull and bear spreads using calls' breakeven point:

$$\begin{aligned}\textit{Asset price} &= \textit{lower strike price} + \textit{lower strike call premium} \\ &\quad - \textit{higher strike call premium} \\ &= \$30 + \$4 - \$2 \\ &= \$32\end{aligned}$$

Knowledge check

Q 13.1: How is a bull spread formed using call options?
Q 13.2: How is a bear spread formed using call options?
Q 13.3: What does a bull spread using call's P&L diagram look like?
Q 13.4: What does a bear spread using call's P&L diagram look like?
Q 13.5: Does a bull spread using calls pay or receive a net payment of premium?
Q 13.6: Does a bear spread using calls pay or receive a net payment of premium?
Q 13.7: What are the Delta and Vega characteristics of a bull spread using calls?
Q 13.8: What are the Delta and Vega characteristics of a bear spread using calls?
Q 13.9: What is the breakeven point for bull and bear spreads using calls?

13.2 BULL AND BEAR SPREADS USING PUTS

Bull and bear spreads can also be formed using put options, as follows:

- Bull spread: Combination of a lower strike long put and higher strike short put
- Bear spread: Combination of a lower strike short put and higher strike long put

Consider the following example:

- Lower strike put: strike price = \$70 and premium = \$6
- Higher strike put: strike price = \$100 and premium = \$18

Figure 13.2 shows the P&L diagrams for bull and bear spreads that are created using puts.

Some observations are as follows:

- Whether formed using calls or puts, bull spreads require long positions in lower strike options and short positions in higher strike options.
- Higher strike put options have higher premiums than lower strike put options, as they have greater moneyness. Hence, the higher strike put premium received will be larger than the lower strike put premium paid. Because of this, a bull spread using puts will provide a net reception of premium, while a bear spread using puts will require a net payment of premium.
- The P&L diagrams for bull and bear spreads using puts are broadly similar to the P&L diagrams for bull and bear spreads using puts.

The exposures of bull and bear spreads using puts are similar to that of bull and bear spreads using calls:

- A bull spread using puts is long Delta. This is because the higher strike short put Delta is positive and, due to its greater moneyness, of greater magnitude than the lower strike long put's negative Delta.
- A bull spread using puts is broadly Vega neutral. This is because the long put is long Vega, and the short put is short Vega.
- Because options are zero-sum games, a bear spread using puts has the opposite exposure of a bull spread using puts: It is short Delta and broadly Vega neutral.

The breakeven point for bull and bear spreads using puts is

Bull and bear spreads using puts breakeven point:

$$\begin{aligned} \textit{Asset price} &= \textit{higher strike price} - \textit{higher strike put premium} \\ &\quad + \textit{lower strike put premium} \end{aligned}$$

For example, if the higher strike is \$50, the lower strike put premium is \$3, and the higher strike put premium is \$6, it follows that the breakeven point is

Bull and bear spreads using puts' breakeven point:

$$\begin{aligned} \textit{Asset price} &= \textit{higher strike price} - \textit{higher strike put premium} \\ &\quad + \textit{lower strike put premium} \\ &= \$50 - \$6 + \$3 \\ &= \$47 \end{aligned}$$

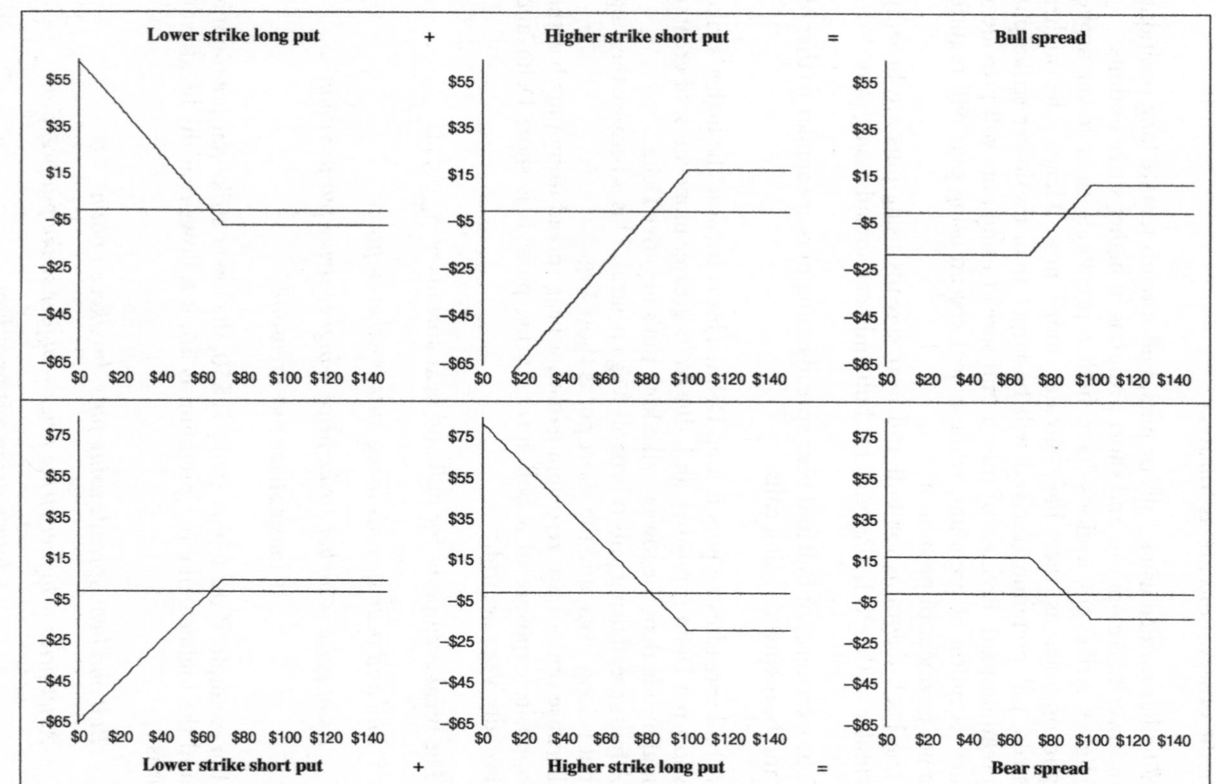

FIGURE 13.2 P&L diagrams for bull and bear spreads using puts

Knowledge check

Q 13.10: How is a bull spread formed using put options?
Q 13.11: How is a bear spread formed using put options?
Q 13.12: What does a bull spread using put's P&L diagram look like?
Q 13.13: What does a bear spread using put's P&L diagram look like?
Q 13.14: Does a bull spread using puts pay or receive a net payment of premium?
Q 13.15: Does a bear spread using puts pay or receive a net payment of premium?
Q 13.16: What are the Delta and Vega characteristics of a bull spread using puts?
Q 13.17: What are the Delta and Vega characteristics of a bear spread using puts?
Q 13.18: What is the breakeven point for bull and bear spreads using puts?

13.3 RISK REVERSALS

In Chapter 12 we learned about protective puts, covered calls, and collars that combine protective puts and covered calls. Recall that a protective put is typically an OTM (low strike) long put that protects a long position in a given asset from declines in the value of the asset, while a covered call is typically an OTM (high strike) short call that can be used to enhance yields or, if used as part of a collar, to finance a protective put.

An investor may form the view that in eagerness to enter into protective puts other investors are paying premiums that are greater than fair value. An investor with this view will want to take short positions in low strike OTM puts to receive the overvalued premiums.

Similarly, an investor may form the view that in their eagerness to enter into covered calls other investors are demanding call premiums that are less than fair value. An investor with this view will want to take long positions in high strike OTM calls to pay the undervalued premiums.

An investor that forms both views will want to enter into both a lower strike OTM short put and a higher strike OTM long call. Such a strategy is known as a "risk reversal."

For example, consider the following scenario:

- Put: strike price = \$50, and premium = \$15
- Call: strike price = \$100, and premium = \$12

Figure 13.3 shows the P&L diagram for a risk reversal.

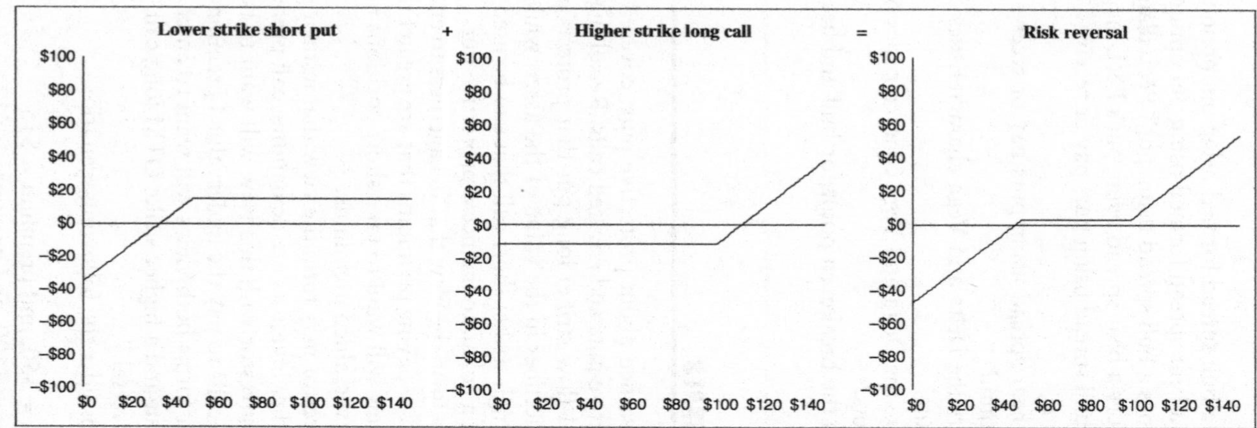

FIGURE 13.3 P&L diagram for a risk reversal

What is the exposure of the risk reversal strategy? To answer this question, recall the exposures of a short put and long call:

- Short put: Long Delta and Short Vega
- Long call: Long Delta and Long Vega

Since a risk reversal is a combination of a short put and long call, a risk reversal is long Delta and broadly Vega neutral.

The risk reversal's breakeven point depends on whether the put premium is greater, less, or equal to the call premium, as follows:

Risk reversal breakeven point when put premium is greater than the call premium:

Asset price = lower strike price − put premium + call premium

Risk reversal breakeven point when put premium is less than the call premium:

Asset price = higher strike price − put premium + call premium

When the put premium is equal to the call premium there are two breakeven points associated with a risk reversal: a lower breakeven point where the risk reversal transitions from losses to zero P&L, and a higher breakeven point where the risk reversal transitions from zero P&L to profits. In between the two breakeven points P&L is zero. In equation form, the breakeven points when the premiums are identical are

Lower risk reversal breakeven point when put premium is equal to the call premium:

Asset price = lower strike price

Higher risk reversal breakeven point when put premium is equal to the call premium:

Asset price = higher strike price

Knowledge check

Q 13.19: What is a "risk reversal" strategy?
Q 13.20: What is the motivation for entering into a risk reversal?

Q 13.21: What does a risk reversal's P&L diagram look like?
Q 13.22: What are the Delta and Vega characteristics of a risk reversal?
Q 13.23: What is the breakeven point for a risk reversal when the put premium is greater than the call premium?
Q 13.24: What is the breakeven point for a risk reversal when the put premium is less than the call premium?
Q 13.25: What are the breakeven points for a risk reversal when the put premium is equal to the call premium?

13.4 BUTTERFLY SPREADS

In Chapter 11 we learned that straddles consist of a call and a put with identical strike prices and strangles consist of a call and a put where the call strike is higher than the put strike.

Consider a straddle whose strike prices are at-the-money (ATM). We can refer to this straddle as an "ATM straddle." Hence:

- A long ATM straddle consists of a long ATM call and a long ATM put.
- A short ATM straddle consists of a short ATM call and a short ATM put.

Further, consider a strangle whose put and call strikes are OTM. We can refer to this strangle as an "OTM strangle." Hence:

- A long OTM strangle consists of a long OTM call and a long OTM put.
- A short OTM strangle consists of a short OTM call and a short OTM put.

Butterfly spreads combine ATM straddles and OTM strangles, as follows:

- Long butterfly spread: combination of a long OTM strangle and a short ATM straddle
- Short butterfly spread: combination of a short OTM strangle and a long ATM straddle

A long butterfly spread can be entered into by an investor that forms the view that OTM strangles are trading below fair value on the market and/or ATM straddles are trading above fair value. The investor will, therefore, want to purchase (i.e., long) undervalued OTM strangles and sell (i.e., short) overvalued ATM straddles.

A short butterfly spread can be entered into by an investor that forms the view that OTM strangles are trading above fair value on the market, and/or ATM straddles are trading below fair value. The investor will, therefore, want to sell (i.e., short) overvalued OTM strangles and purchase (i.e., long) undervalued ATM straddles.

For example, consider the following scenario:

- ATM Call: strike = \$75 and premium = \$23
- ATM Put: strike = \$75 and premium = \$21
- OTM Call: strike = \$100 and premium = \$13
- OTM Put: strike = \$50 and premium = \$11

Figure 13.4 shows the P&L diagrams for long and short butterfly spreads.

Figure 13.4 demonstrates that the long butterfly spread is profitable if the underlying asset price is near-the-money, and suffers a limited loss if the underlying asset price increases or decreases dramatically.

Both a straddle and strangle are broadly Delta neutral; hence, long and short butterfly spreads are also broadly Delta neutral. A long strangle is characterized by long Vega, and a short straddle is characterized by short Vega. However, the Vegas of an ATM straddle and an OTM strangle do not offset each other. Instead:

- Long butterfly spread: short Vega
- Short butterfly spread: long Vega

Why? Because while a long OTM strangle is positively volatility sensitive and a short ATM straddle is negatively volatility sensitive, the sensitivity of the short ATM straddle is much greater than the sensitivity of the long OTM strangle, as the magnitude of Vega is greatest for near-the-money options and smaller for OTM and ITM positions.[2] Because of this, a long butterfly spread is short Vega, and a short butterfly spread is long Vega.

A butterfly spread's two breakeven points are

Lower butterfly spread breakeven point:

$$\begin{aligned} \textit{Asset price} = {} & \textit{ATM strike price} + \textit{OTM put premium} \\ & + \textit{OTM call premium} - \textit{ATM put premium} \\ & - \textit{ATM call premium} \end{aligned}$$

[2]The relationship between moneyness and the magnitude of Vega is discussed in Section 10.2.4 of Chapter 10.

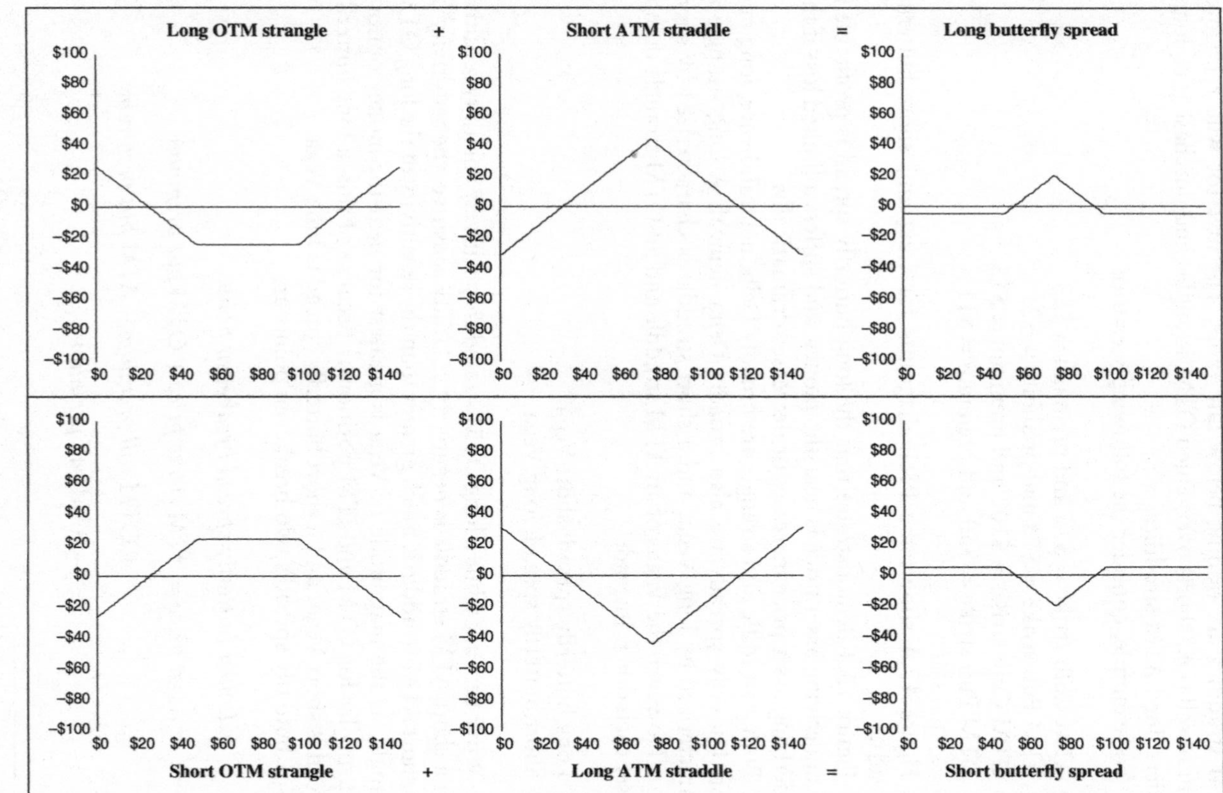

FIGURE 13.4 P&L diagrams for long and short butterfly spreads

Higher butterfly spread breakeven point:

Asset price = ATM strike price – OTM put premium
– OTM call premium + ATM put premium
+ ATM call premium

Let's calculate the higher and lower breakeven points using the example explored earlier. The breakeven points are:

Lower butterfly spread breakeven point:

Asset price = ATM strike price + OTM put premium
+ OTM call premium – ATM put premium
– ATM call premium
= $75 + $11 + $13 – $21 – $23
= $55

Lower butterfly spread breakeven point:

Asset price = ATM strike price – OTM put premium
– OTM call premium + ATM put premium
+ ATM call premium
= $75 – $11 – $13 + $21 + $23
= $95

Knowledge check

Q 13.26: What is a "long butterfly spread" strategy?
Q 13.27: What is a "short butterfly spread" strategy?
Q 13.28: What is the motivation for entering into a long butterfly spread?
Q 13.29: What is the motivation for entering into a short butterfly spread?
Q 13.30: What does a long butterfly spread's P&L diagram look like?
Q 13.31: What does a short butterfly spread's P&L diagram look like?
Q 13.32: What are the Delta and Vega characteristics of a long butterfly spread?

Q 13.33: What are the Delta and Vega characteristics of a short butterfly spread?

Q 13.34: What are the breakeven points for long and short butterfly spreads?

13.5 CONDOR SPREADS

A condor spread is similar to a butterfly spread with the following key difference: While a butterfly spread is a combination of an ATM straddle and an OTM strangle, a condor spread is a combination of two OTM strangles, where one of the strangles is *deeper* OTM than the other strangle. A deeper-OTM strangle has strike prices that are farther from the underlying asset price than a less-deep-OTM strangle.

Condor spreads combine deeper-OTM strangles with less-deep-OTM strangles, as follows:

- Long condor spread: combination of a long deeper-OTM strangle and a short less-deep-OTM strangle
- Short condor spread: combination of a short deeper-OTM strangle and a long less-deep-OTM strangle

For example, consider the following scenario:

- Less-deep-OTM Call: strike = $85 and premium = $15
- Less-deep-OTM Put: strike = $65 and premium = $18
- Deeper-OTM Call: strike = $100 and premium = $13
- Deeper-OTM Put: strike = $50 and premium = $11

Figure 13.5 shows the P&L diagrams for long and short condor spreads.

Figure 13.5 demonstrates that the long condor spread is profitable when the underlying asset price is near-the-money, and suffers a small loss if the underlying asset price increases or decreases dramatically. Figure 13.5 also demonstrates that the short condor spread suffers losses when the underlying asset price is near-the-money and earns a small profit if the underlying asset price increases or decreases dramatically.

A strangle is broadly Delta neutral; hence, long and short condor spreads are also broadly Delta neutral. A short strangle is short Vega, and a long strangle is long Vega. However, the Vegas of the two strangles do not offset each other, as the magnitude of the less-deep-OTM strangle's Vega is larger than the Vega of the deeper-OTM strangle. Hence:

- Long condor spread: short Vega
- Short condor spread: long Vega

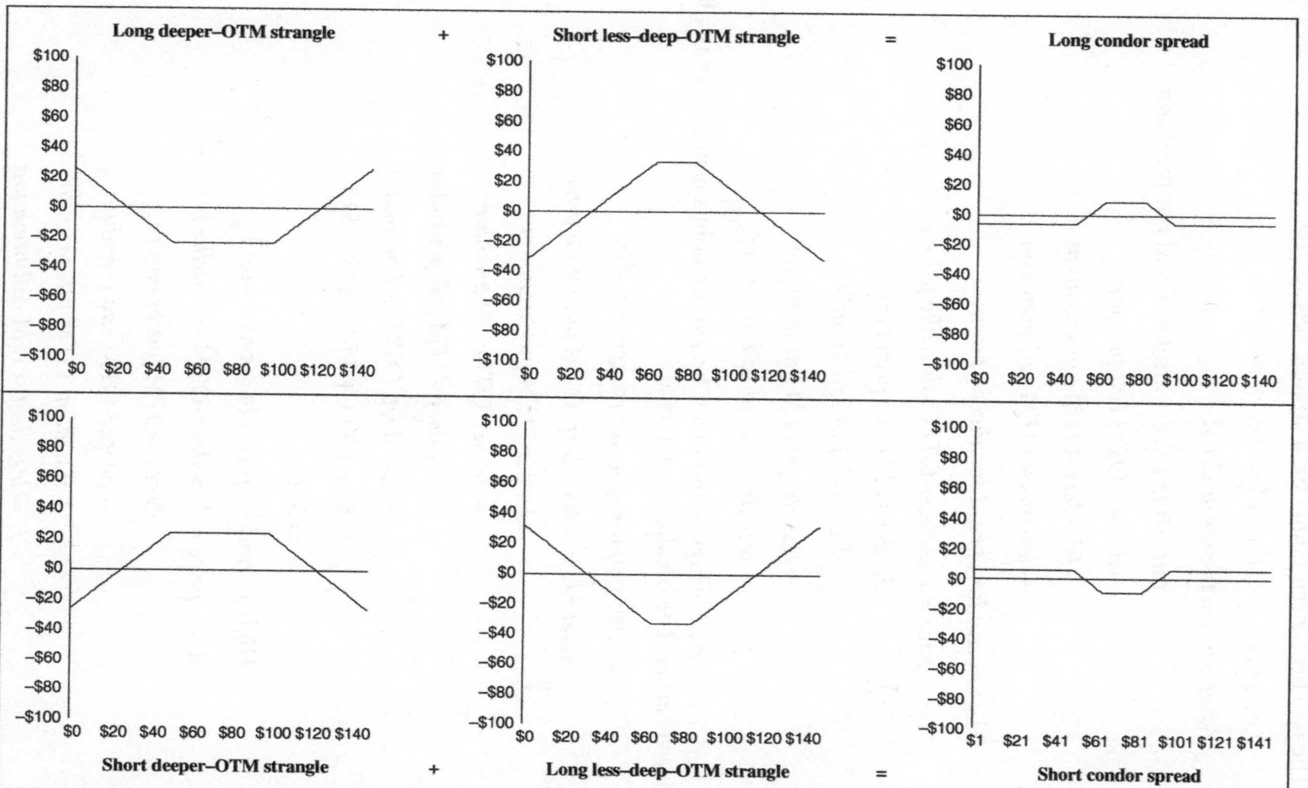

FIGURE 13.5 P&L diagrams for long and short condor spreads

The two breakeven points for a condor spread are

Lower condor spread breakeven point:

Asset price = less-deep-OTM

put strike price + deeper-OTM put premium

+ deeper-OTM call premium

– less-deep-OTM put premium

– less-deep-OTM call premium

Higher condor spread breakeven point:

Asset price = less-deep-OTM call strike price –

deeper-OTM put premium

– deeper-OTM call premium

+ less-deep-OTM put premium

+ less-deep-OTM call premium

Let's calculate the higher and lower breakeven points using the example explored earlier. The breakeven points are

Lower condor spread breakeven point:

Asset price = less-deep-OTM put strike price +

deeper-OTM put premium

+ deeper-OTM call premium

– less-deep-OTM put premium

– less-deep-OTM call premium

= \$65 + \$11 + \$13 – \$18 – \$15

= \$56

Higher condor spread breakeven point:

Asset price = less-deep-OTM call strike price –

deeper-OTM put premium

– deeper-OTM call premium

+ less-deep-OTM put premium

+ less-deep-OTM call premium

= \$85 – \$11 – \$13 + \$18 + \$15

= \$94

Knowledge check

Q 13.35: What is a "long condor spread" strategy?
Q 13.36: What is a "short condor spread" strategy?
Q 13.37: What does a long condor spread's P&L diagram look like?
Q 13.38: What does a short condor spread's P&L diagram look like?
Q 13.39: What are the Delta and Vega characteristics of a long condor spread?
Q 13.40: What are the Delta and Vega characteristics of a short condor spread?
Q 13.41: What are the breakeven points for long and short condor spreads?

KEY POINTS

- Bull and bear spreads are formed using either call or put options. A bull spread using calls is a combination of a lower strike long call and higher strike short call. A bear spread using calls is a combination of a lower strike short call and higher strike long call. A bull spread using puts is a combination of a lower strike long put and higher strike short put. A bear spread using puts is a combination of a lower strike short put and higher strike long put.
- A bull spread provides similar exposure to a collar, and a bear spread provides opposite exposure. A bull spread using calls will have a net payment of premium, and a bear spread using calls will have a net reception. A bull spread using puts will have a net reception of premium, and the bear spread using puts will have a net payment. A bull spread is long Delta and broadly Vega neutral, and a bear spread is short Delta and broadly Vega neutral.
- A "risk reversal" trading strategy is formed through entering into a lower strike short put and a higher strike long call, and can be implemented to take advantage of the view that protective puts are overvalued and covered calls are undervalued. A risk reversal is long Delta and is broadly Vega neutral. A risk's reversals breakeven point depends on whether the call premium is greater, less, or equal to the put premium.
- A long butterfly spread is formed through entering into a combination of a long out-of-the-money (OTM) strangle and a short at-the-money (ATM) straddle. A short butterfly spread is formed through entering into a combination of a short OTM strangle and a long ATM straddle.

- A long butterfly spread may be entered into by an investor that forms the view that OTM strangles are trading below fair value on the market, and/or ATM straddles are trading above fair value. A short butterfly spread may be entered into by an investor that forms the view that OTM strangles are trading above fair value on the market, and/or ATM straddles are trading below fair value. Condor spreads are similar to butterfly spreads; however, they consist of long and short positions in less-deep-OTM and deeper-OTM strangles.
- Long and short butterfly spreads and condor spreads are broadly Delta neutral. Long butterfly spreads and condor spreads are short Vega, and short butterfly spreads and condor spreads are long Vega. Both butterfly spreads and condor spreads have two breakeven points.

PART Five

Swaps

CHAPTER 14

Interest Rate Swaps

INTRODUCTION

In this and the subsequent chapter we will explore a type of derivative security known as a "swap." Broadly, a swap is an exchange of cash flows between two counterparties over a number of periods of time. This chapter explores the most important swap product, the interest rate swap. We will learn about the characteristics of an interest rate swap, how an interest rate swap's cash flows are calculated, and how interest rate swaps can be used to transform cash flows. The subsequent chapter explores other swap varieties.

After you read this chapter, you will be able to

- Describe the characteristics of an interest rate swap.
- Distinguish between fixed and floating interest rate swap legs and rates.
- Understand how the fixed rate is determined.
- Calculate the cash flows associated with an interest rate swap.
- Explain how interest rate swaps can transform cash flows.

14.1 INTEREST RATE SWAP CHARACTERISTICS

An interest rate swap is an agreement in which two counterparties agree to periodically exchange fixed and floating rates of interest over a number of periods of time. One of the swap counterparties, known as the long interest rate swap position, agrees to periodically receive a floating rate and pay a fixed rate. The other swap counterparty, known as the short interest rate swap position, agrees to periodically receive a fixed rate and pay a floating rate. The exchange of fixed rate for floating rate is broadly illustrated in Figure 14.1.

Additional interest rate swap characteristics are as follows:

- The fixed rate is agreed-upon at the initiation of the interest rate swap. The fixed rate does not change during the life of the swap.

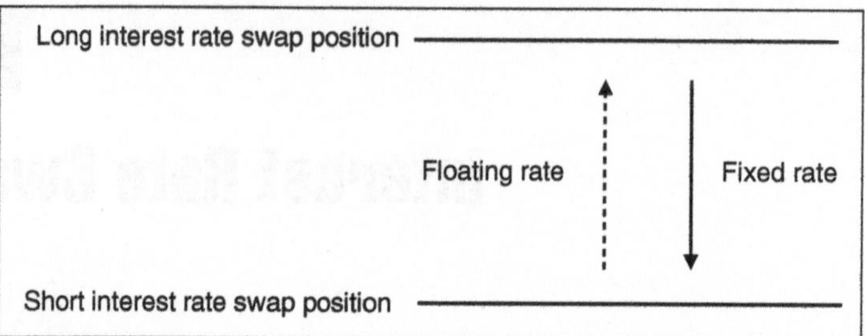

FIGURE 14.1 The exchange of fixed rate for floating rate in an interest rate swap

- The floating rate fluctuates over time. The most commonly used floating rate is the London Interbank Offered Rate (LIBOR). LIBOR is a benchmark rate that is formed through a survey of the rates at which banks borrow from each other.[1] Other organizations provide alternatives to LIBOR, examples of which are EURIBOR and TIBOR.[2]
- The maturity of the swap is referred to as its "tenor." The tenor is determined by agreement between the two counterparties. Common interest rate swap tenors are 5- and 10-year tenors.

The convention is that neither the long nor short position to an interest rate swap pays or receives a premium at initiation. The fact that there is no premium at initiation indicates that an interest rate swap is designed to have zero value for both counterparties at initiation.

To ensure that an interest rate swap has zero value at initiation, a fixed rate is set such that it is perceived as "fair" to both counterparties, i.e., ensures that neither counterparty's position is an asset nor a liability at initiation. There is only one fixed rate that is fair to both counterparties: a fixed rate equal to the counterparties' expectations of the floating rate. After all, the fixed rate is being exchanged for a floating rate; hence, a "fair" fixed rate is one that is equal to the expected levels of the floating rate.

[1]Historically, LIBOR was managed by the British Bankers Association (BBA). However, following a scandal, LIBOR is no longer managed by the BBA. Instead, it is now managed by the Intercontinental Exchange (ICE); and, therefore, is now formally known as ICE LIBOR. See www.theice.com/iba/libor for more information about LIBOR.

[2]See www.emmi-benchmarks.eu and www.zenginkyo.or.jp/en/tibor to learn about EURIBOR and TIBOR, respectively.

After initiation LIBOR will, inevitably, either increase or decrease. This benefits one of the counterparties and harms the other. Hence the interest rate swap's value will no longer be zero for both counterparties. Instead it will be one of the following:

- Asset: The interest rate swap value for the counterparty that benefits from the LIBOR change will be positive (an asset).
- Liability: The interest rate swap value for the counterparty that is harmed by the asset price change will be negative (a liability).

Consider the following interest rate swap example:

- Counterparty A is the long position.
- Counterparty B is the short position.
- The floating rate is LIBOR.
- The fixed rate is 3%.
- The swap tenor is three years.

Since Counterparty A is the long position, and Counterparty B is the short position, Counterparty A receives LIBOR and pays 3% throughout the life of the swap. Conversely, Counterparty B receives 3% and pays LIBOR. The impact of the future level of LIBOR for each counterparty is detailed in Table 14.1.

We see from this example that the long interest rate swap position benefits if LIBOR increases, while the short interest rate swap position benefits if LIBOR decreases. This suggests the following:

- Enter into a long interest rate swap if one has the view that LIBOR will increase.
- Enter into a short interest rate swap if one has the view that LIBOR will decrease.

TABLE 14.1 The impact of the future level of LIBOR for interest rate swap counterparties

LIBOR level	Impact on Counterparty A (long)	Impact on Counterparty B (short)
LIBOR > 3%	Receives higher rate than it pays	Receives lower rate than it pays
LIBOR < 3%	Receives lower rate than it pays	Receives higher rate than it pays
LIBOR = 3%	Receives and pays the same rate	Receives and pays the same rate

This example may suggest that the cash flows associated with an interest rate swap are straightforward. In reality, the cash flows are complex due to a number of conventions. These include conventions related to the frequency of the cash flows, the method through which rates are converted into cash flows, and the process through which the floating rate is identified, among others. The next section explores these conventions in detail.

Knowledge check

Q 14.1: What is an "interest rate swap"?
Q 14.2: Does the long interest rate swap receive or pay fixed or floating rates?
Q 14.3: Does the short interest rate swap receive or pay fixed or floating rates?
Q 14.4: When is the fixed rate determined by an interest rate swap?
Q 14.5: What is LIBOR?
Q 14.6: What is swap "tenor"?
Q 14.7: Is there a premium payment associated with a swap?
Q 14.8: How is the fixed rate set at swap initiation?
Q 14.9: What is the value of an interest rate swap at initiation?

14.2 INTEREST RATE SWAP CASH FLOWS

In this section we will learn how to calculate the cash flows associated with an interest rate swap. To calculate the cash flows, we require familiarity with the following concepts:

- The frequency of payments
- The notional principal
- Annualized rates versus periodic rates
- Day count conventions
- Accrual factors
- How the floating rate is specified

We next explore each of these concepts in detail.

14.2.1 Frequency of payments

The exchange of cash flows in an interest rate swap may take place more than once per year. Further, the frequency of the payments may be different for the fixed leg than it is for the floating leg. In the United States, the typical convention for the frequency of payments is as follows:

- Fixed leg: Semi-annual (i.e., twice per year)
- Floating leg: Quarterly (i.e., four times per year)

14.2.2 Notional principal

Interest rate swaps are quoted as rates, such as a rate of 1%. However, the actual exchanges of cash flows are in cash, not percentages. To allow the counterparties to identify the cash flows every interest rate swap will specify a dollar amount, referred to as the "notional principal." A cash payment associated with an interest rate swap is identified through multiplying the rate by the notional principal. Unlike a bond, where there is a payment of face value at bond maturity, in an interest rate swap the notional principal is not exchanged.[3] Instead, its purpose is to enable the counterparties to identify the cash payments.

14.2.3 Annualized and periodic rates, day count conventions, and accrual factors

Both fixed and floating rates of interest are quoted as annualized rates. However, as we've learned, the frequencies of the cash flows for a typical U.S. interest rate swap are either semi-annual (for the fixed leg) or quarterly (for the floating leg). Because of this, we have to transform the annualized rates into periodic rates.

We do not transform the annualized fixed rate into the semi-annual fixed rate through simply dividing by two. Neither do we transform the annualized floating rate into the quarterly floating rate through simply dividing by four. Instead, we transform the annualized rate into the periodic rate through multiplying the annualized rate by a factor known as an "accrual factor." The convention through which the accrual factor is calculated is referred to as the "day count convention." In the United States, the day count convention used for the floating leg differs from the day count convention used for the fixed leg. Let's explore each.

Floating leg day count convention

In the U.S., the day count convention typically used to calculate the floating leg accrual factor is referred to as "Actual/360," "Act/360," or "A/360," as it is calculated using the actual number of days in the quarter in the numerator and an assumed 360-day year in the denominator. Hence, the accrual

[3]Cross-currency swaps include an exchange of notional principal. We will explore cross-currency swaps in Chapter 15.

factor used to transform the annualized floating rate into the quarterly floating rate is:

$$\textit{Floating leg accrual factor} = \textit{days in quarter}/360$$

For example, if the actual number of days in the quarter is 91, then the floating leg accrual factor is:

$$\begin{aligned}\textit{Floating leg accrual factor} &= \textit{days in quarter}/360\\ &= 91/360\\ &= 0.2528\end{aligned}$$

Hence, the annualized floating rate is multiplied by 0.2528 to identify the quarterly floating rate.

Fixed leg day count conventions

The day count convention used to calculate the fixed leg accrual factor is referred to as "30/360," as it is calculated assuming 30 days per month (or 180 days semi-annually) in the numerator and an assumed 360-day year in the denominator. Hence, the accrual factor used to transform the annualized fixed rate into the semi-annual fixed rate is:

$$\begin{aligned}\textit{Fixed leg accrual factor} &= 180/360\\ &= 0.5\end{aligned}$$

Hence, the annualized fixed rate is multiplied by 0.5 to identify the semi-annual fixed rate.

If the cash flow is scheduled to take place over the weekend or on a holiday, the numerator may be adjusted to reflect the fact that the cash flow won't be delivered until the next business day.

14.2.4 Specification of the floating rate

We've learned that the floating interest rate is typically based on LIBOR, a benchmark of the rate at which banks borrow from each other. LIBOR is available in different currencies and for different lengths of time. The currencies are U.S. Dollar (USD), Swiss Franc (CHF), Euro (EUR), British Pound (GBP), and Japanese Yen (JPY). The rates, while expressed in annualized terms, have tenors that include overnight, one week, one month, two months, three months, six months, and one year.[4] Hence the specification of the floating rate is never simply "LIBOR" but must include the currency

[4]Source: www.theice.com/iba/libor.

and tenor. For typical U.S. interest rate swaps, the floating rate is 3-month USD LIBOR.

Further, the floating rate in a typical interest rate swap is not the floating rate on the day the floating payment is due. Instead, it is the floating rate reported one period earlier. Hence, the floating payment is the one reported at the beginning and not the end of the given quarter. LIBOR reported at the beginning of a quarter is referred to as "LIBOR-in-advance," and the LIBOR reported at the end of a quarter is referred to as "LIBOR-in-arrears." Typical U.S. interest rate swaps use a "LIBOR-in-advance" convention.

Knowledge check

Q 14.10: What is the typical U.S. convention for the frequency of fixed leg payments?
Q 14.11: What is the typical U.S. convention for the frequency of floating leg payments?
Q 14.12: What is "notional principal"?
Q 14.13: What is the purpose of notional principal?
Q 14.14: Are rates typically quoted as annualized or periodic rates?
Q 14.15: What is an "accrual factor"?
Q 14.16: What is a "day count convention"?
Q 14.17: What is the typical U.S. day count convention for fixed leg payments?
Q 14.18: What is the typical U.S. day count convention for floating leg payments?
Q 14.19: What is "Actual/360"?
Q 14.20: What is "30/360"?
Q 14.21: How is the floating leg accrual factor calculated?
Q 14.22: How is the fixed leg accrual factor calculated?
Q 14.23: What is "LIBOR-in-advance"?
Q 14.24: What is "LIBOR-in-arrears"?
Q 14.25: What is the typical U.S. convention for the specification of LIBOR?

14.3 CALCULATING INTEREST RATE SWAP CASH FLOWS

This section explores a detailed interest rate swap cash flow example. Consider the following swap:

- The tenor of the swap is two years.
- The notional principal is $10 million.

- The floating leg has quarterly payments and uses the A/360 day count convention.
- The fixed leg has semi-annual payments and uses the 30/360 day count convention.
- The annualized fixed rate is 1.75%.
- The floating rate is 3-month USD LIBOR-in-advance.
- There are eight floating-leg cash flows over the two-year tenor that will take place at the end of each quarter. The LIBOR observations and the number of days in each quarter over the two-year tenor are detailed in Table 14.2.
- There are four fixed-leg cash flows over the two-year tenor. These cash flows will take place at the following times:
  - After 6 months (i.e., end of quarter 2)
  - After 12 months (i.e., end of quarter 4)
  - After 18 months (i.e., end of quarter 6)
  - After 24 months (i.e., end of quarter 8)
- We assume throughout that the cash flows are scheduled to take place on business days.

Let's calculate the cash flows associated with both legs of this interest rate swap. The detailed steps through which we will perform these calculations are as follows:

- Step 1: Calculate the floating leg payment.
  - Step 1.1: Calculate the floating rate accrual factor.
  - Step 1.2: Calculate the quarterly floating rate.
  - Step 1.3: Calculate the floating payment.

TABLE 14.2 LIBOR observations

Month	Quarter	Days in quarter	3-month USD LIBOR-in-advance
3	1	91	0.53%
6	2	92	0.45%
9	3	91	1.34%
12	4	91	1.45%
15	5	91	1.76%
18	6	92	2.14%
21	7	91	2.11%
24	8	91	3.21%

- Step 2: Calculate the fixed leg payment.
  - Step 2.1: Calculate the fixed rate accrual factor.
  - Step 2.2: Calculate the semi-annual fixed rate.
  - Step 2.3: Calculate the fixed payment.
- Step 3: Calculate the net cash flows.
  - Step 3.1: Calculate the net long position cash flows.
  - Step 3.2: Calculate the net short position cash flows.

14.3.1 Floating leg payments

Step 1 is the calculation of the floating leg payments. All calculations of the floating leg payments are shown in Table 14.3. To calculate the floating leg payments, we proceed as follows for each quarter:

- Step 1.1: Calculate the floating rate accrual factor.
- Step 1.2: Calculate the quarterly floating rate.
- Step 1.3: Calculate the floating payment.

Let's explore these calculations in detail.

Step 1.1: Calculate the floating rate accrual factor: To calculate the floating rate accrual factor, recall that the day count convention is A/360. Hence, we divide the number of days in the given quarter by 360. For example, there are 92 days in quarter 2. Therefore:

$$\begin{aligned}\textit{Floating leg accrual factor} &= \textit{days in quarter}\\ &= 92/360\\ &= 0.2556\end{aligned}$$

Step 1.2: Calculate the quarterly floating rate: The quarterly floating rate is equal to the annualized floating rate multiplied by the floating rate accrual factor. For example, in quarter 8 the annualized floating rate is 3.21%, and the floating rate accrual factor is 0.2528. Therefore:

$$\begin{aligned}&\textit{Quarterly floating rate}\\ &= \textit{annualized floating rate} \times \textit{floating rate accrual factor}\\ &= 3.21\% \times 0.2528\\ &= 0.8114\%\end{aligned}$$

Step 1.3: Calculate the floating payment: The floating payment is equal to the quarterly floating rate multiplied by the notional principal.

TABLE 14.3 Calculation of floating leg payments

Month	3	6	9	12	15	18	21	24
Quarter	1	2	3	4	5	6	7	8
Annualized floating rate	0.5300%	0.4500%	1.3400%	1.4500%	1.7600%	2.1400%	2.1100%	3.2100%
Days in quarter	91	92	91	91	91	92	91	91
Floating rate accrual factor	0.2528	0.2556	0.2528	0.2528	0.2528	0.2556	0.2528	0.2528
Quarterly floating rate	0.1340%	0.1150%	0.3387%	0.3665%	0.4449%	0.5469%	0.5334%	0.8114%
Floating payment	$13,397.22	$11,500.00	$33,872.22	$36,652.78	$44,488.89	$54,688.89	$53,336.11	$81,141.67

For example, in quarter 3, the quarterly floating rate is 0.3387% and the notional principal is \$10,000,000. Hence, the floating payment is:

$$\begin{aligned} \textit{Floating payment} &= \textit{quarterly floating rate} \times \textit{notional principal} \\ &= 0.3387\% \times \$10,000,000 \\ &= \$33,872.22 \end{aligned}$$

14.3.2 Fixed leg payments

Step 2 is the calculation of the fixed leg payments. All calculations of the fixed leg payments are shown in Table 14.4. To calculate the fixed leg payments, we proceed as follows:

- Step 2.1: Calculate the fixed rate accrual factor.
- Step 2.2: Calculate the semi-annual fixed rate.
- Step 2.3: Calculate the fixed payment.

Let's explore these calculations in detail.

Step 2.1: Calculate the fixed rate accrual factor: To calculate the fixed rate accrual factor, recall that the day count convention is 30/360. Under this convention, we assume 30 days per month or 180 days per semi-annual period. Hence the accrual factor is 0.5 throughout.

Step 2.2: Calculate the semi-annual rate: The semi-annual fixed rate is equal to the annualized fixed rate multiplied by the fixed rate accrual factor. The annualized fixed rate and the fixed rate accrual factors are the same each period. The annualized fixed rate is 1.75%, and the fixed rate accrual factor is 0.5. Therefore, we calculate the semi-annual fixed rate as follows:

$$\begin{aligned} \textit{Semi-annual fixed rate} &= \textit{annualized fixed rate} \times \textit{fixed rate accrual factor} \\ &= 1.75\% \times 0.5 \\ &= 0.875\% \end{aligned}$$

TABLE 14.4 Calculation of fixed leg payments

Month Quarter	3 1	6 2	9 3	12 4	15 5	18 6	21 7	24 8
Annualized fixed rate		1.7500%		1.7500%		1.7500%		1.7500%
Fixed rate accrual factor		0.5000		0.5000		0.5000		0.5000
Semi-annual fixed rate		0.8750%		0.8750%		0.8750%		0.8750%
Fixed payment		\$87,500.00		\$87,500.00		\$87,500.00		\$87,500.00

Step 2.3: Calculate the fixed payment: The fixed payment is equal to the semi-annual fixed rate multiplied by the notional principal. Both the semi-annual fixed rate and the notional principal are the same each period. The semi-annual fixed rate is 0.875%, and the notional principal is $10,000,000. Hence, the fixed payment is:

$$
\begin{aligned}
\textit{Fixed payment} &= \textit{semi-annual fixed rate} \times \textit{notional principal} \\
&= 0.875\% \times \$10,000,000 \\
&= \$87,500
\end{aligned}
$$

14.3.3 Net cash flows

Step 3 is the calculation of the net cash flows received by each position. To calculate the net amounts received by both the long and short interest rate swap positions, we proceed as follows:

- Step 3.1: Calculate the net long position cash flows.
- Step 3.2: Calculate the net short position cash flows.

All calculations are shown in Table 14.5.

Let's explore these calculations in detail.

Step 3.1: Calculate the net long position cash flows. The long interest rate swap position receives floating and pays fixed. Hence, the net received by the long interest rate swap position is:

$$\textit{Net long position cash flow} = \textit{floating payment} - \textit{fixed payment}$$

For example, in quarter 3 the floating payment is $33,872.22, and there is no fixed payment. Hence, the net received by the long interest rate swap position is:

$$
\begin{aligned}
\textit{Net long position cash flow} &= \textit{floating payment} - \textit{fixed payment} \\
&= \$33,872.22 - 0 \\
&= \$33,872.22
\end{aligned}
$$

Step 3.2: Calculate the net short position cash flows. The short interest rate swap position receives fixed and pays floating. Hence, the net received by the short interest rate swap position is:

$$\textit{Net short position cash flow} = \textit{fixed payment} - \textit{floating payment}$$

TABLE 14.5 Calculation of net cash flows

Month	3	6	9	12	15	18	21	24
Quarter	1	2	3	4	5	6	7	8
Floating leg								
Annualized floating rate	0.5300%	0.4500%	1.3400%	1.4500%	1.7600%	2.1400%	2.1100%	3.2100%
Actual days in quarter	91	92	91	91	91	92	91	91
Floating rate accrual factor	0.2528	0.2556	0.2528	0.2528	0.2528	0.2556	0.2528	0.2528
Quarterly floating rate	0.1340%	0.1150%	0.3387%	0.3665%	0.4449%	0.5469%	0.5334%	0.8114%
Floating payment	$13,397.22	$11,500.00	$33,872.22	$36,652.78	$44,488.89	$54,688.89	$53,336.11	$81,141.67
Fixed leg								
Annualized fixed rate		1.7500%		1.7500%		1.7500%		1.7500%
Fixed rate accrual factor		0.5000		0.5000		0.5000		0.5000
Semi-annual fixed rate		0.8750%		0.8750%		0.8750%		0.8750%
Fixed payment		$87,500.00		$87,500.00		$87,500.00		$87,500.00
Net cash flows								
Net cash flow received by long	$13,397.22	$(76,000.00)	$33,872.22	$(50,847.22)	$44,488.89	$(32,811.11)	$53,336.11	$(6,358.33)
Net cash flow received by short	$(13,397.22)	$76,000.00	$(33,872.22)	$50,847.22	$(44,488.89)	$32,811.11	$(53,336.11)	$6,358.33

For example, in quarter 2 the fixed payment is \$87,500, and the floating payment is \$11,500. Hence, the net received by the long interest rate swap position is:

$$\begin{aligned} \textit{Net short position cash flow} &= \textit{floating payment} - \textit{fixed payment} \\ &= \$87,500 - \$11,500 \\ &= \$76,000 \end{aligned}$$

Knowledge check

Q 14.26: What are the steps through which the floating leg payments are calculated?

Q 14.27: What are the steps through which the fixed leg payments are calculated?

Q 14.28: What are the steps through which the net interest rate swap cash flows are calculated?

14.4 HOW INTEREST RATE SWAPS CAN TRANSFORM CASH FLOWS

In this section we will explore a core purpose of interest rate swaps: to enable borrowers and lenders to transform the nature of their cash flows. To understand the discussion in this section, let's first note the following preliminary concepts:

Risk-free rates and credit spreads

The interest rate that borrowers pay lenders can be perceived as being made up of two components: the risk-free interest rate and the credit spread. The risk-free interest rate (known as the "IR") is the interest rate a risk-free borrower pays when they borrow money. The credit spread (known as the "SPRD") is additional interest, on top of the risk-free rate, that a credit-risky borrower pays to compensate the lender for accepting their credit risk. For example, a credit-risky borrower may pay an interest rate of 8% in a market where the risk-free interest rate is 3%. In this scenario, we can perceive this borrower's interest rate as consisting of IR = 3% and SPRD = 5%.

LIBOR is a proxy for the risk-free rate

LIBOR is a benchmark of the rate at which banks borrow from each other. While not entirely risk-free, particularly during times of crisis such as during 2007–2008, LIBOR is sufficiently close to risk-free that it is perceived as a proxy for the risk-free rate, i.e., for the IR.

Borrowing fixed versus borrowing floating

There are, broadly, two types of cash flows associated with debt transactions:

- Borrowers paying lenders a fixed rate: For example, a corporate bond typically has a fixed interest rate, referred to as the coupon rate. The fixed rate comprises both the IR and SPRD elements. For example, a credit-risky corporate bond may have a fixed coupon of 5.5% in a market where a risk-free bond with similar characteristics has a fixed coupon of 2%. The fixed rate of 5.5% can be perceived as being made up of a fixed IR of 2% and a fixed SPRD of 3.5%.
- Borrowers paying lenders a floating rate: For example, private loans typically have an interest rate consisting of LIBOR and a fixed SPRD, for example, LIBOR + 7%. LIBOR is the IR element of the loan interest, and the additional 7% represents the SPRD. Hence, if LIBOR is 8%, then the total rate is 8% + 7% = 15%. If LIBOR is 2%, then the total rate is 2% + 7% = 9%. Because the total rate can vary, the borrower is paying a floating rate.

Based on the above, there are four cash flows that a typical borrower or lender may experience:

- Borrower paying floating: pays floating IR + fixed SPRD
- Lender receiving floating: receives floating IR + fixed SPRD
- Borrower paying fixed: pays fixed IR + fixed SPRD
- Lender receiving fixed: receives fixed IR + fixed SPRD

Interest rate swaps are used to transform the IR elements of cash flows. To demonstrate, in the next subsections we will explore how an interest rate swap can facilitate each of the following:

- Borrower transformed from paying floating to paying fixed
- Lender transformed from receiving floating to receiving fixed
- Borrower transformed from paying fixed to paying floating
- Lender is transformed from receiving fixed to receiving floating

14.4.1 Floating to fixed rate borrowing

Consider a borrower with a floating rate obligation consisting of floating IR and fixed SPRD. This obligation is depicted in Figure 14.2.

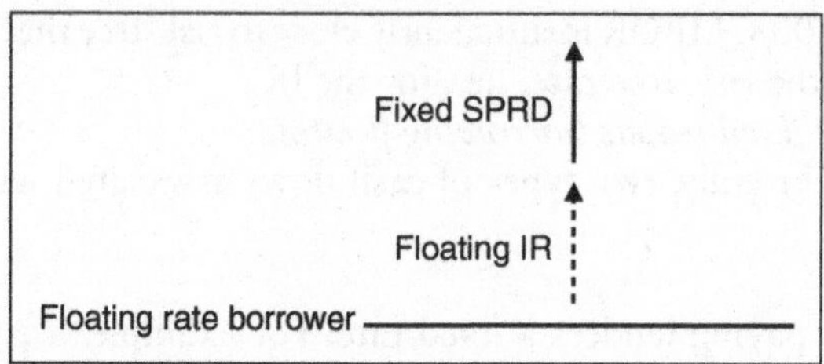

FIGURE 14.2 Floating rate borrower

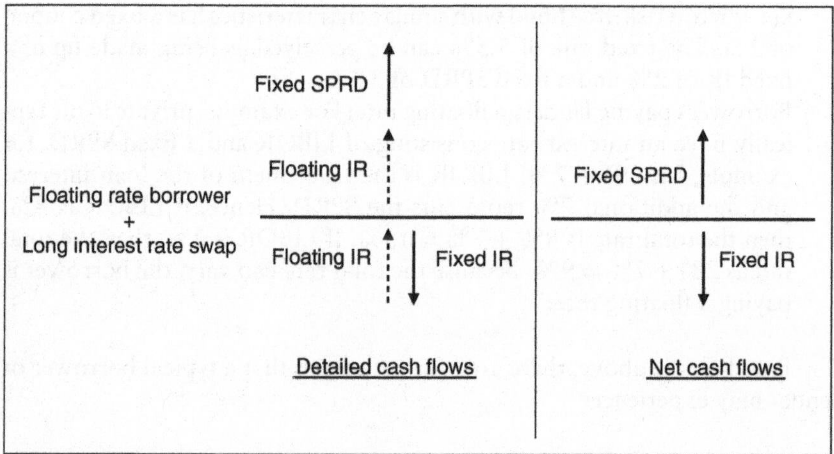

FIGURE 14.3 Transformation of floating rate borrowing into fixed rate borrowing

Should the floating IR increase, the borrower pays more. Should the floating IR decrease, the borrower pays less. To transform this floating rate borrowing into fixed rate borrowing, the borrower should enter into a long interest rate swap—in other words, the borrower should enter into a receive-floating-pay-fixed interest rate swap. The new position, consisting of the original obligation and the interest rate swap, is depicted in Figure 14.3.

With this strategy, the floating IR obligation is offset by the receive-floating leg of the interest rate swap. The borrower is left paying fixed SPRD and fixed IR, similar to a fixed rate obligation. Hence, the net result is that the borrower has transformed its position from floating rate borrowing to fixed rate borrowing.

14.4.2 Floating to fixed rate lending

Consider a lender receiving a floating rate, as depicted in Figure 14.4.

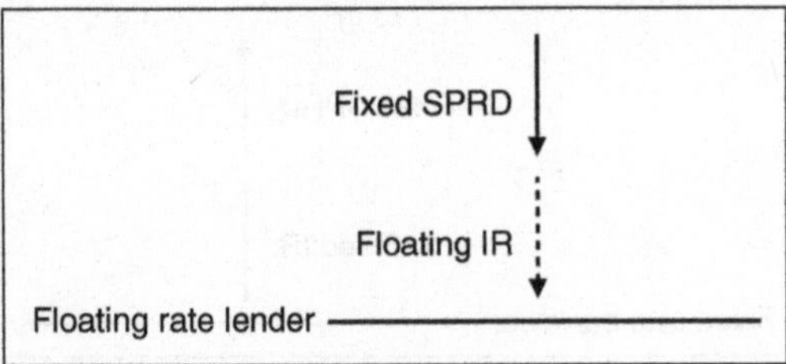

FIGURE 14.4 Floating rate lender

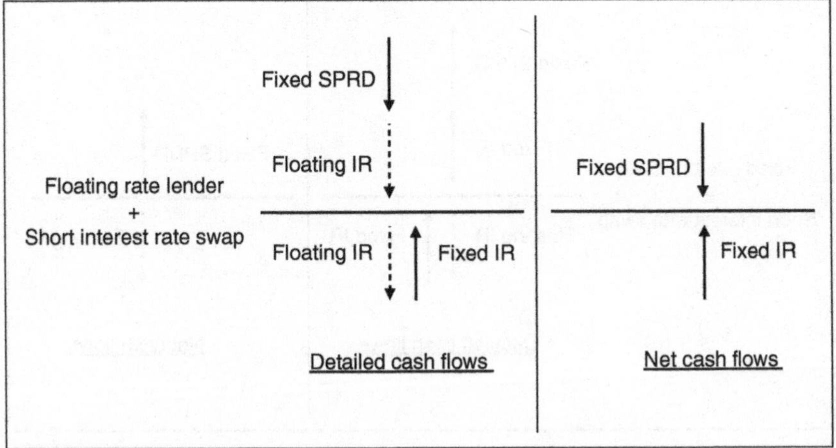

FIGURE 14.5 Transformation of floating rate lending into fixed rate lending

Should the floating IR increase, the lender receives more. Should the floating IR decrease, the lender receives less. To transform this floating rate lending into fixed rate lending, the lender should enter into a short interest rate swap. In other words, the lender should enter into a receive-fixed-pay-floating interest rate swap. The new position, consisting of the original position and the interest rate swap, is depicted in Figure 14.5.

With this strategy, the floating IR reception is offset by the pay-floating leg of the interest rate swap, and the lender is left receiving the fixed leg of the interest rate swap. The net result is that the lender has transformed its position from floating rate lending to fixed rate lending.

14.4.3 Fixed to floating rate borrowing

Consider a borrower with a fixed rate obligation consisting of fixed IR and fixed SPRD. This obligation is depicted in Figure 14.6.

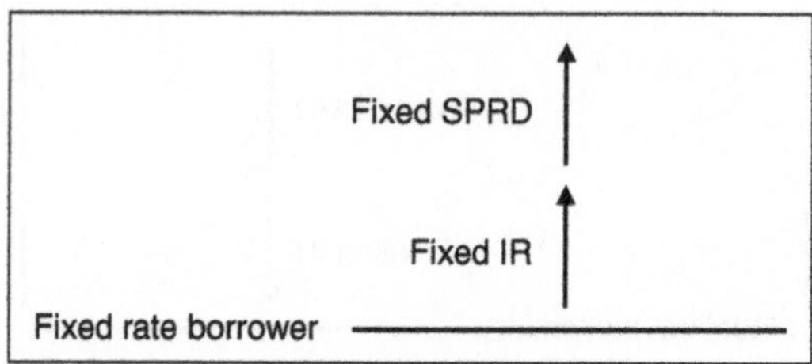

FIGURE 14.6 Fixed rate borrower

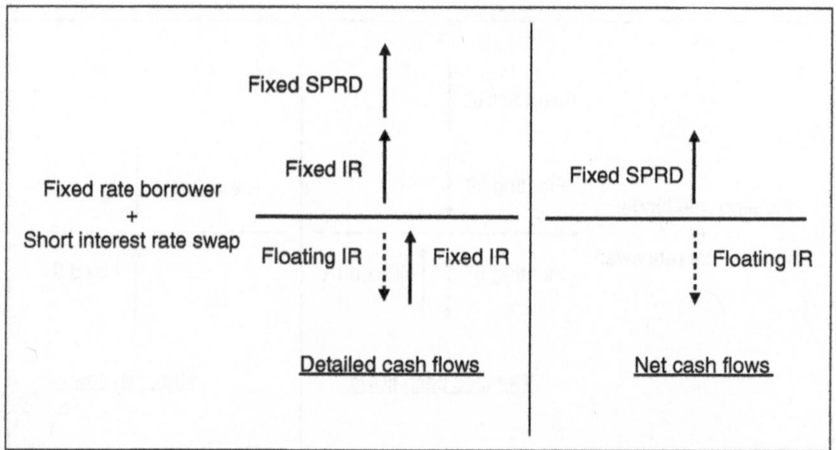

FIGURE 14.7 Transformation of fixed rate borrowing into floating rate borrowing

Should the floating IR decrease, the borrower's fixed IR will be less attractive. Should the floating IR increase, the borrower's fixed IR will be more attractive. To transform this fixed rate borrowing into floating rate borrowing, the borrower should enter into a short interest rate swap, i.e., a receive-fixed-pay-floating interest rate swap. The new position, consisting of the original obligation and the interest rate swap, is depicted in Figure 14.7.

With this strategy, the fixed IR obligation is offset by the receive-fixed leg of the interest rate swap. The borrower is left paying fixed SPRD and floating IR, similar to their obligation in a floating rate obligation. Hence, the net result is that the borrower has transformed its position from fixed rate borrowing into floating rate borrowing.

14.4.4 Fixed to floating rate lending

Consider a lender receiving a fixed rate. This reception is depicted in Figure 14.8.

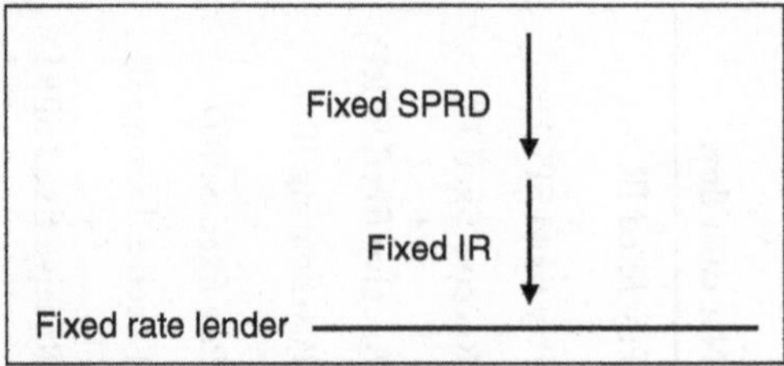

FIGURE 14.8 Fixed rate lender

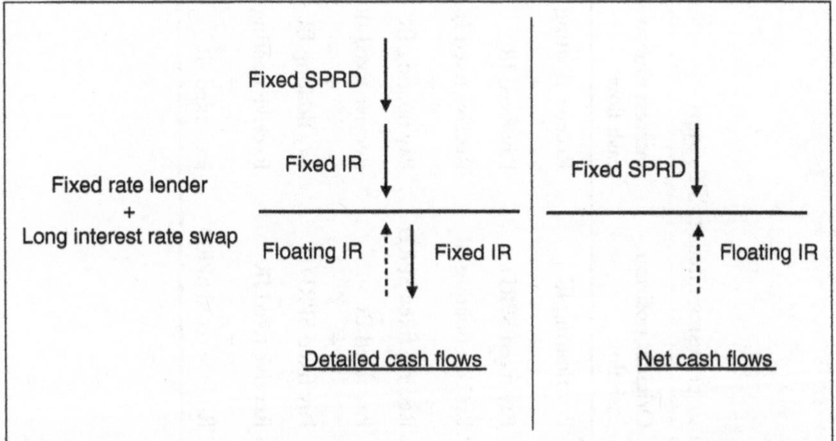

FIGURE 14.9 Transformation of a fixed rate lending into floating rate lending

Should the floating IR increase, the lender's fixed IR is less attractive. Should the floating IR decrease, the lender's fixed IR is more attractive. To transform this fixed rate lending into floating rate lending, the lender should enter into a long interest rate swap, i.e., a receive-floating-pay-fixed interest rate swap. The new position, consisting of the original position and the interest rate swap, is depicted in Figure 14.9.

With this strategy, the fixed IR reception is offset by the pay-fixed leg of the interest rate swap, and the lender is left receiving the floating leg of the interest rate swap. The net result is that the lender has transformed its position from fixed rate lending into floating rate lending.

14.4.5 Comparison of cash flow transformation strategies

Table 14.6 compares the cash flow transformation strategies discussed in this section.

TABLE 14.6 Comparison of cash flow transformation strategies using interest rate swaps

Original position	Transformed position	Interest rate swap recommendation	Original position cash flow	Interest rate swap cash flow	Net cash flow
Floating rate borrower	Fixed rate borrower	Long interest rate swap	Pay floating IR + Pay fixed SPRD	Receive floating IR + Pay fixed IR	Pay fixed IR + Pay fixed SPRD
Floating rate lender	Fixed rate lender	Short interest rate swap	Receive floating IR + Receive fixed SPRD	Receive fixed IR + Pay floating IR	Receive fixed IR + Receive fixed SPRD
Fixed rate borrower	Floating rate borrower	Short interest rate swap	Pay fixed IR + Pay fixed SPRD	Receive fixed IR + Pay floating IR	Pay floating IR + Pay fixed SPRD
Fixed rate lender	Floating rate lender	Long interest rate swap	Receive fixed IR + Receive fixed SPRD	Receive floating IR + Pay fixed IR	Receive floating IR + Receive fixed SPRD

Knowledge check

Q 14.29: What is "IR"?
Q 14.30: What is "SPRD"?
Q 14.31: Is LIBOR a proxy for IR or SPRD?
Q 14.32: What are the IR and SPRD characteristics of a borrower paying floating?
Q 14.33: What are the IR and SPRD characteristics of a lender receiving floating?
Q 14.34: What are the IR and SPRD characteristics of a borrower paying fixed?
Q 14.35: What are the IR and SPRD characteristics of a lender receiving fixed?
Q 14.36: What interest rate swap will transform a borrower paying floating into a borrower paying fixed?
Q 14.37: What interest rate swap will transform a lender receiving floating into a lender receiving fixed?
Q 14.38: What interest rate swap will transform a borrower paying fixed into a borrower paying floating?
Q 14.39: What interest rate swap will transform a lender receiving fixed into a lender receiving floating?

KEY POINTS

- An interest rate swap is an agreement in which two counterparties agree to periodically exchange fixed and floating rates of interest over a number of periods of time. The long position receives floating and pays fixed. The short position receives fixed and pays floating.
- Neither the long nor short position to an interest rate swap pays or receives a premium at initiation. Hence, the counterparties agree to a fixed rate that is perceived as fair to both.
- In the United States the typical convention is semi-annual 30/360 fixed payments and quarterly 3-month USD LIBOR-in-advance Actual/360 floating payments. The notional principal is used to identify the cash flows.
- A multi-step process can be used to calculate interest rate swap cash flows. The process involves calculating the floating leg payments, the fixed leg payments, and the net cash flows received by each position.
- A core purpose of interest rate swaps is to allow borrowers and lenders to transform the nature of their cash flows. Floating-rate borrowers and fixed-rate lenders transform their positions through entering into long interest rate swaps. Fixed-rate borrowers and floating-rate lenders transform their positions through entering into short interest rate swaps.

CHAPTER 15

Credit Default Swaps, Cross-Currency Swaps, and Other Swaps

INTRODUCTION

The previous chapter explored interest rate swaps. This chapter explores several additional types of swaps. We will learn about credit default swaps, which are the exchange of periodic payments of spread in return for a payment contingent on a credit event. We will learn about cross-currency swaps, which are the exchange of interest payments in different currencies. This chapter also briefly introduces equity swaps and commodity swaps.

After you read this chapter, you will be able to

- Describe credit default swaps.
- Understand the concepts of protection buyer, protection seller, and credit default swap spread.
- Explain the key determinants of the credit default swap spread.
- Show how exposures can be transformed using a credit default swap.
- Describe cross-currency swaps.
- Contrast cross-currency swaps to interest rate swaps.
- Show how cash flows can be transformed using a cross-currency swap.
- Describe equity swaps and commodity swaps.

15.1 CREDIT DEFAULT SWAP CHARACTERISTICS

A credit default swap is an agreement between two counterparties to exchange periodic payments of spread in return for a payment contingent on a credit event. The two counterparties are known as the "protection buyer" and the "protection seller." The protection buyer makes periodic payments to the protection seller. In return, the protection seller agrees to make a payment should a reference asset issued by a reference entity experience a credit event.

For example, the reference entity may be a certain corporation, the reference asset may be a bond issued by the corporation, and the credit event may be the corporation's bankruptcy.

While the inclusion of the word "protection" in the counterparties' names suggests that the protection buyer holds a position that it is protecting, in reality regulators typically allow investors to hold "naked" credit default swaps, i.e., they allow investment in a credit default swap even when the investor does not hold a position that requires protection.

The payments made by the protection buyer to the protection seller are known as the credit default swap "spread." While the expression "spread" is used, the payments made by the protection buyer do not include any rate other than the spread. The protection buyer typically makes quarterly spread payments to the protection seller.

The spread is quoted in annualized percentage terms. The spread is agreed-upon at initiation and is fixed during the tenor of the credit default swap. The agreement will specify the tenor and the day count convention through which the quoted annualized spread can be transformed into a quarterly spread. The credit default swap agreement will also specify a notional principal through which to convert the spread into cash flows.

For example, consider the following credit default swap:

- Spread of 1%
- Five-year tenor
- Notional principal of $10 million
- Day count convention is A/360
- Number of days in given quarter is 92

In this example, the accrual factor is 92/360 = 0.2556, and the spread payment in the given quarter is:

$$\begin{aligned} \textit{Quarterly spread payment} &= \textit{credit default spread} \times \textit{accrual factor} \\ &\quad \times \textit{notional principal} \\ &= 1\% \times 0.2556 \times \$10{,}000{,}000 \\ &= \$25{,}556.56 \end{aligned}$$

The payments of spread typically end once there is a credit event. Further, upon the occurrence of a credit event the protection seller makes a large payment to the protection buyer, typically calculated as follows:

- The "recovery rate" associated with the reference asset is identified. The recovery rate is the value of the reference asset following the credit event expressed as a percentage of its face value.

- The percentage loss that the reference asset experiences due to the credit event is calculated as 100% of the reference asset's face value minus the recovery rate, i.e., 100% – *recovery rate.*
- The percentage loss is multiplied by the notional principal to identify the payment that the protection seller makes to the protection buyer.

For example, if the notional principal is $10M and the recovery rate is 65%, then the payment made by the protection seller should a credit event occur is:

$$\begin{aligned} \textit{Protection seller payment upon credit event} &= (100\% - \textit{recovery rate}) \\ &\quad \times \textit{notional principal} \\ &= (100\% - 65\%) \times \$10{,}000{,}000 \\ &= \$3{,}500{,}000 \end{aligned}$$

The above is a broad description of the characteristics of the cash flows associated with a credit default swap. In practice, heavily standardized contracts and protocols add levels of complexity to credit default swap cash flows.[1] For example, a common practice is for the protection buyer to pay a fixed spread of 1% or 5%. Because of this convention, reconciling payments take place up front should the fixed spread differ from the agreed-upon spread. Further, the identification of the recovery rate may be through a "credit event fixing", which is a formalized one-time auction process through which the recovery value of the reference asset is determined.[2] In addition, there are careful definitions of how a credit event is defined and by whom.

There are also other variations of credit default swaps. For example, in a "binary" or "digital" credit default swap the payment upon a credit event is the full notional principal. There are also a number of varieties of basket, multi-name, and index credit default swaps that reference multiple reference assets rather than a single reference asset.

Knowledge check

Q 15.1: What is a "credit default swap"?
Q 15.2: What payments does the protection buyer make?

[1]To learn more about credit default swap conventions, see www2.isda.org/asset-classes/credit-derivatives.
[2]To learn more about credit event fixings, see www.creditfixings.com.

Q 15.3: What payment does the protection seller make?
Q 15.4: Does a protection buyer have to hold a position that they are protecting?
Q 15.5: What is the "credit default swap spread"?
Q 15.6: What is the typical frequency of the spread payments?
Q 15.7: Is the credit default swap spread typically quoted as an annualized or periodic rate?
Q 15.8: When is the credit default swap spread set?
Q 15.9: Does the credit default swap spread remain fixed over its tenor?
Q 15.10: How is the quarterly spread payment calculated?
Q 15.11: What is a "recovery rate"?
Q 15.12: What is the protection seller's payment once a credit event occurs?
Q 15.13: What credit default swap convention requires there to be reconciling payments upfront?
Q 15.14: What is a "binary" credit default swap?
Q 15.15: Do credit default swaps ever reference multiple reference assets?

15.2 KEY DETERMINANTS OF THE CREDIT DEFAULT SWAP SPREAD

The level of the credit default swap spread is a function of two key factors:

- Probability of credit event: The greater the probability of a credit event, the more likely the protection seller will have to make a payment; hence, the higher the spread the protection seller will demand.
- Recovery rate: The smaller the recovery rate, the larger the payment that the protection seller will have to make should a credit event occur; hence, the higher the spread the protection seller will demand.

The credit default swap spread is agreed-upon at initiation based on the counterparties' views of the probability of the credit event's occurring and the recovery rate. The credit default swap spread is then fixed during the swap's tenor. Hence, once initiated, the protection buyer and protection seller are value sensitive to changes in both the probability of the credit event's occurring and the recovery rate, as presented in Table 15.1.

Due to these sensitivities a credit default swap can be used to gain exposure to changes in probability in credit events' occurring and recovery rates.

TABLE 15.1 Credit default swap sensitivity

Position	Value sensitivity to changes in the probability of a credit event	Sensitivity to changes in the recovery rate
Protection buyer	Positively sensitive	Negatively sensitive
Protection seller	Negatively sensitive	Positively sensitive

These exposures parallel the exposures associated with bond positions, as follows:

- A protection seller's exposures are similar to the exposures faced by an investor in a bond issued by the given reference entity, i.e., a long bond position. After all both benefit when the probability of a credit event decreases and the recovery rate is higher.
- A protection buyer's exposures are similar to the exposures faced by a short bond position in a bond issued by the given reference entity. After all, both benefit when the probability of a credit event increases and the recovery rate is lower.

A credit default swap can also be used to transform an investor's existing exposures, as follows:

- An investor holding a long bond position is negatively exposed to increases in the probability of a credit event and decreases in the recovery rate. To offset these exposures, a long bond position can enter into a credit default swap as a protection buyer. Since a protection buyer benefits when the probability of a credit event increases and recovery rate decreases, the investor's portfolio will be broadly neutral to changes in these factors.
- An investor holding a short bond position is negatively exposed to decreases in the probability of a credit event and increases in the recovery rate. To offset these exposures, a short bond position can enter into a credit default swap as a protection seller. Since the protection seller benefits when the probability of a credit event decreases and when recovery rate increases, the investor's portfolio will be broadly neutral to changes in these factors.

These strategies are summarized in Table 15.2.

TABLE 15.2 Exposure transformation strategies using credit default swaps

Exposures and recommendations	Long bond	Short bond
Exposure to probability of credit event	Negatively sensitive	Positively sensitive
Exposure to recovery rate	Positively sensitive	Negatively sensitive
Recommended credit default swap	Protection buyer	Protection seller
Credit default swap position's exposure to probability of credit event	Positively sensitive	Negatively sensitive
Credit default swap position's exposure to recovery rate	Negatively sensitive	Positively sensitive
Net portfolio exposure to probability of credit event	Neutral	Neutral
Net portfolio exposure to recovery rate	Neutral	Neutral

Knowledge check

Q 15.16: What is the relationship between the credit default swap spread and the probability of a credit event?

Q 15.17: What is the relationship between the credit default swap spread and the recovery rate?

Q 15.18: What is a protection buyer's value sensitivity to changes in the probability of a credit event?

Q 15.19: What is a protection seller's value sensitivity to changes in the probability of a credit event?

Q 15.20: What is a protection buyer's value sensitivity to changes in the recovery rate?

Q 15.21: What is a protection seller's value sensitivity to changes in the recovery rate?

Q 15.22: To what bond position is a protection seller's exposures parallel?

Q 15.23: To what bond position is a protection buyer's exposures parallel?

Q 15.24: What credit default swap position can be used to offset a long bond position?

Q 15.25: What credit default swap position can be used to offset a short bond position?

15.3 CROSS-CURRENCY SWAP CHARACTERISTICS

A cross-currency swap is an agreement similar to an interest rate swap with one key difference: Unlike an interest rate swap in which the notional principal is in the same currency for both legs, in a cross-currency swap the notional principal for each of the swap legs is in a different currency. For example, one leg of a cross-currency may specify the notional principal in U.S. dollars, while the notional principal for the other leg is in euros.

Three types of cross-currency swaps are as follows:

- Fixed rate in one currency for floating rate in the other currency
- Floating rate in one currency for floating rate in the other currency
- Fixed rate in one currency for fixed rate in the other currency

Unlike interest rate swaps where notional principal is not exchanged at initiation or expiration, in a cross-currency swap notional principal *is* exchanged both at initiation and expiration. At initiation, the notional principals associated with the legs of a cross-currency swap are typically set equal to each other based on the exchange rate at initiation. At expiration, the notional principals can deviate significantly from each other in value.

Knowledge check

Q 15.26: What is a cross-currency swap?
Q 15.27: What are three types of cross-currency swaps?
Q 15.28: When is notional principal exchanged in a cross-currency swap?
Q 15.29: What is the relationship between the notional principals of the two cross-currency swap legs at initiation?

15.4 TRANSFORMING CASH FLOWS USING A CROSS-CURRENCY SWAP

Let's explore the following example to illustrate how cross-currency swaps can be used to transform cash flows: A European governmental agency transacts exclusively in EUR (i.e., euros). The agency wishes to borrow €1 billion (i.e., one billion EUR) to fund its operations, and since it is a governmental agency, it is able to borrow at the risk-free interest rate. The agency has identified British lenders and, to accommodate them, the agency has chosen to borrow in GBP (i.e., British pounds) instead of EUR.

The EUR/GBP exchange rate is 0.7. In other words, one EUR is worth 0.7 GBP. Hence the agency wishes to borrow £700 million (i.e., seven hundred million GBP), the equivalent of €1 billion at initiation. The coupon rate is 2% with semi-annual payments and two years until maturity.

The cash flows that the agency faces in this example due to this £700M bond are illustrated in Figure 15.1. The agency, as a borrower, initially receives £700M. The borrower then has the following obligations: Coupon payments equal to 2%/2 × £700M = £7M every half year, and a final repayment of £700M at maturity.

The governmental agency transacts exclusively in EUR, yet has chosen to borrow GBP. This leads to three challenges:

- The agency will receive £700M at initiation, yet requires EUR to fund its operations and not GBP. Hence, the agency must convert the £700M to GBP.
- The agency has £7M interest payments semi-annually. This requires the agency to semi-annually convert EUR into GBP in order to have the necessary cash to make these GBP payments. If GBP increases in value relative to EUR, the agency will face higher interest costs.
- The agency must make a £700M principal payment at maturity. This requires the agency to convert EUR into GBP in order to have the necessary cash to make this GBP payment. If GBP increases in value relative to EUR, the agency will face higher costs in EUR.

A cross-currency swap can help the agency with these challenges. Continuing the example, the agency negotiates a cross-currency swap. One leg's notional principal is £700M, and, since the EUR/GBP exchange rate is 0.70, the other leg's notional principal is €1B. Both legs have fixed rates, quoted on an annualized basis and paid semi-annually. The fixed rate associated with the GBP leg is 2%, while the fixed rate associated with the EUR leg is 3%. The agency enters into the receive-GBP-pay-EUR cross-currency swap position. The detailed cash flows are illustrated in Figure 15.2, and the net cash flows are illustrated in Figure 15.3.

As illustrated in Figure 15.3, the net cash flows are an initial reception of €1B, semi-annual payments of €15M, and a final payment of €1B. In other

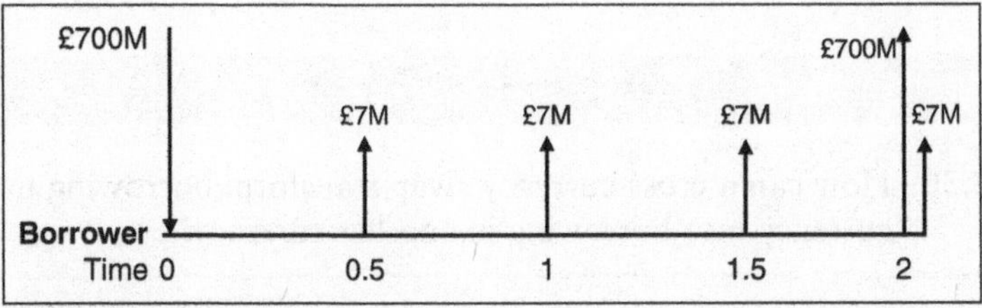

FIGURE 15.1 GBP borrower

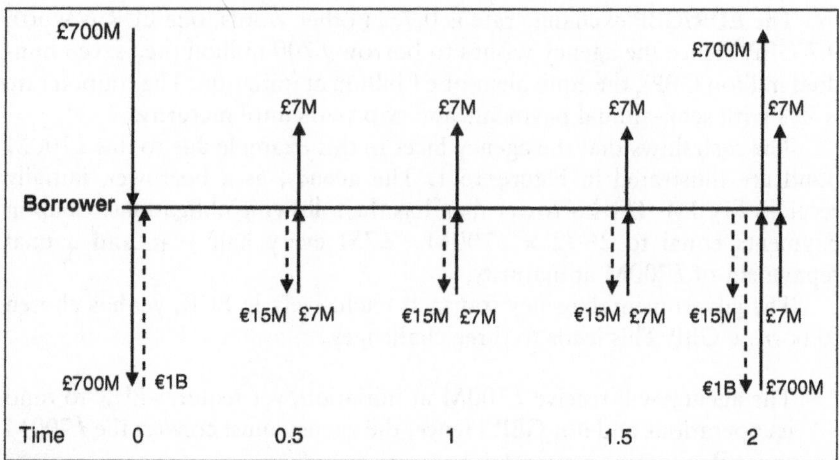

FIGURE 15.2 Transformation of GBP borrowing into EUR borrowing: detailed cash flows

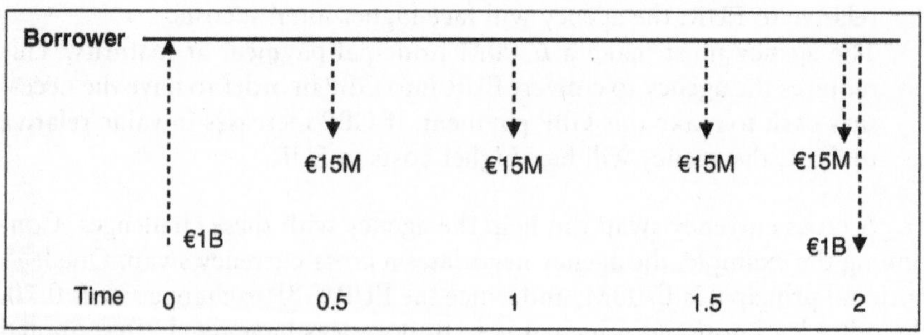

FIGURE 15.3 Transformation of GBP borrowing into EUR borrowing: net cash flows

words, the cross-currency swap has effectively converted GBP borrowing into EUR borrowing. This solves the agency's challenges: The agency now receives EUR at initiation, which it requires to fund its operations. Further, the agency makes EUR interest and principal payments and, therefore, does not face GBP/EUR currency risk.

Knowledge check

Q 15.30: How can a cross-currency swap transform borrowing in one currency into borrowing in another currency?

15.5 OTHER SWAP VARIETIES

This and the previous chapter have explored interest rate swaps, credit default swaps, and cross-currency swaps. There are other types of swaps as well. Two examples are equity swaps and commodity swaps.

An equity swap is an agreement in which two counterparties agree to swap equity returns for an interest rate. Hence, one of the counterparties receives equity returns and pays an interest rate while the other counterparty receives the interest rate and pays equity returns. The equity returns may be those of a well-known index, such as the S&P 500, or may be the returns on a single stock or a customized basket of stocks. The interest rate can be floating or fixed. In some equity swaps, known as "equity-for-equity" swaps, each of the counterparties receives one equity return and pays another equity return.

A commodity swap is an agreement in which two counterparties agree to swap commodity returns for an interest rate. Hence one of the counterparties receives commodity returns and pays an interest rate, while the other counterparty receives the interest rate and pays commodity returns. A variation of a commodity swap is an agreement where one of the counterparties receives the return on a refined commodity and pays the return on an unrefined version of the same commodity plus a spread, while the other counterparty receives the return on the unrefined commodity plus a spread and pays the return on the refined commodity. For example, when the two legs are crude oil versus refined oil, such a swap is known as a "crack spread swap"; and when the two legs are natural gas versus electricity, such a swap is known as a "spark spread swap."

Knowledge check

Q 15.31: What is an equity swap?
Q 15.32: What is an equity-for-equity swap?
Q 15.33: What is a commodity swap?
Q 15.34: What is a crack spread swap?
Q 15.35: What is a spark spread swap?

KEY POINTS

- A credit default swap is an agreement between two counterparties to exchange periodic payments of spread in return for a payment contingent on a credit event. The protection buyer makes periodic payments of spread to the protection seller. In return, the protection seller agrees to make a large lump-sum payment should a reference asset experience a credit event.

- Key determinants of the credit default swap spread are the probability of the credit event and the recovery rate. The credit default swap spread is fixed during the swap tenor, and the protection buyer and protection seller are sensitive to changes in the probability of the credit event and the recovery rate. Due to these sensitivities a credit default swap can be used to gain exposures to changes in probability in credit events and recovery rates.
- A cross-currency swap is similar to an interest rate swap; however, the notional principal for each of the swap legs is in a different currency. Each of the two legs may be either fixed or floating. Notional principal is exchanged both at initiation and expiration.
- A cross-currency swap can be used to transform borrowing in one currency into borrowing in another currency.
- An equity swap is an agreement in which two counterparties agree to swap equity returns for an interest rate. A commodity swap is an agreement in which two counterparties agree to swap the returns associated with a given commodity for an interest rate.

APPENDIX

Solutions to Knowledge Check Questions

A.1 CHAPTER 1: FORWARDS AND FUTURES

A 1.1: An agreement between two counterparties that obligates them to transact in the future
A 1.2: To purchase an asset from the short position at a future point in time
A 1.3: To sell an asset to the long position at a future point in time
A 1.4: The future point in time at which the transaction occurs in a forward
A 1.5: The price at which the underlying asset is purchased in a forward
A 1.6: The cash flow that occurs at expiration
A 1.7: $S_T - F$
A 1.8: When the price of the asset received is greater than the forward price paid
A 1.9: When the price of the asset received is less than the forward price paid
A 1.10: When the price of the asset received is equal to the forward price paid
A 1.11: Profit and loss: the difference between the cash flows at initiation and expiration
A 1.12: $S_T - F$
A 1.13: When the price of the asset received is greater than the forward price paid
A 1.14: When the price of the asset received is less than the forward price paid
A 1.15: When the price of the asset received is equal to the forward price paid
A 1.16: $F - S_T$
A 1.17: When the forward price received is greater than the price of the asset delivered
A 1.18: When the forward price received is less than the price of the asset delivered

A 1.19: When the forward price received is equal to the price of the asset delivered
A 1.20: $F - S_T$
A 1.21: When the forward price received is greater than the price of the asset delivered
A 1.22: When the forward price received is less than the price of the asset delivered
A 1.23: When the forward price received is equal to the price of the asset delivered
A 1.24: The underlying asset price at expiration
A 1.25: P&L
A 1.26: See Figure 1.8
A 1.27: Underlying asset price is greater than the forward price
A 1.28: Underlying asset price is less than the forward price
A 1.29: See Figure 1.10
A 1.30: Underlying asset price is less than the forward price
A 1.31: Underlying asset price is greater than the forward price
A 1.32: An agreement where the profit that one of the counterparties receives is exactly equal to the loss that the other counterparty suffers
A 1.33: The net of the P&L across the two counterparties is always zero
A 1.34: The risk of suffering a loss because a counterparty does not fulfill its obligations
A 1.35: Careful screening of counterparties, use of legal contracts, netting agreements, margin requirements, periodic cash resettlement, and the use of CCPs
A 1.36: A central counterparty clearinghouse: an organization that can become the counterparty to each of the original counterparties to a derivatives transaction
A 1.37: They maintain high credit ratings
A 1.38: A standardized forward contract that trades on an exchange
A 1.39: They are both agreements between two counterparties that obligate them to transact in the future.
A 1.40: Futures contracts trade on exchanges and are heavily standardized and regulated.
A 1.41: Trading that takes place through networks of dealers that are employed by financial institutions
A 1.42: The price at which the asset is purchased in a futures contract
A 1.43: No
A 1.44: Single stock futures
A 1.45: The Commodities Futures Trading Commission (CFTC)

A.2 CHAPTER 2: CALL OPTIONS

A 2.1: An agreement between two counterparties in which one of the counterparties has the right to purchase an underlying asset from the other counterparty in the future
A 2.2: Purchase an underlying asset in the future
A 2.3: To sell the underlying asset to the long call should the long call choose to exercise its right to purchase
A 2.4: "Take advantage of"
A 2.5: The price at which the long position has the right to purchase the underlying asset
A 2.6: Another name for the strike price
A 2.7: The fee that the long call pays the short call to obtain its right to purchase
A 2.8: Another name for the call premium
A 2.9: Long call
A 2.10: Short call
A 2.11: Short call
A 2.12: At initiation
A 2.13: An option that provides the right to exercise at expiration or earlier
A 2.14: An option that provides the right to exercise at expiration
A 2.15: Both
A 2.16: When the underlying asset price is greater than the strike price
A 2.17: When the underlying asset price is less than or equal to the strike price
A 2.18: $S_T - K$
A 2.19: Zero
A 2.20: The difference between the underlying asset price and the strike price
A 2.21: When the underlying asset price is greater than the strike price
A 2.22: $\max(S_T - K, 0)$
A 2.23: P&L takes into account the premium that is paid by the long call at initiation
A 2.24: $S_T - K - c_0$
A 2.25: $-c_0$
A 2.26: $\max(S_T - K, 0) - c_0$
A 2.27: $K - S_T$
A 2.28: Zero
A 2.29: $\min(K - S_T, 0)$
A 2.30: P&L takes into account the premium that the short position receives at initiation

A 2.31: $K - S_T + c_0$
A 2.32: c_0
A 2.33: $\min(K - S_T, 0) + c_0$
A 2.34: See Figure 2.3
A 2.35: $S_T > K + c_0$
A 2.36: $S_T < K + c_0$
A 2.37: $S_T = K + c_0$
A 2.38: See Figure 2.5
A 2.39: $S_T < K + c_0$
A 2.40: $S_T > K + c_0$
A 2.41: $S_T = K + c_0$
A 2.42: Any profit that one of the counterparties receives is exactly equal to the loss that the other counterparty suffers
A 2.43: Whether a long option position will earn a positive payoff if it chooses to exercise
A 2.44: In-the-money. An option where the long position will earn a positive payoff through exercising the option
A 2.45: At-the-money. An option where the long position will earn a payoff of zero through exercising the option
A 2.46: Out-of-the-money. An option where the long position does not exercise as the long position would earn a negative payoff through exercising the option
A 2.47: $S_T > K$
A 2.48: $S_T = K$
A 2.49: $S_T < K$
A 2.50: Neither counterparty gets to choose whether to exercise
A 2.51: Destruction of optionality value and earlier payment of strike price
A 2.52: The value of having the right to decide whether to exercise or not
A 2.53: The investor receives any benefit that flows from the underlying asset
A 2.54: When the underlying asset pays no income before expiration
A 2.55: A strategy of selling call options where the underlying assets pay dividends to naïve investors that fail to take advantage of their ability to exercise early when they should
A 2.56: See Table 2.7
A 2.57: See Table 2.7

A.3 CHAPTER 3: PUT OPTIONS

A 3.1: An agreement between two counterparties in which one of the counterparties has the right to sell an underlying asset to the other counterparty in the future

A 3.2: A call option provides the right to purchase while a put option provides the right to sell
A 3.3: Sell an underlying asset in the future
A 3.4: Purchase an underlying asset in the future should the long put choose to exercise its right to sell
A 3.5: The fee that the long put pays the short put to obtain its right to sell
A 3.6: Another name for the put premium
A 3.7: Long put
A 3.8: Short put
A 3.9: Short put
A 3.10: At initiation
A 3.11: When the strike price received by the long put is greater than the price of the underlying asset it delivers
A 3.12: When the strike price is less than or equal to the underlying asset price
A 3.13: $K - S_T$
A 3.14: Zero
A 3.15: The difference between the strike price and the underlying asset price
A 3.16: When the underlying asset price is less than the strike price
A 3.17: $\max(K - S_T, 0)$
A 3.18: The long put's P&L takes into account the premium that it pays at initiation
A 3.19: $K - S_T - p_0$
A 3.20: $-p_0$
A 3.21: $\max(K - S_T, 0) - p_0$
A 3.22: $S_T - K$
A 3.23: Zero
A 3.24: $\min(S_T - K, 0)$
A 3.25: The short put's P&L takes into account the premium that the short put receives at initiation
A 3.26: $S_T - K + p_0$
A 3.27: p_0
A 3.28: $\min(S_T - K, 0) + p_0$
A 3.29: See Figure 3.3
A 3.30: $S_T < K - p_0$
A 3.31: $S_T > K - p_0$
A 3.32: $S_T = K - p_0$
A 3.33: See Figure 3.5
A 3.34: $S_T > K - p_0$
A 3.35: $S_T < K - p_0$
A 3.36: $S_T = K - p_0$
A 3.37: Any profit that one of the counterparties receives is exactly equal to the loss that the other counterparty suffers

A 3.38: $S_T < K$
A 3.39: $S_T = K$
A 3.40: $S_T > K$
A 3.41: Destruction of optionality value and delivery of a more expensive asset
A 3.42: Earlier reception of the strike price
A 3.43: American-style put options have higher premiums than otherwise identical European-style put options
A 3.44: See Table 3.7
A 3.45: See Table 3.7

A.4 CHAPTER 4: USEFUL QUANTITATIVE CONCEPTS

A 4.1: The frequency with which a stated interest rate is assumed to be invested during a given year
A 4.2: Infinitely
A 4.3: An interest rate that is compounded an infinite number of times per year
A 4.4: $PV = \frac{FV}{\left(100\%+\frac{r}{m}\right)^{m \cdot t}}$
A 4.5: $FV = PV \cdot \left(100\% + \frac{r}{m}\right)^{m \cdot t}$
A 4.6: EXP( )
A 4.7: e^{A+B}
A 4.8: 1
A 4.9: e^{-A}
A 4.10: $PV = FV \cdot e^{-r \cdot t}$
A 4.11: $FV = PV \cdot e^{r \cdot t}$
A 4.12: The natural logarithm function
A 4.13: LN( )
A 4.14: $r = \frac{ln\left(\frac{FV}{PV}\right)}{t}$
A 4.15: The degree to which the returns associated with an asset are dispersed over time
A 4.16: Volatility
A 4.17: Step 1: Calculate the average return. Step 2: Calculate each return's deviation from the average return. Step 3: Calculate the square of each deviation. Step 4: Calculate the average of the squared deviations (variance). Step 5: Calculate the square root of the variance
A 4.18: Standard deviation that is calculated using an entire population of observations
A 4.19: Standard deviation that is calculated using a sample from a larger population

A 4.20: Sample standard deviation calculates the average squared deviations through dividing by the number of observations minus one. Population standard deviation divides by the number of observations

A 4.21: The average of the squared deviations

A 4.22: $\sigma = \sqrt{\frac{\sum_{i=1}^{n}(r_i - \bar{r})^2}{n-1}}$

A 4.23: STDEV.S( )

A 4.24: Investments with higher standard deviation are riskier

A 4.25: Returns are normally distributed

A 4.26: 50%

A 4.27: 50%

A 4.28: 68.27%

A 4.29: 95.45%

A 4.30: 99.73%

A 4.31: The standard deviation of annual returns

A 4.32: $\sigma_{annualized} = \sigma_x \times \sqrt{y}$

A 4.33: NORM.S.DIST( )

A 4.34: Returns are normally distributed, the average return is zero, and the standard deviation of returns is 100%

A 4.35: N (given return)

A 4.36: 1 – N (given return)

A 4.37: They are equivalent

A 4.38: $z\text{-}score = \frac{\text{Given return} - \text{average return}}{\text{standard deviation of return}}$

A 4.39: Input the z-score into the standard normal cumulative distribution function

A.5 CHAPTER 5: INTRODUCTION TO PRICING AND VALUATION

A 5.1: The price at which counterparties transact

A 5.2: The value of holding a given position

A 5.3: Forward price

A 5.4: Forward value

A 5.5: Initiation

A 5.6: A forward price is chosen that is agreeable, or "fair," to both counterparties

A 5.7: No

A 5.8: Zero

A 5.9: Yes

A 5.10: When changes in the determinants of its value result in positive value

A 5.11: When changes in the determinants of its value result in negative value
A 5.12: They are the negative of each other
A 5.13: Strike price or exercise price
A 5.14: Option value
A 5.15: Initiation
A 5.16: No
A 5.17: No
A 5.18: They should be equal to each other at initiation
A 5.19: Long position
A 5.20: Short position
A 5.21: They are the negative of each other
A 5.22: See Table 5.1
A 5.23: $f_t = S_t - F \cdot e^{-r_t \cdot (T-t)}$
A 5.24: $-f_t$
A 5.25: $F = S_0 \cdot e^{r_0 \cdot (T-t_0)}$
A 5.26: $c_t = S_t \cdot \mathrm{N}(d_1) - K \cdot e^{-r_t \cdot (T-t)} \cdot \mathrm{N}(d_2)$
A 5.27: $-c_t$
A 5.28: $p_t = K \cdot e^{-r_t \cdot (T-t)} \cdot \mathrm{N}(-d_2) - S_t \cdot \mathrm{N}(-d_1)$
A 5.29: $-p_t$
A 5.30: $d_1 = \dfrac{ln\left(\frac{S_t}{K}\right)+\left(r_t+\frac{\sigma_t^2}{2}\right)\cdot(T-t)}{\sigma_t \cdot \sqrt{T-t}}$
A 5.31: $d_2 = d_1 - \sigma_t \cdot \sqrt{T-t}$
A 5.32: Identify the inputs, calculate d_1 and d_2, calculate $\mathrm{N}(d_1)$ and $\mathrm{N}(d_2)$, and calculate c_t
A 5.33: Identify the inputs, calculate d_1 and d_2, calculate $\mathrm{N}(d_1)$ and $\mathrm{N}(d_2)$, and calculate $-c_t$
A 5.34: Identify the inputs, calculate d_1 and d_2, calculate $\mathrm{N}(-d_1)$ and $\mathrm{N}(-d_2)$, and calculate p_t
A 5.35: Identify the inputs, calculate d_1 and d_2, calculate $\mathrm{N}(-d_1)$ and $\mathrm{N}(-d_2)$, and calculate $-p_t$
A 5.36: The option is European-style; the underlying asset pays no income; there are no "frictions" such as transaction costs or taxes; the risk-free interest rate is known and constant; the underlying asset volatility is known and constant; and returns are normally distributed
A 5.37: Many options are American-style. Many options are written on underlying assets that pay income. There are frequently significant frictions. The risk-free rate and volatility are unlikely to be constant. Returns may not be normally distributed
A 5.38: Yes

A 5.39: The underlying asset volatility identified through reverse-engineering the Black-Scholes model
A 5.40: Using sophisticated numerical analysis techniques
A 5.41: A graph of the implied volatility across time to expiration
A 5.42: It is a useful tool through which to learn about the market's expectation of underlying asset volatility in the future
A 5.43: The market expects volatility to increase
A 5.44: The market expects volatility to decrease
A 5.45: A smile-shaped graph of implied volatility across strike prices
A 5.46: A skew-shaped graph of implied volatility across strike prices
A 5.47: A three-dimensional graph of implied volatility across both time to expiration and strike price
A 5.48: We should output the same implied volatility regardless of the strike price when reverse-engineering the Black-Scholes model. Volatility smiles and skews show that the implied volatility, in fact, varies as a function of the strike price. This effect may occur because the Black-Scholes model is imperfect or because the premium is incorrectly valued by the market.

A.6 CHAPTER 6: UNDERSTANDING PRICING AND VALUATION

A 6.1: Option value is the present value of the probability of the option ending up ITM multiplied by the expected payoff at expiration should the option end up ITM
A 6.2: Forward value is the present value of the expected payoff at expiration
A 6.3: An investment that provides a future cash flow that investors are completely certain they will receive
A 6.4: An investment that provides a future cash flow where investors are uncertain about the amount they will receive
A 6.5: An investor that demands a rate of return greater than the risk-free rate when investing in a risky investment
A 6.6: An investor that demands the risk-free rate even when investing in a risky investment
A 6.7: The risk-free rate
A 6.8: The risk-free rate
A 6.9: A rate of return greater than the risk-free rate
A 6.10: The risk-free rate
A 6.11: To compensate for taking risk

A 6.12: Because a risk-neutral investor does not demand compensation for accepting risk
A 6.13: Risk-averse
A 6.14: Synthetically replicating a position using a continuously rebalanced portfolio consisting of the underlying asset and a bond
A 6.15: Because any deviation will be exploited until it no longer exists
A 6.16: Since valuation is the same regardless of risk characteristics, we can value positions from the perspective of a risk-neutral world and form expectations and discount using the risk-free rate
A 6.17: No
A 6.18: Valuation from the perspective of a risk-neutral world that forms expectations and discounts using the risk-free rate
A 6.19: $\text{prob}(S_T > K) = \text{N}(d_2)$
A 6.20: $\text{prob}(S_T < K) = \text{N}(-d_2)$
A 6.21: $\text{E}[S_T] = S_t \cdot e^{r_t \cdot (T-t)}$
A 6.22: $E[S_T | S_T > K] = S_t \cdot e^{r_t \cdot (T-t)} \cdot \frac{\text{N}(d_1)}{\text{N}(d_2)}$
A 6.23: $E[S_T | S_T < K] = S_t \cdot e^{r_t \cdot (T-t)} \cdot \frac{\text{N}(-d_1)}{\text{N}(-d_2)}$
A 6.24:
$$\begin{aligned} c_t &= \text{PV}(\textit{probability of call ending up ITM} \\ &\quad \times \textit{expected long call payoff when ITM}) \\ &= \text{PV}(\text{prob}(S_T > K) \cdot \text{E}[S_T - K | S_T > K]) \\ &= \text{PV}(\text{prob}(S_T > K) \cdot (\text{E}[S_T | S_T > K] - K)) \\ &= \text{PV}\left(\text{N}(d_2) \cdot \left(S_T \cdot e^{r_t \cdot (T-t)} \cdot \frac{\text{N}(d_1)}{\text{N}(d_2)} - K\right)\right) \\ &= e^{-r_t \cdot (T-t)} \cdot \text{N}(d_2) \cdot \left(S_T \cdot e^{r_t \cdot (T-t)} \cdot \frac{\text{N}(d_1)}{\text{N}(d_2)} - K\right) \\ &= e^{-r_t \cdot (T-t)} \cdot \text{N}(d_2) \cdot S_t \cdot e^{r_t \cdot (T-t)} \cdot \frac{\text{N}(d_1)}{\text{N}(d_2)} - K \cdot e^{-r_t \cdot (T-t)} \cdot \text{N}(d_2) \\ &= S_t \cdot \text{N}(d_1) - K \cdot e^{-r_t \cdot (T-t)} \cdot \text{N}(d_2) \end{aligned}$$
A 6.25: $e^{-r_t \cdot (T-t)}$ is present value, $\text{N}(d_2)$ is probability of the call ending up ITM, and $S_t \cdot e^{r_t \cdot (T-t)} \cdot \frac{\text{N}(d_1)}{\text{N}(d_2)} - K$ is the expected long call payoff when ITM
A 6.26:
$$\begin{aligned} p_t &= \text{PV}(\textit{probability of put ending up ITM} \\ &\quad \times \textit{expected long put payoff when ITM}) \\ &= \text{PV}(\text{prob}(S_T < K) \cdot \text{E}[K - S_T | S_T < K]) \\ &= \text{PV}(\text{prob}(S_T < K) \cdot (K - \text{E}[S_T | S_T < K])) \\ &= \text{PV}\left(\text{N}(-d_2) \cdot \left(K - S_t \cdot e^{r_t \cdot (T-t)} \cdot \frac{\text{N}(-d_1)}{\text{N}(-d_2)}\right)\right) \\ &= e^{-r_t \cdot (T-t)} \cdot \text{N}(-d_2) \cdot \left(K - S_t \cdot e^{r_t \cdot (T-t)} \cdot \frac{\text{N}(-d_1)}{\text{N}(-d_2)}\right) \\ &= K \cdot e^{-r_t \cdot (T-t)} \cdot \text{N}(-d_2) - e^{-r_t \cdot (T-t)} \cdot \text{N}(-d_2) \cdot S_T \cdot e^{r_t \cdot (T-t)} \cdot \frac{\text{N}(-d_1)}{\text{N}(-d_2)} \\ &= K \cdot e^{-r_t \cdot (T-t)} \cdot \text{N}(-d_2) - S_t \cdot \text{N}(-d_1) \end{aligned}$$

A 6.27: $e^{-r_t \cdot (T-t)}$ is present value, $N(-d_2)$ is probability of the put ending up ITM, and $K - S_t \cdot e^{r_t \cdot (T-t)} \cdot \frac{N(-d_1)}{N(-d_2)}$ is the expected long put payoff when ITM

A 6.28:
$$\begin{aligned} f_t &= PV(\textit{expected long forward payoff}) \\ &= PV(E[S_T - F]) \\ &= PV(E[S_T] - F) \\ &= PV(S_t \cdot e^{r_t \cdot (T-t)} - F) \\ &= e^{-r_t \cdot (T-t)} \cdot (S_t \cdot e^{r_t \cdot (T-t)} - F) \\ &= S_t \cdot e^{r_t \cdot (T-t)} \cdot e^{-r_t \cdot (T-t)} - F \cdot e^{-r_t \cdot (T-t)} \\ &= S_t - F \cdot e^{-r_t \cdot (T-t)} \end{aligned}$$

A 6.29: $e^{-r_t \cdot (T-t)}$ is present value and $S_t \cdot e^{r_t \cdot (T-t)} - F$ is the expected long forward payoff

A 6.30: Since $f_0 = S_0 - F \cdot e^{-r_0 \cdot (T-t_0)} = 0$, it follows $F = \frac{S_0}{e^{-r_0 \cdot (T-t_0)}} = S_0 \cdot e^{r_0 \cdot (T-t_0)}$

A.7 CHAPTER 7: THE BINOMIAL OPTION PRICING MODEL

A 7.1: As a number of discrete points in time

A 7.2: The underlying asset price will either increase or decrease by specified factors between today and expiration

A 7.3: Factors by which the underlying asset price will increase or decrease, respectively

A 7.4: $D = 1/U$

A 7.5: The long call pays the short call a premium at initiation and receives either $\max(S_U - K, 0)$ or $\max(S_D - K, 0)$ at expiration. Must be European-style

A 7.6: Since the one-period binomial option pricing model only models initiation and expiration, there is no opportunity for early exercise

A 7.7: Step 1: Structure a portfolio consisting of a portion of the underlying asset and a short call so that it has the same payoff whether the underlying asset price increases or decreases. Step 2: Discount the portfolio's payoff to the present using the risk-free rate. Step 3: Solve for the option value

A 7.8: Because through doing so it will be possible to structure the portfolio so that it has the same payoff whether the underlying asset price increases or decreases

A 7.9: Because if a portfolio has identical payoffs in both scenarios it is a risk-free investment as its future payoff is known with certainty. This allows us to discount it to the present using the risk-free interest rate and solve for the option value

A 7.10: $c = \begin{pmatrix} max(S_0 \cdot U - K, 0) \cdot \omega \\ +max(S_0 \cdot D - K, 0) \cdot (1 - \omega) \end{pmatrix} \cdot e^{-r \cdot T/n}$ where $\omega = \frac{e^{r \cdot T/n} - D}{U - D}$

A 7.11: $U = e^{\sigma \cdot \sqrt{T/n}}$

A 7.12: $p = \begin{pmatrix} max(K - S_0 \cdot U, 0) \cdot \omega \\ +max(K - S_0 \cdot D, 0) \cdot (1 - \omega) \end{pmatrix} \cdot e^{-r \cdot T/n}$ where $\omega = \frac{e^{r \cdot T/n} - D}{U - D}$

A 7.13: American-style

A 7.14: Initiation, the midpoint between initiation and expiration, and expiration

A 7.15: Step 1: Build the two-period binomial "tree". Step 2: Identify the potential payoffs at expiration. Step 3: Calculate the midpoint node values. Step 4: Calculate option value at initiation

A 7.16: In each of the periods the underlying asset either increases by U or decreases by D

A 7.17: We use the one-period model to identify the value at each of the midpoint nodes, as from the perspective of each of the midpoint nodes there are two potential payoffs in the subsequent period

A 7.18: We use the one-period model to identify the value of the node at initiation, as from the perspective of the initial node there are two potential payoffs in the subsequent period

A 7.19: The value identified for each of the midpoint nodes takes into account the potential for early exercise

A 7.20: If the early payoff is greater than the value of holding the option, then the early payoff is recorded as the node value. If early payoff is less than the value of holding the option, then the value of holding the option is recorded as the node value

A 7.21: T/n years

A 7.22: The value identified using the Black-Scholes model

A.8 CHAPTER 8: INTRODUCTION TO THE GREEKS

A 8.1: Various measures of forward and option sensitivity to changes in the underlying asset price and volatility, the risk-free interest rate, and the time to expiration

A 8.2: As most of their names are Greek letters

A 8.3: The estimated dollar change in position value per one dollar increase in the underlying asset price

A 8.4: The estimated change in position Delta per one dollar increase in the underlying asset price

A 8.5: The estimated dollar change in position value per one percent increase in the underlying asset volatility

A 8.6: The estimated dollar change in position value per one percent increase in the risk-free interest rate
A 8.7: The estimated dollar change in position value per one day decrease in the time to expiration
A 8.8: Delta, Vega, Rho, Theta
A 8.9: Gamma
A 8.10: Underlying asset price
A 8.11: Underlying asset price
A 8.12: Underlying asset volatility
A 8.13: Risk-free interest rate
A 8.14: Time to expiration
A 8.15: They don't change during the life of the agreement
A 8.16: Increase
A 8.17: Increase
A 8.18: Increase
A 8.19: Increase
A 8.20: Decrease
A 8.21: Through multiplying the given Greek by the given multiple-unit change
A 8.22: Above
A 8.23: Using the first derivatives of the Black-Scholes model with respect to the source of sensitivity
A 8.24: First derivatives provide an estimate of change in value that is often not completely accurate
A 8.25: 1
A 8.26: 0
A 8.27: 0
A 8.28: $\frac{F \cdot (T-t) \cdot e^{(-r_t \cdot (T-t))}}{100}$
A 8.29: $\frac{-F \cdot r_t \cdot e^{(-r_t \cdot (T-t))}}{365}$
A 8.30: $N(d_1)$
A 8.31: $\frac{N'(d_1)}{S_t \cdot \sigma_t \cdot \sqrt{T-t}}$
A 8.32: $\frac{S_t \cdot \sqrt{T-t} \cdot N'(d_1)}{100}$
A 8.33: $\frac{K \cdot (T-t) \cdot e^{(-r_t \cdot (T-t))} \cdot N(d_2)}{100}$
A 8.34: $\frac{\left(\begin{array}{c} -S_t \cdot \sigma_t \cdot \frac{N'(d_1)}{2 \cdot \sqrt{T-t}} \\ -K \cdot r_t \cdot e^{(-r_t \cdot (T-t))} \cdot N(d_2) \end{array} \right)}{365}$
A 8.35: $-N(-d_1)$
A 8.36: $\frac{N'(d_1)}{S_t \cdot \sigma_t \cdot \sqrt{T-t}}$

A 8.37: $\frac{S_t \cdot \sqrt{T-t} \cdot N'(d_1)}{100}$

A 8.38: $\frac{-K \cdot (T-t) \cdot e^{(-r_t \cdot (T-t))} \cdot N(-d_2)}{100}$

A 8.39: $\frac{\left(\begin{array}{c} -S_t \cdot \sigma_t \cdot \frac{N'(d_1)}{2 \cdot \sqrt{T-t}} \\ +K \cdot r_t \cdot e^{(-r_t \cdot (T-t))} \cdot N(-d_2) \end{array} \right)}{365}$

A 8.40: $N'(d_1) = e^{-\frac{d_1^2}{2}} / \sqrt{2 \cdot \pi}$

A 8.41: The negative of the value of the Greeks for the corresponding long position

A 8.42: Holding everything else equal, as the underlying asset price increases by one dollar, by how many dollars will the position change in value?

A 8.43: Holding everything else equal, as the underlying asset price increases by one dollar, by how much will its Delta change in value?

A 8.44: Holding everything else equal, as the underlying asset volatility increases by 1% above its current volatility, by how many dollars will the position change in value?

A 8.45: Holding everything else equal, as the risk-free interest rate increases by 1% above the current risk-free interest rate, by how many dollars will the position change in value?

A 8.46: Holding everything else equal, as the time to expiration decreases by one day, by how many dollars will the position change in value?

A.9 CHAPTER 9: UNDERSTANDING DELTA AND GAMMA

A 9.1: Whether a given Greek is positive, negative, or zero

A 9.2: Changes in the position's value are positively related to changes in the underlying asset price

A 9.3: Changes in the position's value are negatively related to changes in the underlying asset price

A 9.4: The position's value does not change as the underlying asset price changes

A 9.5: Changes in the position's Delta are positively related to changes in the underlying asset price

A 9.6: Changes in the position's Delta are negatively related to changes in the underlying asset price

A 9.7: The position's Delta does not change as the underlying asset price changes

A 9.8: "Sensitivity" measures what happens to one variable as another variable changes; "risk" indicates that there is uncertainty about whether the change will take place and the magnitude of the change

A 9.9: Yes
A 9.10: Yes
A 9.11: Long Delta Gamma neutral
A 9.12: Short Delta Gamma neutral
A 9.13: Long Delta long Gamma
A 9.14: Short Delta short Gamma
A 9.15: Short Delta long Gamma
A 9.16: Long Delta short Gamma
A 9.17: Because they are purchasing counterparties that receive the underlying asset and, therefore, are positively sensitive to changes in its price
A 9.18: Because they are selling counterparties that deliver the underlying asset and, therefore, are negatively sensitive to changes in its price
A 9.19: Long and short forwards
A 9.20: Increases from 0 to 1 as the underlying asset price increases
A 9.21: Decreases from 0 to −1 as the underlying asset price increases
A 9.22: Increases from −1 to 0 as the underlying asset price increases
A 9.23: Decreases from 1 to 0 as the underlying asset price increases
A 9.24: A position with Delta that is universally the same number across the underlying asset price
A 9.25: Because the counterparties to a forward are both obligated to transact; hence, the counterparties fully experience gains or losses as the underlying asset price changes.
A 9.26: Because the long position to an option is not obligated to transact; hence, sensitivity is a function of the likelihood of the transaction taking place
A 9.27: When Delta is constant across the underlying asset price, the position is Gamma neutral. When Delta is positively sensitive to changes in the underlying asset price, the position is long Gamma. When Delta is negatively sensitive to changes in the underlying asset price, the position is short Gamma
A 9.28: Because Delta is always 1
A 9.29: Because Delta is always −1
A 9.30: Because Delta increases from 0 and 1 as the underlying asset price increases
A 9.31: Because Delta decreases from 0 to −1 as the underlying asset price increases
A 9.32: Because Delta increases from −1 to 0 as the underlying asset price increases
A 9.33: Because Delta decreases from 1 to 0 as the underlying asset price increases
A 9.34: Forward positions
A 9.35: Highest near-the-money, approaches zero deep-OTM and deep-ITM

A 9.36: Lowest near-the-money, approaches zero deep-OTM and deep-ITM
A 9.37: Highest near-the-money, approaches zero deep-OTM and deep-ITM
A 9.38: Lowest near-the-money, approaches zero deep-OTM and deep-ITM
A 9.39: Because Delta is not sensitive to changes in the underlying asset price when deep-OTM and deep-ITM
A 9.40: Because Delta is very sensitive to changes in the underlying asset price when near-the-money
A 9.41: Because call and put Delta change in identical fashion as the underlying asset price increases

A.10 CHAPTER 10: UNDERSTANDING VEGA, RHO, AND THETA

A 10.1: Changes in the position's value are positively related to changes in the underlying asset volatility
A 10.2: Changes in the position's value are negatively related to changes in the underlying asset volatility
A 10.3: The position's value does not change as the underlying asset volatility changes
A 10.4: Changes in the position's value are positively related to changes in the risk-free interest rate
A 10.5: Changes in the position's value are negatively related to changes in the risk-free interest rate
A 10.6: The position's value does not change as the risk-free interest rate changes
A 10.7: The position's value will increase as time to expiration decreases
A 10.8: The position's value will decrease as time to expiration decreases
A 10.9: The position's value will not change as time to expiration decreases
A 10.10: Yes
A 10.11: Yes
A 10.12: No
A 10.13: Vega neutral, long Rho, short Theta
A 10.14: Vega neutral, short Rho, long Theta
A 10.15: Long Vega, long Rho, short Theta
A 10.16: Short Vega, short Rho, long Theta
A 10.17: Long Vega, short Rho, long or short Theta
A 10.18: Short Vega, long Rho, long or short Theta
A 10.19: Symmetrical
A 10.20: Symmetrical
A 10.21: Asymmetrical
A 10.22: Asymmetrical

A 10.23: Asymmetrical
A 10.24: Asymmetrical
A 10.25: As their symmetrical payoffs mean that change in volatility can lead to offsetting benefit and harm
A 10.26: As their asymmetrical payoffs mean that wider dispersion of the underlying asset returns caused by increased volatility is beneficial while increased volatility has no potential for harm
A 10.27: As their asymmetrical payoffs mean that wider dispersion of the underlying asset returns caused by increased volatility is harmful while increased volatility has no potential for benefit
A 10.28: As an option's asymmetry is most acute near-the-money
A 10.29: Forward price/strike price decreases
A 10.30: As they are purchasing counterparties for whom the present value of the forward price/strike that is paid decreases as the risk-free interest rate increases
A 10.31: As they are selling counterparties for whom the present value of the forward price/strike that is received decreases as the risk-free interest rate increases
A 10.32: As the time to expiration decreases the present value of the forward price/strike price will increase
A 10.33: The present value of the forward price/strike that is paid increases as time to expiration decreases
A 10.34: The present value of the forward price/strike that is received increases as time to expiration decreases
A 10.35: As time to expiration decreases, optionality value erodes
A 10.36: No impact
A 10.37: Decreases value as the optionality value has eroded
A 10.38: Increases value as liability smaller since the optionality provided has eroded
A 10.39: Because their value decreases as time to expiration decreases because the present value of the forward price to be paid increases
A 10.40: Because their value increases as time to expiration decreases because the present value of the forward price to be received increases
A 10.41: Because their value decreases as time to expiration decreases because the present value of the strike price to be paid increases and because the optionality value that the long call holds decreases
A 10.42: Because their value increases as time to expiration decreases because the present value of the strike price to be received increases and because the short call's liability due to providing optionality decreases
A 10.43: On the one hand, their value increases as time to expiration decreases because the present value of the strike price to be received increases. On the other hand, their value decreases as

time to expiration decreases because the optionality value that the long put holds decreases. Whether long or short Theta depends on which effect is more impactful

A 10.44: On the one hand, their value decreases as time to expiration decreases because the present value of the strike price to be paid increases. On the other hand, their value increases as time to expiration decreases because the short put's liability due to providing optionality decreases. Whether long or short Theta depends on which effect is more impactful

A.11 CHAPTER 11: PRICE AND VOLATILITY TRADING STRATEGIES

A 11.1: A view about whether the underlying asset price will increase or decrease in the future
A 11.2: A view about whether the underlying asset volatility will increase or decrease in the future
A 11.3: Positive value sensitivity to underlying asset price change
A 11.4: Negative value sensitivity underlying asset price change
A 11.5: Positive value sensitivity to underlying asset volatility change
A 11.6: Negative value sensitivity to underlying asset volatility change
A 11.7: Long Delta and Long Vega
A 11.8: Long Delta and Short Vega
A 11.9: Long Delta and Vega neutral
A 11.10: Short Delta and Long Vega
A 11.11: Short Delta and Short Vega
A 11.12: Short Delta and Vega neutral
A 11.13: Delta neutral and Long Vega
A 11.14: Delta neutral and Short Vega
A 11.15: None
A 11.16: Long call
A 11.17: Short put
A 11.18: Long forward
A 11.19: Long put
A 11.20: Short call
A 11.21: Short forward
A 11.22: Price neutral volatility bullish or bearish
A 11.23: Long call and long put with identical strike prices
A 11.24: Short call and short put with identical strike prices
A 11.25: Long straddle pays and short straddle receives
A 11.26: Broadly Delta neutral

A 11.27: Broadly Delta neutral
A 11.28: Long Vega
A 11.29: Short Vega
A 11.30: The magnitude of the call Delta and put Delta may not be identical
A 11.31: Delta is an inaccurate estimate
A 11.32: At-the-money Delta-neutral-straddle
A 11.33: $K = S_t \cdot e^{\left(r_t + \frac{\sigma_t^2}{2}\right)\cdot(T-t)}$
A 11.34: 0.5, assuming European-style where underlying asset pays no income
A 11.35: Larger
A 11.36: See Figure 11.1
A 11.37: See Figure 11.1
A 11.38: *Underlying asset price = strike price – call premium – put premium*
A 11.39: *Underlying asset price = strike price + call premium + put premium*
A 11.40: Lower strike long put and a higher strike long call
A 11.41: Lower strike short put and a higher strike short call
A 11.42: Long strangle pays and the short strangle receives
A 11.43: As OTM options are cheaper than ATM options
A 11.44: Broadly Delta neutral
A 11.45: Broadly Delta neutral
A 11.46: Long Vega
A 11.47: Short Vega
A 11.48: See Figure 11.2
A 11.49: See Figure 11.2
A 11.50: *Underlying asset price = put strike price – call premium – put premium*
A 11.51: *Underlying asset price = call strike price + call premium + put premium*
A 11.52: Long straddle or long strangle
A 11.53: Short straddle or short strangle

A.12 CHAPTER 12: SYNTHETIC, PROTECTIVE, AND YIELD-ENHANCING TRADING STRATEGIES

A 12.1: The concept that a forward or option position can be synthetically created through holding combinations of other traded positions
A 12.2: Through combining a traded long call and a traded short put
A 12.3: Through combining a traded short call and a traded long put

A 12.4: Through combining a traded long forward and a traded long put
A 12.5: Through combining a traded short forward and a traded short put
A 12.6: Through combining a traded short forward and a traded long call
A 12.7: Through combining a traded long forward and a traded short call
A 12.8: A forward price/strike price equal to the forward price/strike price of the intended synthetic position
A 12.9: Expiration date equal to the expiration date of the intended synthetic position
A 12.10: See Figure 12.1
A 12.11: See Figure 12.1
A 12.12: See Figure 12.2
A 12.13: See Figure 12.2
A 12.14: See Figure 12.3
A 12.15: See Figure 12.3
A 12.16: Identical
A 12.17: No premium
A 12.18: Equivalent to each other
A 12.19: At-the-money-forward. A strike price equal to the forward price of a forward initiated today
A 12.20: $K = F = S_t \cdot e^{r_t \cdot (T-t)}$
A 12.21: ATM: Long position indifferent about exercising or not. ATMF: Call price is equal to put price. ATM DNS: Absolute call Delta is equal to absolute put Delta
A 12.22: Larger
A 12.23: Smaller
A 12.24: Identical to each other
A 12.25: 1, 0, 0
A 12.26: *Long Put Delta = Long Call Delta* – 1
A 12.27: *Long Call Gamma = Long Put Gamma*
A 12.28: *Long Call Vega = Long Vega*
A 12.29: The strategy of taking advantage of discrepancies between the cost of entering into corresponding traded and synthetic positions
A 12.30: Long forward, short call, long put
A 12.31: Short forward, long call, short put
A 12.32: Short forward, long call, short put
A 12.33: Long forward, short call, long put
A 12.34: Long forward, short call, long put
A 12.35: Short forward, long call, short put
A 12.36: Adding a long put to a portfolio consisting of an asset
A 12.37: To protect a position in an asset from losses
A 12.38: OTM
A 12.39: Long call

A 12.40: Because the long put requires payment of a premium
A 12.41: *Asset price = asset purchase price + put premium*
A 12.42: Higher
A 12.43: Adding a short call to a portfolio consisting of an asset
A 12.44: To enhance yield
A 12.45: OTM
A 12.46: Short put
A 12.47: The short call's losses negate the asset's upside
A 12.48: *Asset price = asset purchase price – call premium*
A 12.49: Lower
A 12.50: Adding a long put and short call to a portfolio consisting of an asset
A 12.51: To protect a position in an asset from losses and to finance the protection
A 12.52: OTM
A 12.53: See Figure 12.4
A 12.54: Positively sensitive to the asset price and broadly volatility neutral
A 12.55: *Asset price = asset purchase price + put premium – call premium*

A.13 CHAPTER 13: SPREAD TRADING STRATEGIES

A 13.1: Combination of a lower strike long call and a higher strike short call
A 13.2: Combination of a lower strike short call and a higher strike long call
A 13.3: See Figure 13.1
A 13.4: See Figure 13.1
A 13.5: Pay
A 13.6: Receive
A 13.7: Long Delta and broadly Vega neutral
A 13.8: Short Delta and broadly Vega neutral
A 13.9: *Asset price = lower strike price + lower strike call premium – higher strike call premium*
A 13.10: Combination of a lower strike long put and higher strike short put
A 13.11: Combination of a lower strike short put and higher strike long put
A 13.12: See Figure 13.2
A 13.13: See Figure 13.2
A 13.14: Receive
A 13.15: Pay
A 13.16: Long Delta and broadly neutral Vega
A 13.17: Short Delta and broadly Vega neutral
A 13.18: *Asset price = Higher strike price – higher strike put premium + lower strike put premium*

A 13.19: Combination of a lower strike OTM short put and a higher strike OTM long call
A 13.20: To take advantage of overvalued OTM puts and undervalued OTM calls
A 13.21: See Figure 13.3
A 13.22: Long Delta and broadly Vega neutral
A 13.23: *Asset price = lower strike price – put premium + call premium*
A 13.24: *Asset price = higher strike price – put premium + call premium*
A 13.25: *Lower*: *Asset price = lower strike price. Higher*: *Asset price = higher strike price*
A 13.26: Combination of a long OTM strangle and a short ATM straddle
A 13.27: Combination of a short OTM strangle and a long ATM straddle
A 13.28: To take advantage of undervalued OTM strangles and overvalued ATM straddles
A 13.29: To take advantage of overvalued OTM strangles and undervalued ATM straddles
A 13.30: See Figure 13.4
A 13.31: See Figure 13.4
A 13.32: Broadly Delta neutral and short Vega
A 13.33: Broadly Delta neutral and long Vega
A 13.34:

Lower: *Asset price = ATM strike price + OTM put premium+ OTM call premium – ATM put premium – ATM call premium*
Higher: *Asset price = ATM strike price – OTM put premium– OTM call premium + ATM put premium + ATM call premium*

A 13.35: Combination of a long deeper-OTM strangle and a short less-deep-OTM strangle
A 13.36: Combination of a short deeper-OTM strangle and a long less-deep-OTM strangle
A 13.37: See Figure 13.5
A 13.38: See Figure 13.5
A 13.39: Broadly Delta neutral and short Vega
A 13.40: Broadly Delta neutral and long Vega
A 13.41:

Lower: *Asset price = less-deep-OTM put strike price + deeper-OTM put premium + deeper-OTM call premium – less-deep-OTM put premium – less-deep-OTM call premium*
Higher: *Asset price = less-deep-OTM call strike price – deeper-OTM put premium – deeper-OTM call premium + less-deep-OTM put premium + less-deep-OTM call premium*

A.14 CHAPTER 14: INTEREST RATE SWAPS

A 14.1: An agreement in which two counterparties agree to periodically exchange fixed and floating rates of interest over a number of periods of time
A 14.2: Receives floating pays fixed
A 14.3: Receives fixed pays floating
A 14.4: At initiation
A 14.5: A benchmark rate that is formed through identifying the rates at which banks borrow from each other
A 14.6: Swap maturity
A 14.7: No
A 14.8: A swap rate is set that is perceived as "fair" through being equal to the expected levels of the floating rate
A 14.9: Zero
A 14.10: Semi-annual
A 14.11: Quarterly
A 14.12: The dollar amount by which rates are multiplied in a swap to identify the cash flows
A 14.13: To identify the swap's cash flows
A 14.14: Annualized
A 14.15: The factor by which an annualized rate is multiplied to transform it into a periodic rate
A 14.16: The convention through which the accrual factor is calculated
A 14.17: 30/360
A 14.18: Actual/360
A 14.19: The day count convention through which accrual factors are calculated using the actual number of days in the period in the numerator and an assumed 360-day year in the denominator
A 14.20: The day count convention through which accrual factors are calculated using 30 days per month in the period in the numerator and an assumed 360-day year in the denominator
A 14.21: *Days in quarter*/360
A 14.22: 180/360, as well as business day adjustments
A 14.23: LIBOR reported at the beginning of a quarter
A 14.24: LIBOR reported at the end of a quarter
A 14.25: 3-month USD LIBOR-in-advance
A 14.26: Calculate the floating rate accrual factor. Calculate the quarterly floating rate. Calculate the floating payment
A 14.27: Calculate the fixed rate accrual factor. Calculate the semi-annual fixed rate. Calculate the fixed payment

A 14.28: Calculate the net long position cash flows. Calculate the net short position cash flows
A 14.29: Risk-free interest rate
A 14.30: Credit spread
A 14.31: IR
A 14.32: Pays floating IR + fixed SPRD
A 14.33: Receives floating IR + fixed SPRD
A 14.34: Pays fixed IR + fixed SPRD
A 14.35: Receives fixed IR + fixed SPRD
A 14.36: Long interest rate swap
A 14.37: Short interest rate swap
A 14.38: Short interest rate swap
A 14.39: Long interest rate swap

A.15 CHAPTER 15: CREDIT DEFAULT SWAPS, CROSS-CURRENCY SWAPS, AND OTHER SWAPS

A 15.1: An agreement between two counterparties to exchange periodic payments of spread in return for a payment contingent on a credit event
A 15.2: Quarterly payments of spread
A 15.3: A payment should a reference asset issued by a reference entity experience a credit event
A 15.4: No
A 15.5: The payments made by the protection buyer to the protection seller
A 15.6: Quarterly
A 15.7: Annualized
A 15.8: At initiation
A 15.9: Yes
A 15.10: *Quarterly spread payment* = *credit default spread* × *accrual factor* × *notional principal*
A 15.11: The value of the reference asset following the credit event expressed as a percentage of its face value
A 15.12: *Protection seller payment upon credit event* = (100% – *recovery rate*) × *notional principal*
A 15.13: The payment of a fixed spread of 1% or 5%
A 15.14: A credit default swap in which the full notional principal is the payment should a credit event occur
A 15.15: Yes
A 15.16: Positive
A 15.17: Negative
A 15.18: Positive

A 15.19: Negative
A 15.20: Negative
A 15.21: Positive
A 15.22: Long bond position
A 15.23: Short bond position
A 15.24: Protection buyer
A 15.25: Protection seller
A 15.26: An agreement similar to an interest rate swap where the notional principal for each of the swap legs is in a different currency
A 15.27: Fixed rate in one currency for floating rate in the other currency, floating rate in one currency for floating rate in the other currency, and fixed rate in one currency for fixed rate in the other currency
A 15.28: At initiation and expiration
A 15.29: Equal to each other based on the exchange rate at initiation
A 15.30: Enter into a cross currency swap that receives the currency that is being borrowed and pays the desired borrowing currency
A 15.31: An agreement in which two counterparties agree to swap equity returns for an interest rate
A 15.32: An equity swap where each of the counterparties receives one equity return and pays another equity return
A 15.33: An agreement in which two counterparties agree to swap commodity returns for an interest rate
A 15.34: An agreement where one of the counterparties receives the return on a refined oil and pays the return on crude oil plus a spread, while the other counterparty receives the return on crude oil plus a spread and pays the return on refined oil
A 15.35: An agreement where one of the counterparties receives the return on electricity and pays the return on natural gas plus a spread, while the other counterparty receives the return on natural gas plus a spread and pays the return on electricity

Index